The Campus Crisis Toolkit

The Campus Crisis Toolkit

Strategies and Solidarity for the Rest of Us

Edited by

Lisa M. Di Bartolomeo and
Kevin M. Gannon

Published by State University of New York Press, Albany

Printed in the United States of America

EU GPSR Authorised Representative:
Logos Europe, 9 rue Nicolas Poussin, 17000, La Rochelle, France
contact@logoseurope.eu

For information, contact State University of New York Press, Albany, NY
www.sunypress.edu

Library of Congress Cataloging-in-Publication Data

Names: Di Bartolomeo, Lisa M., editor. | Gannon, Kevin M., editor.
Title: The campus crisis toolkit : strategies and solidarity for the rest of us / edited by Lisa M. Di Bartolomeo and Kevin M. Gannon.
Description: Albany : State University of New York Press, [2026]. | Includes bibliographical references and index.
Identifiers: ISBN 9798855805772 (hardcover : alk. paper) | ISBN 9798855807035 (epub) | ISBN 9798855805796 (PDF) | ISBN 9798855805789 (pbk. : alk. paper)
Further information is available at the Library of Congress.

Contents

Editors' Note

Readers will likely note that more recent campus crises—in particular, the wave of campus protests against the destruction of Gaza and the newest iterations of the Trump regime's war on higher education—are not explicitly addressed in the present volume. This absence is not because of any desire not to confront these difficult (to say the least) subjects, but rather the extended nature of the manuscript-to-print timeline. All but the final stages of the work on the volume's manuscript was completed prior to the dramatic escalation of campus unrest in the spring of 2024, and the volume's final draft was undergoing final edits before the presidential election. Of course, none of the issues raised by this volume's authors has become less relevant, even if they may seem overshadowed in the public eye as of late. It is one of the dismaying realities of the present moment that critical analyses of campus crises in higher education remain urgently relevant. If anything, recent events highlight the need for ongoing struggle—in both theory and praxis—to continue resisting the manifold attacks on higher education and the people who make it work. This volume is a waystation, but not the final stop, in those efforts. We invite readers to approach it in that spirit.

Acknowledgments

First and foremost, we'd like to thank our friends and colleagues who shared their stories: whether those stories found their way into this volume or not. If it weren't for their brave willingness to offer their experiences and lend their voices, we would not have a book. Our contributors' unselfishness regarding their emotional, psychological, and professional trauma will, we hope, help others enduring similar travails, and we are deeply grateful for that.

When Lisa lost her job, our mutual friend and colleague, Derek Krissoff, reached out to her and suggested putting together a volume along the lines of this current version. Over the course of conversations, Derek brought in Kevin, and a partnership was born. Without Derek's initial push (and later connection), we might never have dared to put such a volume together; more than anyone, we'd like to recognize Derek, a publishing guru and all-around mensch, for his foundational help.

Derek also recommended that we work with SUNY Press and Rebecca Colesworthy—a recommendation that has proved fruitful and supportive. Rebecca understood and shared our vision from the start and has helped us bring it to realization. We are grateful for both her sure editorial hand and shared commitment to this project and the ideals that animate it.

Lisa would also like to thank a few people, including Kevin. Kevin has been a patient expert on this team, offering insight born of his greater publishing experience, and has been an excellent partner in dividing and sharing the work. Lisa would also like to thank her colleagues at WVU: those who remain and those who moved on, either by force or by choice. We all believed in a place and did our best for our students, and it is no shame on us that an entire administration failed us, our students, our university, and our state. That the maker of that failure kept his job and his huge salary and perks without facing any consequences is galling; that he continues to claim that he was *right* to slash and burn West Virginia's flagship, land-grant institution is infuriating. When the fury threatens to take over, Lisa does her best to remember the wonderful students, colleagues, and friends of her nearly two decades as a professor at her alma mater.

Kevin would like to thank Lisa, who has been the ideal coconspirator on this project, and whose unflinching commitment to what higher education could and should be (and at WVU, should have been) is inspiring. He is also grateful for her patience and flexibility when life intervened in the writing and editing schedule. Kevin's colleagues at Queens University of Charlotte have helped him find a professional home there, and he is deeply appreciative of their unwavering commitment to students and the larger campus community. Finally, Kevin would like to thank his children, Sova and Leo, for continually reminding him of what's truly important and who higher education is for.

Finally, we want to acknowledge and celebrate the efforts and dedication of faculty, staff, and students across higher education. Despite the loud voices insisting on the opposite, you and our and your work matter, deeply and fundamentally. We hope this book is of service to you and that you find affirmation, support, and inspiration from its chapters.

Join a union. Start a union. Raise hell. Solidarity forever!

Introduction

LISA M. DI BARTOLOMEO AND KEVIN M. GANNON

These are difficult times for higher education and those who learn and work within it. The COVID-19 pandemic not only disrupted college and universities' operations, but for many of them, it also triggered a crisis (or accelerated an already-existing one) in student enrollment and retention. The pandemic also intensified the austerity policies already championed by administrators and consultants committed to neoliberal economic ideology; the result has been the evisceration of curricula and (certain) academic programs, coupled with the continuing and intensifying adjunctification of the faculty. The hard right turn in both US and international politics has not only lent momentum to those curricular and programmatic cuts, but it's also produced a cadre of self-styled "culture warriors" avowedly dedicated to rolling back the hard-won (yet still incomplete) gains in educational access, diversity, and opportunity that marked the previous few decades. A modern-day McCarthyism grips academia, where diversity, equity, and inclusion (DEI) plays the role that the so-called communist menace did decades ago. In this hysterical and vicious campaign, faculty, staff, and students find themselves threatened by implicit discrimination, explicit hostility, and danger—and all too often, both. As if all these factors were not enough, the flood tide of US gun violence continues to wash over college campuses; repeated mass shootings mean our campuses are now marked by features such as lockdown drills and flyers listing steps to take during a shooting posted on classroom walls.

Amid budget cuts, threats to both instruction and instructors, academic and cultural barriers placed in front of students (and certain communities of students in particular), a surging authoritarian movement, and the looming threats of both metaphorical and literal violence, faculty, staff, and students still do the work of higher education on campuses across the country (and the world). But never has that work felt more fraught, precarious, and besieged than this moment. Higher education—defined as both a whole sector and complex ecosystem of diverse institutions—is in crisis. Indeed, even "crisis" may not be the word to fully describe this moment. It's more accurate, we think, to see the entire spectrum of problems we face as an interlocking, mutually reinforcing system—a "polycrisis." The distinguishing feature of a polycrisis, according to historian Adam Tooze, is that "disparate shocks interact so that the whole is worse than the sum of its parts."[1] We would submit that "the whole is worse than the sum of its parts" is a fitting description of the current higher-ed landscape, fraught and riddled with difficulties as it is.

But how did we get to this polycrisis moment? US higher education has long been the envy of the world, and rightfully so: college educates rather than simply trains; it develops minds rather than simply preparing automata for the job market. International and domestic students and scholars have flocked to US universities and colleges in search of academic freedom, intellectual rigor, and important research—features that have enabled them to discover, develop, and thrive. Students have moved into residence halls hoping to discover their best selves as they interact with professors and peers, staff, and community. Yet higher ed is about to fail all those people, in part because we all trusted our administrators to work in good faith, our leaders to behave with integrity and foresight, and our colleagues to pay attention. Sadly, that trust was misplaced, leading to the current crises across academe.

As academics, one of our reflexive responses to complex problems is to do our research, to turn to the literature on the subject. But there is precious little literature on strategies for crisis management—especially in book or monograph form—to be found for the higher-ed context, and what does exist is aimed at the narrow audience of senior administrators (presidents, vice presidents, and boards) at larger institutions.[2] This volume is explicitly aimed at (and is authored by) *the rest of us*—the faculty, staff, and students who comprise the lion's share of campus populations. It is *our* values, livelihoods, and prospects for success that are most threatened by these crises—and, often, also threatened by top-level administrators' responses to those crises.

The essays in this volume address a particular aspect of the polycrisis (examples include declarations of financial exigency, program closures and faculty layoffs, campus closures, political interference, outbreaks of violence) but use the authors' own experiences—and those of their colleagues and students—to specifically discuss response strategies, what worked and what didn't, and reflections drawn from those experiences. In this regard, the individual chapters will provide an extensive and useful toolkit for readers who find themselves in similar, if not identical, situations on their own campus. If crisis hasn't come to your campus yet—don't worry, it will. And when it does, this book will help.

Again, we'd like to underscore the fact that this volume is designed for our students, our colleagues, and our peers—academics across the country who care deeply about the educational mission to which they have dedicated their careers at the types of colleges and universities that make up the bulk of the US higher education sector: community colleges, smaller teaching- and undergraduate-oriented institutions, and regional and comprehensive public universities. This book is for those of us who care not only about practical political considerations but also about teaching, learning, and student success. It is impossible to separate the waves of crises washing across our campuses from the crises our students are experiencing; indeed, there is significant overlap between the two. Students pay attention. They see what is being done to their programs and their mentors. They see millions of dollars of their tuition money misspent with no accountability. They have been at the forefront of movements to save their majors and programs across the nation. It falls to educators to center the student experience even as many of us face "non-renewal" or "Reductions in Force (RIFs)," threats to tenure and academic freedom, interference with our curricula and pedagogies, and even threats to our very persons. Students also suffer from the short-sighted but long-running evisceration of higher ed. Keeping them front of mind when addressing the challenges we face can ensure our concerns are heard favorably by the nonacademic public who send their kids to college, worry about high tuition costs, and see the effects of the erosion of excellence on the nation's campuses.

Therefore, in its orientation toward faculty, staff, and even student audiences, this volume is quite intentional about its "for the rest of us" purpose. It's sobering to acknowledge that the overwhelming majority of teachers and other staff at colleges and universities across the country will find significant value in a collection like this, but that realization underscores the necessity for the volume and the power of the intervention we are trying to make in the current discourse in and around higher education. The collective goal of all the contributors is to offer practical strategies and tools aimed at helping readers who find themselves confronting similar challenges, difficulties, or full-blown crises.

The contributors to this volume write from a variety of perspectives, backgrounds, and institutions to offer a helpful toolkit for, about, and by campuses in crisis. Few academics have any training in how to deal with assaults on academic freedom, tenure, shared governance, or their very employment. Most faculty spent years surviving grad school, only to land in an academic job market that provides a scant few tenure-track positions alongside a demoralizing sea of contingent-labor positions. Few faculty or staff have the wherewithal to know exactly what happens when outside consultants arrive on campus, or how to effectively respond to program and budget cuts. But rather than become simply a litany of complaints and despair, this book consists of an empowering set of essays that provide practical advice, constructive criticism, and object lessons. We hope the strategies, initiatives, and actions described in these pages can help readers who are confronting their own campus crises, no matter what form they may take. Only by combining theory and practice, only by honestly reckoning with the difficult terrain we occupy, and only in solidarity with one another—faculty, staff, and students—can we face the higher-ed polycrisis with any hope of overcoming it.

This book won't save US higher education. It will, however, be of invaluable assistance to those of you who will.

Notes

1. Adam Tooze, "Welcome to the World of the Polycrisis," *Financial Times*, Oct. 28, 2022. https://www.ft.com/content/498398e7-11b1-494b-9cd3-6d669dc3de33; Also see chapter 25 in this volume.

2. See, for example, Ralph Gigliotti, *Crisis Leadership in Higher Education: Theory and Practice* (Rutgers University Press, 2019) and Eugene L. Zdziarski, Norbert W. Dunkel, J. Michael Rollo, eds. *Campus Crisis Management: A Comprehensive Guide for Practitioners* (London: Routledge, 2021).

Part 1

West Virginia University as Case Study

This section focuses on West Virginia University (WVU) as a case study, offering a range of perspectives on the "academic transformation" (or #academicdecimation, as it came to be called) wrought by President E. Gordon Gee and his administration in 2023–2024. We chose to begin our toolkit with this quintessential "canary in a coalmine," an image apropos for a state long beset by internal colonization and extractive exploitation. WVU dug itself into a deep budget hole and a crisis of shared governance—exacerbated by some forces beyond its control—in ways examined here by Lisa Corrigan; an author who wishes to remain anonymous given their particular work; and Lisa M. Di Bartolomeo. But rather than rehashing what was already widely reported in the national (and even international) media, this section also offers perspectives from faculty and students who were on the front lines: creating a union on campus, dealing with threats to their visa status, documenting what was being lost, and sharing tips on dealing with the media during their time in the spotlight. What happened at WVU was the genesis of the present volume, so we thought it appropriate to start there, particularly because one of us, Lisa, fell victim to Gee's destructive cuts and lost her job and her program.

1

"Mountaineers Go First"

The WVU Mistake

Lisa M. Di Bartolomeo

No doubt those reading this chapter already know something about the substantial faculty and staff cuts at West Virginia University (WVU) as part of the so-called Academic Transformation of AY 2023–2024. We gained a national spotlight thanks to the sweeping and poorly planned nature of the cuts, which were more like a frenzied knife attack than a surgically precise or strategically considered effort at streamlining the institution. This chapter offers an overview of the events at WVU, which are significant not only in our own institutional context but also as perhaps the most visible and (in)famous examples of the types of crises the other authors in this volume explore. Here, then, is the story of what many of us call "academic decimation."

In 2014, E. Gordon Gee returned to WVU's presidency (he had previously served as the university's president in the early 1980s as well), following the departure of then-president James Clements for Clemson University in late 2013. (Full disclosure: I was faculty senate chair and one of the two voting faculty members on the Board of Governors [BoG] when Clements announced he was leaving.) The BoG was looking for someone who could take the helm immediately while we conducted a national search. The board quickly settled on Gee as someone with nationally recognized experience and a history with WVU. Although the BoG at first only considered Gee as an interim president, he was quickly offered the permanent job, which he accepted, without a national search. Many of us thought he would be good for WVU, considering his national profile and legendary fundraising prowess. I personally believed he would work hard at WVU to cement his professional legacy and help us achieve R1 status.

Hiring Gee was a risk. Anyone who follows higher education administration has likely heard of his notorious exploits at other institutions, from lavish spending on travel, parties, and renovations to his campus homes to problematic off-the-cuff remarks.[1] But the board considered WVU extremely fortunate to have him agree to a permanent return. Faculty seemed mostly pleased to have a serious, nationally known leader, one renowned for being a financial rainmaker;[2] staff appreciated his well-publicized attention (he ran an ongoing video series in which he would do various jobs around campus, from line cook to bus driver, focusing on the often-forgotten folks who make an institution run); and students generally enjoyed his selfie-taking antics and his surprise late-night appearances at bars and parties. Gee also went on a charm offensive to win over state legislators and the governor, playing on the historic power that WVU has held in the imagination and its statewide sports fandom. That was our honeymoon period. But hiring a president so focused on his own personal vision and ~~fixation~~ on "transformation" should have served as an alarm bell. Good presidents focus on the good of the institution to establish their success, rather than on their own personal brand or making headlines for being "visionary."[3]

Apart from attaining R1 status and significant fundraising goals, Gee also set his sights on what he called the "Freedom Agenda," an effort to divorce WVU, Marshall University, and the WV School of Osteopathic Medicine from the state-level oversight of the West Virginia Higher Education Policy Commission (WVHEPC), claiming that because these three schools were larger than any of the other institutions of higher education in the state, they deserved greater freedom to determine their own course and exemptions from much of the reporting WVHEPC expected. Much of the new freedom centered on personnel decisions and gave these institutions greater autonomous authority on their campuses, especially concerning administration and finance. One selling point Gee used on campus was that the "Freedom Agenda" would enable administration to be more nimble in its decision-making, especially around hiring, evaluation, and promotion, without undue state interference. The "Freedom

Agenda," particularly its changes to staff contracts and the move away from established government-employee norms at a state institution, should have served as a bellwether for Gee's real "agenda": the wholesale reinvention of employee contracts, and empowerment of administration to fire people virtually at will.

Within a few months of taking command at WVU, Gee removed the sitting provost and appointed then–law school dean, Joyce McConnell, in her stead. McConnell served from 2014 until her departure in 2019 to become the president of Colorado State University. Thereupon Gee appointed as provost Maryanne Reed, then the dean of the Reed College of Media (no relation). Reed was the focus of significant faculty opposition from the moment her appointment was mentioned. This opposition centered on two aspects: her limited leadership experience and her lack of a terminal degree. Reed College enrolled 1,024 total students in 2019, the second lowest enrollment of any college at WVU, and had only 25 faculty and staff—the equivalent of a department in other units—under her leadership, and she holds only an MS in journalism (not a terminal degree in that field).[4] But Gee ignored faculty opposition, as well as calls for a national, competitive search, and stuck with Reed.[5] The campus had no choice but to accept her appointment, though this instance was an ominous warning sign that Gee would ultimately ignore faculty input when it conflicted with his own desires. In this instance, it was clear that he wanted Reed as his chief academic officer—indeed, many faculty believed he chose her because she would be willing to be the face of the decisions Gee wanted to make. (Interestingly, as of this writing, no budget or personnel cuts have come for the small unit where she served as dean.)

In December 2020, shortly after Reed became provost, she and Gee "issued a charge to transform WVU."[6] It was soon clear that "transformation" would be synonymous with retrenchment. By November 2021, program cuts were already being approved by the BoG, including the MA program in Spanish and fifteen undergraduate degree programs. One popular and nationally recognized program, the BA in puppetry, was saved from the chopping block in part because of a nationwide outcry. At the outset, these cuts affected the College of Creative Arts more than others, and resulted in a recombination of some majors into a new program, which may have masked their true scope. The focus of those cuts meant that many faculty and students failed to hear the warning bells—except when it came to the puppetry program. Because puppetry was granted a reprieve, perhaps we deluded ourselves that, with enough pushback, administration would back down from a fight. Naturally, we all thought we would be able to push back hard enough should our programs be on the line. Our naïveté led us to drop our guard; as it turns out, that was our downfall.

By the time the COVID-19 epidemic hit in the spring of 2020, WVU had already been experiencing years of declining enrollments over and above national trends.[7] COVID exacerbated those trends, even as its attendant federal funding papered over some of WVU's budgetary shortfalls with its emergency appropriations. That situation was not unique to WVU; many other institutions floated on federal support during that time. Those monies enabled the WVU administration to paint a rosy picture of financial health—and that picture appeared sufficiently sanguine as to not alarm the BoG. Instead, because WVU had repeatedly set unrealistic enrollment targets that it repeatedly failed to hit, while spending profligately on the dream of "if you build it, they will come," the institution fell deeper and deeper into debt, and no one steering the ship seemed to notice or care. Some have suggested that WVU lacked coherent data and the ability to analyze its own situation, which is truly damning, as demonstrated in chapter 4 of this volume, "Fighting the Lies: A Brief History of the 'WVU Facts' Report."

By the time of the pandemic, the administration was working hard to revise the institutional promotion and tenure guidelines, justified by what they claimed was a changing academic reality. A committee was formed that met extensively for more than a year to discuss best practices, represent a variety of stakeholders, and plan for the future. (Full disclosure: I was a vocal member of this committee.) The committee made a number of recommendations, few of which were included in the final draft that the provost's office presented to the faculty for approval. In particular, that draft included changes to the very concept of tenure, providing for posttenure review and making it easier to dismiss any faculty for a variety of reasons. As a result, the faculty soundly rejected the proposed revisions to the P & T document in the spring of 2023, leaving the provost's office angry and without the tools they had sought to manage faculty. This moment seemed to confirm the faculty's worst fears, given the previous portents. But we patted ourselves on the back for having asserted ourselves and voted down the new document. Now the provost's office turned their attention to a more troubling "academic transformation" by requesting program reviews using an external consultant, the rpkGroup.[8]

Much has been written about these consultants' reviews—the extreme vetting and self-defense that a variety of programs (many in the arts and humanities) were required to perform over the summer of 2023, in months when many faculty are off contract and unpaid, and when many use the time for scholarly endeavors or family activities.[9] A web search for news about the "WVU mistake," "academic decimation, and "WVU cuts" will yield significant coverage of this process by local, statewide, and national media outlets. There is not enough space in this volume to detail all the cuts or to list all the press attention; suffice it to say that the cuts led to mass opposition and protests from faculty, staff, students, alumni, community members, and national professional organizations over the course of several weeks from August through September 2023, processes that continued for several months.

On September 7, 2023, the WVU Faculty Assembly (a body consisting of all full-time faculty) overwhelmingly voted "No Confidence" in the Gee-Reed administration, by a 797 to 100 margin.[10] The vote was immediately rejected by the BoG (indeed, within moments of the vote's announcement, the board chair released a prepared statement of full-throated support for Gee) and the Gee-Reed administration. They likewise ignored the thousands of emails, letters, phone calls, and other contacts protesting the proposed cuts. In the end, though some of the cuts were (perhaps temporarily) softened, WVU terminated its entire World Languages Department, its PhD program in mathematics (the only one in the state), its master's in public administration, its jazz studies program—over thirty total. Over three hundred faculty and staff lost their jobs (and that number continues to climb) via Reductions in Force (RIFs), forced early retirements (in which faculty members retired sooner than planned in hopes that their sacrifice would save colleagues' jobs), nonrenewals of term faculty and staff, and other administrative measures. It's worth stressing that many of the affected programs were the only ones of their kind in the entire state, and that WVU is both the Morrill Act Land-Grant institution (a fact Gee never failed to trumpet) *and* the doctoral flagship in our small state. As a land-grant institution, WVU is not only morally but also legally obligated to provide excellent education for West Virginia's residents. In addition, numerous faculty have since chosen to leave for a number of reasons: they feel their jobs will be the next to go, they no longer trust the administration, they no longer have faith in the academic, moral, and financial health of the university, or because one partner in a relationship lost their job, and both partners were forced to leave to find jobs together. Even within the programs that remained, there seemed to be little rhyme or reason as to which faculty or staff survived. For instance, why keep Arabic but not Russian for some remaining language instruction? Why cut extremely popular teachers whose classes were heavily enrolled? Why excise graduate programs that existed nowhere else in the state and required few or no additional resources? Why did some underperforming programs survive when others, seemingly healthy, went to the wall? Even STEM and professional programs were axed; the resulting faculty cuts inevitably mean increased teaching loads and a threat to our R1 status. The criteria by which the RIFs, nonrenewals, and cuts were determined were established during the process itself—that is, even as units and programs were targeted, they were being asked to justify their existences within a murky and rapidly changing evaluative framework. No one could hope to adapt or get ahead of such hidden and mutable metrics. The game isn't a game when there are no rules. Academia isn't Calvinball.

We should have been frightened when required to perform these "vetting" exercises. Instead, we executed them in good faith, believing—foolishly—that the strong cases we were making for our survival would be seriously evaluated on their merits and the available evidence. But we didn't know that the die was already cast. A harbinger was rpkGroup referring to us as the "University of West Virginia" in some early presentations, making clear that they had merely recycled what they had told other schools (as this misnomer signals an obvious cut-and-paste job from documents prepared for their previous clients), not bothering to ascertain even the basic details of the current university with which they were "working."

From the "WVU mistake" and the leadership's numerous failures along the way (failure to address failing enrollments; failure to curtail wanton spending on new buildings and residence halls; failure to curb administrative bloat, a hiring spree, and swollen salaries at the top), there are lessons to learn and warning signals to notice. What we endured at WVU is not and will not be unique; we were simply a worst-case scenario of leadership dereliction. No two experiences are the same, and I wouldn't wish on my worst enemy what my colleagues and I endured over the past year. But some of my observations may help you sharpen the focus on the distress signals that exist on your campus.

Consultants. An obvious flashing red light is the presence on your campus of consultants, particularly those who are looking at the academic program side of the enterprise. Their work may be heralded as an effort to streamline programs or create efficiencies—these words should strike fear in your heart. When rpkGroup came to Morgantown, few knew what they'd already done elsewhere—recommending cuts and closures, eliminating faculty lines, etc., and most of us had only limited interactions with them. Take every opportunity to meet with these visitors; press them hard on their qualifications and goals, what they've been tasked to do, and what results their work has had on other campuses. If there are no such opportunities, create them. Demand meetings; ask these questions and push for answers, and publicize their work on your campus. You'll regret passively accepting their visits and the giant paychecks your institution pays them. RpkGroup has a national reputation for recommending precisely the kinds of cuts WVU implemented; when they came to campus, we should have taken to the ramparts. Instead, each of us in our own programs believed that *others* would be faced with hard choices, not us—our programs were mission critical. What we didn't realize was that rpkGroup and the provost's office had already determined the outcome, which favored "valuable" majors: preprofessional and workforce preprograms and those seen as the big money-makers. There was no attention to whether a program was unique in the state, reached underserved students, or, indeed, was actually profitable. Instead, it was about rpkGroup's, and Gee's, vision of transformation for the sake of transformation—and the $45 million budget deficit provided the perfect excuse to excise programs at odds with that vision.

P & T Guideline Revisions. Another warning sign is an effort by your leadership to revise personnel documents. Of course, such revisions are necessary from time to time, and updates can reflect campus realities. But once you begin to see proposals that might make it easier for the administration to fire faculty—whether tenured or nontenure track—you should worry. Join the committee or group working on such changes, and when, inevitably, administration chooses faculty-unfriendly changes over your objections, raise a stink. Passivity ensures that your administration will enact their changes regardless of the negative impact on faculty retention and recruitment. Such erosion of employment protections not only harms your individual campus but also becomes part of the landslip of academic freedom and job security across the country. Each institution stealing a piece of job security eases the way for the next one to go even further.

Shared Governance Issues. Yet another warning sign, much more difficult to mark than expensive consultants or ham-handed attacks on tenure, is an unhealthy culture of shared governance. Many of us at WVU believed we had a strong relationship with administration. Because of an earlier scandal over a degree unjustly granted to a well-connected person (the Bresch degree scandal of 2007–8), WVU had revised its board membership to ensure greater faculty and staff voice at the highest level.[11] Additionally, a registrar was hired to close the loopholes that had allowed that unearned degree to be awarded in the first place. As a result of the scandal and its aftermath, faculty were convinced that they were vigilant watchdogs equipped with mechanisms to ensure good stewardship. Under the succession of presidents that followed, that belief seemed reasonable. When Gee arrived on campus, he charmed many of us into believing that he had WVU's best interests at heart, that he saw WVU as his crowning legacy, atoning for his various missteps over his decades in leadership. His focus on state outreach, student success, and achieving R1 status while recommitting to the land-grant mission turned out to be a dangerous lullaby, singing us to sleep as he made important changes throughout the institution. By the time we woke up, it was too late.

Maintaining strong oversight and involvement in the daily operations of a campus requires skepticism. Obviously, having a friendly relationship with your institution's leaders is helpful, not only for your own career but also for your institution, fostering cooperation and an open dialogue. But I speak from bitter experience when I say that even when you speak truth to power, power often ignores that truth, and instead plays on your love of high-level access. Too many faculty leaders, including me, chose chumminess over critique, advancement over accountability—all to our own and our institutions' detriment. No matter how charming, how convincingly they cosplay at being faculty, or how they stoke our own ambitions, we cannot ever forget that the administration is not our friend. Trust me when I say that even a friendship you once believed in will not save your job or those of your colleagues in the end.

Your campus may experience some of these warnings, or none of them. Each institution is different in its structure, culture, and challenges. However, our experience at WVU is the canary in the coal mine for higher education—a harbinger of crisis, suffering, and a messy aftermath that will almost certainly befall others. A few years ago, WVU's marketing team (again with highly paid outside consultants) created a new catchphrase for their marketing campaign: Mountaineers Go First. In the case of campus crisis, WVU has, indeed, gone first—into diminishment, loss, and uncertainty. I hope that you, my academic colleagues, learn from our example, and actively work to defend your institutions before it's too late. No one can save us but ourselves.

Notes

1. Here is only a small sample: https://bleacherreport.com/articles/1345902-osu-president-gordon-gees-spending-scandal-shows-hypocrisy-of-ncaa-regulations; https://www.register-herald.com/opinion/wvu-troubles-not-surprising-with-gee-s-history-of-lavish-spending/article_b6550eac-4126-11ee-83a5-5304f56f5d9a.html; https://westvirginiawatch.com/2023/08/22/wvu-troubles-not-surprising-with-gees-history-of-lavish-spending/; https://www.wsj.com/articles/SB115924190013574035; https://www.usatoday.com/story/sports/college/2012/09/24/ohio-state-president-gordon-gee-spends-millions-to-travel-entertain/1590261/; https://www.cleveland.com/morris/2011/03/osu_president_gees_joke_reveal.html; https://www.wosu.org/news/2012-01-13/gee-apologizes-for-polish-comment; https://sports.yahoo.com/osus-gee-apologizes-inappropriate-remarks-183117632—ncaaf.html.

2. See, for example: https://www.dispatch.com/story/news/education/2012/11/09/ohio-state-s-gee-given/23584895007/; https://www.wvgazettemail.com/news/education/wvu-closes-in-on-1-billion-fundraising-goal/article_6af12bc4-cf19-58f6-b338-44fc733bbdc2.html; https://www.espn.com/college-sports/story/_/id/9342172/ohio-state-gordon-gee-retire-wake-controversy.

3. https://www.mindingthecampus.org/2023/05/08/gee-whiz-wvu-confronts-the-real-world/.

4. https://institutionalresearch.wvu.edu/files/d/57f8e8b6-28c6-43b5-83df-3e3b8e76584b/wvu_enrollment_trends_fall-2019.xls.

5. https://wvmetronews.com/2021/12/06/wvu-faculty-senate-rejects-no-confidence-motion-in-gee-reed-administration/; https://www.theintermountain.com/news/local-news/2021/12/wvus-gee-is-facing-no-confidence-vote/; https://www.newsandsentinel.com/news/business/2021/12/wvu-president-gee-facing-no-confidence-vote-in-faculty-senate/.

6. https://provost.wvu.edu/academic-transformation.

7. See https://www.wvhepc.edu/resources/data-and-publication-center/data-center-enrollment/ for enrollment data. For 2019–2020, WVU enrolled 26,869 students; in 2020–2021, 26,377 students; in 2021–2022, 25,483; in 2022–2023, 24,788, and in 2023, the most recent year for which data is available at this writing, enrollment was 24,213 students.

8. It is outside the scope of this chapter, but worth mentioning is the fact that the VP for enrollment management, Sharon Martin, increased her pay dramatically even as WVU's enrollments repeatedly fell. For instance, in 2019, her actual pay was $301,250, while in 2023, she made $417,356.14. Keeping in mind the enrollment decrease cited above, enrollments fell by 9.8 percent over that time while Martin's pay increased by 38.5 percent. https://openpayrolls.com/employee/sharon-l-martin-4511.

9. See, for instance, https://www.nytimes.com/2023/08/20/opinion/west-virginia-university-cuts.html; https://truthout.org/articles/colleges-say-theyre-cash-

strapped-yet-pay-top-dollar-for-anti-union-consultants/; https://newrepublic.com/article/176202/west-virginia-university-higher-education-enrollment-cliff-cuts; https://outsidethebeltway.com/when-does-a-university-stop-being-a-university/ and others.

10. This count is not a total but only the count of those present and voting.

11. https://www.nytimes.com/2008/01/22/us/22heather.html.

2

Speculative Finance/Speculative Fiction

The Financialization of Higher Ed

Lisa M. Corrigan

On December 18, 2020, when E. Gordon Gee, president of West Virginia University (WVU), issued a call for "Academic Transformation" to the West Virginia Board of Governors, few could have foreseen then what the consequences would be for the faculty, staff, and students at the state's only Research I university. As I have written elsewhere, the academic transformation of West Virginia's top research university has systematically dismantled much of the liberal arts, mathematical sciences, public policy, and foreign language programs, despite their profitability.[1] Citing the pandemic as one exigency that forced a reassessment, Gee described the context for academic transformation as follows: "With a declining high school population, limited instructional support and growing skepticism in the public about the value of a college degree, higher education is facing an existential crisis. In such an environment, universities like ours must restate our relevance to current and future students and their families, stake our claim as a leader in innovative and purposeful research, and be ready and willing to adapt to an ever-changing landscape."[2] Gee cited the declining enrollment—what management consultants call the "enrollment cliff"—along with rising college costs and what he characterized as the public's disdain for college education. Calling the moment an "existential crisis," Gee sought to brand "academic transformation" as a data-driven process and WVU as a nimble and forward-thinking organization, rather than an institution deeply in debt ($55 million) due, in part, to projects authorized by Gee himself.[3] The Eberly College of Arts and Sciences took the hardest hit, reducing or eliminating assets and faculty lines in the Center for Women's and Gender Studies, chemistry, communication studies, English, mathematical and data sciences, philosophy, public administration, and world languages, literatures, and linguistics.[4] In the spring of 2023, 132 faculty lines were cut, with 12 graduate programs discontinued and a 3 percent tuition increase approved. An additional twenty-eight majors and 143 faculty lines were eliminated in the fall of 2023 to the outcry of faculty and students and amidst a 600-person faculty vote of no confidence for Gee and a student walkout.[5]

To accomplish academic transformation, WVU retained the services of rpkGroup, a Washington, D.C., Beltway consultancy group deeply invested in efforts to privatize public education.[6] Dubbed "change management," rpkGroup's intervention was pitched as a project of financial maximization in the face of fiscal mismanagement. With a client list that demonstrates how widespread "change management" rebranding has been (particularly since the COVID-19 crisis began), rpkGroup worked with Gee and other university administrators across the country to implement a fiscal and political agenda that has restructured university priorities and funding in ways that have accelerated the privatization of higher education white hastening the decline of the humanities and liberal arts.[7] They do so through what they call "centering academic affairs in the higher education business model" as they produce (often tenuous) financial rather than educational justifications for fiscal cuts to the teaching and research aspects of university life. Declining enrollment made a handy rationale for major financial divestment and university leaders such as Gee (led by consultants) engaged in speculative rhetoric that identified factors contributing to transformation—declining consumer confidence in their institutions, their educational offerings, and cost—while promising a new, transformed institutional culture that would restore confidence. Indeed, Gee and those like him were deeply invested in producing speculative fictions that have attempted to build new worlds in higher education.

The centrality of rpkGroup and fiscal language to Gee's justification of what became a massive crisis at WVU highlights two central coconstitutive processes that undergird the forms of "academic transformation" currently assaulting higher education in the United States (and elsewhere):

speculative finance and speculative fiction. This chapter uses WVU as a paradigmatic case to understand how consultants and administrators have (re)shaped narratives speculating about the future of higher ed to disassemble notions of the "public good" and advance instead notions of capital and profit. With the ultimate goal of privatization, the speculative rhetorical and financial goals of this process capture and redeploy what LiPuma and Lee (2004) call the "technologies, processes, and ideological norms associated with finance and debt" to fundamentally shift popular conceptions of public higher education shifting risk from creditors to debtors and transforming the subjectivity of state employees, students, and communities as the market subsumes any democratic goals of public higher education.[8] Caught between the Scylla of uncertainty on the one hand and the Charybdis of scarcity on the other, higher ed is buckling without a coherent political strategy to move forward. The "change management" sector is happy to step in with speculative rhetoric to help move privatizers further into public higher education to facilitate this wealth transfer.

Indeed, Gee's influence at WVU exposed how and why higher education became a speculatory market for consultants at the exact time that a global pandemic was forcing a massive shift in public education's delivery. Gee's "academic transformation" at WVU is a paradigmatic case for the challenges facing defenders of public higher education because it highlights the *role of speculation* in (1) the narrative of exigencies supposedly driving the decision making to make such tremendous cuts at WVU and (2) the debt bundling and risk shifting of the financial accounting as consultants urged corporate investment in the place of humanities programs. Gee's framework for "academic transformation" and the backlash to it, made the invisible operations of finance capital in the neoliberal university visible, highlighting how "neoliberal finance aims to colonize all possible futures for the sake of a profit-oriented present that becomes a temporal prison for laborers trapped in precarious positions."[9]

On September 29, 2022, in his "State of the University Address," Gee gave no sense of scale about the massive cuts being planned at WVU, but his speech laid out a foundational speculative fiction about WVU that served to create a permission structure for transformation.[10] Given in Washington, D.C., Gee lavished praise on West Virginia's congressional delegation, including Senator Shelley Capito, Senator Joe Manchin, and Congressman David McKinley who were in attendance and who are credited with legislative accomplishments that have benefited WVU.

Gee described the context of higher ed and the role of the congressional delegation, clearly laying out the research/investment priorities of WVU that are coterminous with the delegation's priorities:

> During the pandemic, our students faced unprecedented worries about educational costs, their own health and safety, and their families' struggles. Thanks to our delegation, higher education funding for institutions and students was included in the majority of emergency COVID-19 bills, enabling our University to meet these challenges and assist our students and their families. More recently, the CHIPS and Science Act passed—strengthening our economy and national security, while expanding the geography of innovation. The science provisions provide historic funding increases for science agencies such as the National Science Foundation, the Department of Energy, the National Institute of Health and NASA. . . . For West Virginia, as a participant in the NSF Established Program to Stimulate Competitive Research, or EPSCoR, the big win is a huge investment in research funding over the next several years.[11]

Connecting WVU's needs and successes with national security funding and energy funding is unsurprising, given West Virginia's proximity to Washington, D.C., and its deep investment in coal. As a discursive artifact, Gee's speech laid out a rationale for change, and as a material artifact, it prefaced unprecedented cuts at WVU. This kind of storytelling is how academic transformation emerges and unfolds across different geographic contexts, and it demonstrates where the financial and political commitments are for the consultants and administrators. Budgets are moral documents, and new budgets tell a story of changing morals.

In the succeeding year, Gee leaned into the transformative rhetoric, describing the vision of higher education as one rooted in nineteenth-century ideals. Using metaphors of progress and time, Gee explained, "As a modern land-grant university, we recognize that the 21st century is vastly different from the 19th century. Our needs have changed. There are new external forces bearing down. Society has evolved and thus, their expectations for a university-educated citizenry and workforce has evolved, as well."[12] Invoking notions of modernity and evolution, Gee painted WVU as a space of advancement, forced to adapt to a changing reality, and he offered four principles to help guide the transformation process:

1. We will expand access to education by improving recruitment and retention and focus on raising scholarship funds.

2. We will advance our R1 mission to deliver solutions to real-world problems.

3. We will grow the academic medical center to improve the health of our people.

4. And we will remain the economic engine of the state by partnering with industry.[13]

While this list seems innocuous, "deliver[ing] solutions to real-world problems," expansion of the medical center, and expanding industry partnerships helps focus on profit-making rather than educating.

Seeing Gee's speculation as a rhetorical process of meaning-making is important, since it produced the exigency for a new economic model for WVU. Given that the transformation process was born from WVU's debt load, it's essential to trace *how* finance capital transforms "debts into tradeable instruments, further appropriating value and transferring it to elites."[14] Debt played a huge role in the conversation about transformation.[15] Said another way, debt provided the rationale *and* the avenue for WVU's transformation from an instrument of public good into a space for privatization through the medical center and the invitation of private industry partners. Gee's storytelling replaced the moral commitment to public education as a public good with a vision of WVU as a privatizing university with commitments to corporate partners. To be sure, this shift was made possible by declining federal funding of higher education, particularly during the George W. Bush years. But the financialization of WVU through consultant optimization is where the democratic function of public education is, in fact, transformed into a rationale that is primarily financial. "Financial instruments are a modality of presentation," as Vint explains. She adds that "financial instruments to be simultaneously representations of and forces materially producing the world as they conceptualize it."[16] As higher ed *itself* becomes a financial instrument through corporatization, representations of public education become ornamental rather than instrumental. This kind of thinking is rapidly undermining the creativity and efficacy of higher education while it also shreds the liberal arts and humanities to turn higher ed into vocational education serving corporate sponsors and consultant vultures. Indeed, Gee's influence at WVU illustrates how higher ed is becoming a GameStop-style speculatory market where the language of choice and financial value replaces civic and democratic ideals and where profit replaces social trust.

Consequences of Financial Speculation in Higher Education

This financial speculation of higher education such as Gee has implemented at WVU isn't totally surprising. As Randy Martin notes, speculative capital financializes everyday life as it overdetermines the social through mortgages, health insurance, student loans, life insurance, and credit card debt, shifting risk to from corporations to consumers and accelerating in the movement from stability to risk as basis for contemporary life.[17] In this manner, speculative finance normalizes various forms of abstract violence: on a personal and intimate level, such violence is inflicted by processes of real subsumption, in which everyday existence becomes saturated by the technologies, processes, and ideological norms associated with finance and debt.[18] Risk is shifted from creditors to debtors, transforming their subjectivity. It's no coincidence that the academic transformation consultants descend onto campus as loan forgiveness is sweeping the country through President Joe Biden's student aid policies.

The displacement of *actual people on campus* is a central thrust of the speculative imaginary of finance capitalists, particularly in higher education. Displacement of people is one form of violence that speculation enacts, and it is a consequence of the convergence of tech panic about artificial intelligence, the "human capital management" products for "HR transformation," the unrestrained fantasy of MOOCs and online instruction, and adjunctification. But they're furthered by the privatization of university catering and food services, janitorial and grounds services, and bookstores, where those workers are not working alongside or with campus faculty or students but are instead subcontracted to the campus to undermine collective bargaining and/or wages: this process is another form of financial violence, especially when the university or college in question is the largest employer in the city.

Perhaps the major lesson from Gee's influence at WVU is that when public research universities retain consultants for "academic transformation," they're really looking to move public assets into the private sphere to invite corporations to occupy academic spaces that have been hollowed out. This financialization is possible because higher ed lacks a narrative to describe its mission to the larger public in a political environment increasingly hostile to education. Instead of offering the public transparency about how their educational model works, consultants produce rationales for the new economic speculation that divests from the humanities and liberal arts, leaving students at these institutions at a major structural disadvantage. Likewise, the speculation of academic transformation produces a future vision of higher education that focuses almost exclusively on the technology sector, military technology, and the energy sector (oil, gas, coal), particularly in schools in poor states that have relatively monocultural economic fields. Indeed, the WVU case garnered so much national attention because it was an example of how the convergence of speculative fiction and finance led to a kind of shock doctrine for the state's only Research 1 institution, undermining the democratic function of public education in such a university.

Notes

1. Lisa M. Corrigan, "The Evisceration of a Public University," *The Nation*, August 16, 2023, https://www.thenation.com/article/society/wvu-cuts-higher-education/.

2. "Academic Transformation at WVU," https://provost.wvu.edu/academic-transformation, accessed June 25, 2024.

3. Estimates range from 34 percent to 55 percent, which PolitiFact suggesting that Gee's personal contribution to the debt problem at WVU was 34 percent See: "E. Gordon Gee's University Projects have Increased WVU's Debt Load by 55%," https://www.politifact.com/factchecks/2023/oct/10/west-virginia-university-faculty-senate/has-president-e-gordon-gee-increased-west-virginia/, accessed July 15, 2024.

4. "Academic Portfolio Review," https://provost.wvu.edu/academic-transformation/academic-program-portfolio-review, accessed July 22, 2024; https://www.nytimes.com/2023/08/18/us/west-virginia-university-budget-cuts-deficit.html.

5. "WVU Faculty Vote No Confidence in Gee, Freeze Academic Transformation Process," September 6, 2023, https://wvpublic.org/wvu-faculty-vote-no-confidence-in-gee-freeze-academic-transformation-process/.

6. "Frequently Asked Questions." https://transformation.wvu.edu/faq, accessed June 25, 2024. "The rpk GROUP has been contracted at an hourly rate and will provide an independent third-party perspective throughout the academic program review process. The rpk GROUP also will vet and verify WVU's methodology and recommendations for program review. Until this work

is completed, the University is unable to provide a total cost estimate on services provided by the rpk GROUP."

7. "Client list," https://rpkgroup.com/clients/, accessed June 25, 2024.

8. Edward LiPuma and Benjamin Lee, *Financial Derivatives and the Globalization of Risk* (Durham, NC: Duke University Press, 2004).

9. David M. Higgins and Hugh C. O'Connell, "Introduction: Speculative Finance/Speculative Fiction," *CR: The New Centennial Review*, 19, no. 1 (2019): 7–8.

10. E. Gordon Gee, "State of the University Address, September 29, 2022, https://presidentgee.wvu.edu/speeches/state-of-the-university-address-in-dc-september-2022, accessed 1 June 2024.

11. Gee, "State of the University Address," 2022.

12. Gee, "State of the University Address," 2023.

13. Gee, "State of the University Address," 2023.

14. Sherryl Vint, "Promissory Futures: Reality and Imagination in Finance and Fiction," *CR: The New Centennial Review*, 19, no. 1 (2019): 23.

15. Mike Tony, "WVU Saddled with Nine Figures in Debt Since University Restructuring Began," *Charleston Gazette-Mail*, September 25, 2023, https://www.wvgazettemail.com/news/education/wvu-saddled-with-nine-figures-in-debt-incurred-since-university-restructuring-process-began/article_8133d1dc-395b-5769-88d3-68663abb1ea1.html.

16. Vint, "Promissory Futures," 20.

17. Randy Martin, *Financialization of Daily Life* (Philadelphia: Temple University Press, 2002).

18. LiPuma and Lee, "Financial Derivatives," 3.

3

Fighting the Lies

A Brief History of the "WVU Facts" Report

Anonymous

Background

In August 2023, the provost's office at West Virginia University put forward a proposal to cut dozens of academic programs and hundreds of faculty positions, tenured and untenured. Despite substantial negative attention in the regional and national press, outrage in the university community, and a lopsided vote of no confidence in the university's president and the proposed cuts, the proposal was approved by the politically appointed Board of Governors in October 2023, and layoffs went through as planned in May 2024. As of this writing, upward of two hundred faculty have been involuntarily removed from their positions. Roughly fifty to one hundred of these came in the form of early retirements, which were counted toward satisfying reduction targets and therefore saved the jobs of other faculty. The administration continues to claim that these retirements were "voluntary" and does not count them as part of the cuts.[1]

There is no reason to believe that the financial and academic spiral of WVU is complete. Indeed, these events are likely only the beginning of a generational tailspin, given declining enrollment and state appropriations in the face of ballooning physical-plant costs, administrative payroll, and debt. For me, however, the WVU disaster is over. I am the lead author of WVU Facts, an anonymous faculty report published on a WordPress site[2] in the run-up to the announcement of cuts. I have since been laid off from my "tenured" job and moved out of state. This essay is my attempt to recount some of the faculty responses to the manufactured crisis at WVU, to measure what went right and what went wrong, and perhaps to draw some lessons for future crises. I have chosen to remain anonymous for several reasons; if you absolutely need to know who I am, you can ask the editors of this book to put you in touch.

I published the initial WVU Facts report in May 2023, following months of discussion with a core of concerned faculty in several different colleges at the university. But the genesis of the project should properly be traced to several years earlier because this type of undertaking requires a degree of social capital among faculty from different areas of the university. There was not a lot of this capital at WVU, but some axes of communication had arisen during prior crises. Between 2019 and 2023, concerned faculty, students, and staff built small networks in response to "Campus Carry" legislation from the far-right state legislature, a unilateral rewriting and weakening of tenure protections from the sham provost's office, and a general lack of shared governance at the institution. Avenues for coordination during these crises included several private and semiprivate Facebook groups, two unionization drives, and the WVU Faculty Senate, a representative body with no real policy power but with a minority of members concerned with governance and academic freedom.

I was at the nexus of many of these groups in early 2023 and was receiving information from people in different parts of the university about the financial state of the institution, the decisions that led to the crisis, and the dishonesty of administrators' explanations. At the same time, state and national media began to report on WVU's situation. I decided to try to gather as much of this information as I could into a report that would summarize the emerging consensus among faculty about the crisis and serve as an accurate source of information for journalists covering the story, as well as the faculty and staff they were interviewing. This is how the WVU Facts report came to be.

The Crisis Narrative

This section draws heavily on the WVU Facts report and the references linked therein. As of July 2025, the report is available online at https://

wvufacts.wordpress.com/2023/05/24/the-wvu-budget-crisis/. We first learned about the budget crisis from administrators in early 2023. At a Faculty Senate meeting in February, Chief Financial Officer Paula Congelio announced that her office had just sort of "lost track" of $14 million worth of graduating students and that there would be a budget shortfall. She claimed that she had "come out right away in fall of 2022" and reported this news. But administrators had said nothing about enrollment problems in the fall, and in September 2022 President Gordon Gee reported that enrollment was fine. Congelio's announcement struck many of us as completely off the wall, not because we doubted the enrollment numbers but because the university's highly paid financial administrators didn't seem remotely competent or aware of what was happening.

The situation quickly worsened. After saying nothing about the budget at the March 2023 faculty senate meeting, Gee announced in his "state of the university" address in late March that the shortfall had grown to $35 million. At a senate meeting a few weeks later, Gee and Vice President of Strategic Initiatives Rob Alsop announced that the number was $55 million. Provost Maryanne Reed announced that $21 million would be cut from the budget during the following academic year. At the May senate meeting, Reed outlined a plan to review financial data for all academic programs and recommend program and personnel cuts by the end of the summer, with the help of external consultants.

In each of these meetings, speeches, and announcements, administrators advanced new and baffling claims that didn't add up, and faculty began investigating. Gee claimed the crisis was due to broad economic and demographic factors that all universities faced, but none of WVU's regional or conference peers were going through anything like the crisis that had emerged overnight at WVU. He claimed that he had foreseen the crisis and called for WVU to be a "leaner" institution when he took over in 2014, but faculty who were there at the time remembered the exact opposite. Alsop claimed administrative positions had already been cut "to the bone," but there were far more high-paid executive positions in the central administration and every college on campus than there had been five to ten years earlier. He claimed that the university's bond ratings showed its fiscal position was sound but also that the annual structural budget deficit would grow to $70 million within the next few years without radical cuts to academics. Reed announced that they were hiring external consultants to gather data on academic programs, but her overpopulated office had already hired external consultants to do exactly this task—and had supposedly been working on it for the previous twenty-eight months.

As state and national media began to pay attention to what was happening at WVU, the chorus of outrageous, inaccurate, and contradictory statements from executives grew to a crescendo. Gee told one media outlet that there was no budget crisis at WVU and that they were cutting academics because he wanted to transform the institution into the land-grant university of the future.[3] When Alsop was asked whether high-paid administrative executives would take pay cuts, he responded that cutting executive pay would "devastate morale" at the institution.[4] He suggested that the faculty were to blame for the university's budget problems. An associate provost claimed repeatedly in the media and at meetings that cutting one particular department would save $5.8 million,[5] but total faculty payroll in the department was nowhere near that number.

A distressing number of media outlets covered this story by interviewing WVU executives and their media spokespeople, then printing whatever they said. This result was to be expected in West Virginia, which has weak institutions in general and a lack of independent, critical media in particular. It was more surprising to see outlets such as *Inside Higher Education*[6] and the *New York Times*[7] uncritically relaying questionable and sometimes outright false statements from administrators.

Puncturing the Narrative Bubble

In private conversations, many of the WVU Faculty I spoke to during this time were livid at the inaccurate and lazy media coverage that allowed the Gee administration to spread its lies unchallenged. And several of those faculty, including me, had hunted down specific pieces of information or past statements that established facts that contradicted the administration's statements. But we needed a way to disseminate the truth, without having access to the same media resources as Gee's well-resourced publicity operation. So I decided to try to put everything together and publish it on the web.

Writing the WVU Facts report was largely a process of stitching together the many pieces of information that colleagues had gathered into a coherent narrative. I wrote the first draft alone because writing by committee is sometimes intractable, and it seemed important to get something out quickly. I took the approach of writing the report roughly in academic style: building a larger narrative by painstakingly establishing collections of "small" facts, with each fact referenced to a verifiable source. The process of finding reliable sources of information about the university turned out to be reasonably straightforward.

The first section of the report focused on the timeline leading up to the announcement of the budget crisis. The WVU Faculty Senate posts minutes of meetings on their website and full videos on YouTube.[8] This access made it possible to nail down exactly what administrators said and when.

Gee and Alsop had repeatedly claimed in Faculty Senate meetings that other universities were in a similar situation to WVU. Most public universities in the US post summary budget documents going back several years on their websites, and this fact allowed us to confirm our peer institutions were not facing anything like the crisis that WVU administrators had created. Gee and Alsop repeatedly implied that the "demographic cliff" associated with declining birth rates in the 2000s was driving the crisis. Multiple government agencies post detailed US demographic data online, which quickly debunked this lie: US birth rates began to decline sharply in 2009, well after current undergraduates were born.

The report also zeroed in on the number of (and compensation for) executive jobs involving program analytics and finance, given the university's failures in these areas. WVU's own website was a major source of information: as with most universities, each college and administrative unit at WVU has a page devoted to their "leadership" team. All of the fifteen to twenty states that we investigated, additionally, make compensation for public university employees a matter of public record that can be searched on state websites. Through these means, I was able to match most of the executive administrators listed on WVU websites with their total compensation and compare it to counterparts at richer and more prestigious public universities. As we suspected, WVU executive pay was out of line even with the inflated salaries at other institutions.

A Faculty Senate subcommittee had been trying to track changes in the numbers of administrators over Gee's tenure, but the administrators we communicated with were not forthcoming about changes in their ranks. In the course of this futile effort, we started using the Internet Archive's Wayback Machine, which stores older versions of websites, to compare the "leadership" pages from 2014 with the 2023 versions. This approach turned out to be fruitful: the number of executive positions in the units we checked had grown by 30 to 50 percent, even as enrollment declined substantially. The Office of Strategic Initiatives, and Alsop's $430k/yr. job as the head of that office, had been created out of whole cloth during this time.

Much of the report was concerned with tracing the origins of the crisis. One colleague who had been at WVU when Gee was hired (without a competitive search) was able to retrieve news stories from 2014 about Gee pledging to grow the university to forty thousand students by 2020. Further searches revealed that local landlords had publicly claimed by 2016 that this goal was unattainable, that enrollments were, in fact, declining, and that Gee had responded with inaccurate claims about enrollment and doubled down on his grandiose goal. Public budget reports and Alsop's own slide presentations filled in the rest of this story: WVU had massively expanded its physical plant through debt and public-private partnerships, from which the university could not divest. As physical-plant expansion proceeded throughout Gee's tenure, WVU's enrollment had fallen by 15 to 20 percent. The annual debt service as of 2022 was the size of the entire budget deficit, but the true total was reflected in depreciation and amortization costs, which had skyrocketed. The budget information on WVU's website was supplemented by a faculty member who filed a FOIA request for budget documents back to 2018.

Gee had also become notorious for ignoring shared governance and appointing cronies and political allies to key positions within the university. Contemporary news reports issued by the university showed that Gee had created a series of jobs for Alsop, a lawyer appointed to WVU's Board of Governors. Throughout his career, Alsop had garnered high-level political appointments from West Virginia machine politicians but, as far as we could tell, had no experience in education or institutional finance. Concerning the appointment of Reed, again the Faculty Senate's archive proved invaluable. A colleague who had been in the senate at the time recalled a contentious exchange with Gee shortly after he unilaterally appointed Reed as provost with no competitive search. She is a WVU lifer with no doctorate and no research experience who wouldn't make it through an initial screening in a provost search as typically conducted. We found footage from a senate meeting of Gee's extraordinarily silly and mendacious responses to questions about this appointment and the process that led to it.

Going Public and Lessons Learned

I shared the initial draft with a small group of trusted colleagues from the networks outlined in section 1, most of whom had contributed ideas or research to the effort. We made a few changes, but I neither requested nor received detailed editing advice; again, it was important to get something into the public sphere immediately and writing by committee was not the right approach. I presented the report as coming from a group of concerned WVU faculty. While I did most of the writing and posting myself, I think this presentation accurately reflects that pulling together the facts about the crisis and forming a holistic picture of the situation were a group effort.

To publish the document, I chose to create a WordPress site, because that platform is fast, easy, and free. My colleagues and I started disseminating the link privately through trusted contacts. I also passed it on to an AFT organizer, who was able to share it more openly without worrying about retaliation. While many faculty were initially scared to link the report on social media, once it got outside faculty networks it reached a critical mass where no individual could get in trouble by sharing a link. In its first week, the WVU Facts report was viewed by about fourteen thousand unique visitors. It became a major topic of conversation on social media and Reddit, and circulated widely among faculty, students, and concerned community members. The report eventually came to the attention of reporters in West Virginia and beyond and started to be mentioned in coverage of the unfolding WVU disaster. Over the next several months, a number of excellent and critical articles appeared in the national media, in particular in the *Chronicle of Higher Education*[9] and the *Wall Street Journal.*[10] These stories dug into the financial history of the crisis and the decisions made by Gee's appointees; they had clearly been influenced by the report. Gee, Reed, and Alsop began trying to publicly defend themselves against the charges in the report and the critical media coverage that followed. So, in that sense, we achieved some success. That said, most media outlets didn't treat the report as a trusted source or cover it too extensively because it was anonymous. Having a name and a face to stand behind the report would likely have helped further its uptake.

The report was written in a pseudo-academic style with copious citation links and a methodical, long-format structure. This style resonated with other academics, who ended up disseminating the report widely through their own networks. But it does not seem to have made much of an impact on politicians, the media, or the public outside of the immediate university community. It's possible that there may have been a way to present the facts in a shorter format that would have had more of an impact on groups outside the academy.

In the end, the WVU facts report helped contribute to the massive negative media coverage of WVU in the months around the announcement of academic cuts. But neither the facts nor the negative coverage actually succeeded in stopping or even slowing those cuts: the Board of Governors changed their rules to allow unilateral administrative closure of programs and layoffs of faculty without declaring financial exigency, the administration pushed the cuts through, college Deans remained silent or even spoke in support of these egregious violations of norms and standards, and several hundred faculty were laid off or forcibly retired in May 2024.

And so the one glaring question left is whether we could have done something differently to change the course of the "Morgantown Massacre." I go back and forth on this question, but most days I feel the answer is pretty firmly no. The only way to halt the Gee administration's offensive would have been through organized labor action or widespread public outrage. And no amount of reporting, publicity, or organizing seems likely to have achieved either of those goals. West Virginia is a so-called right to work state, where no public employee can be compelled to join a union, and no public entity such as WVU is compelled to recognize a union. If a large majority of faculty had joined the union and engaged in labor action, it could have disrupted the university's operations and forced the administration to negotiate. But a large proportion of WVU faculty are either scared to associate with a union because they are untenured and can be terminated without cause or are not traditional academics at all and are unconcerned with tenure and shared governance. So, organizing anything more than a tiny minority of faculty there was probably never a realistic goal. In terms of public outrage, West Virginia is a poor, rural, undereducated state with a large majority of low-information voters. Most voters there simply don't care about public universities, except for sports teams. Even if they did care, it would likely do more harm than good: political conditions in the state are more conducive to a right-wing culture war on universities than any kind of support for faculty.

We are left, then, with this somewhat depressing conclusion: the WVU facts report was a reasonably effective way to disseminate information about administrative malfeasance and incompetence to a large audience but was unable to change the conditions on the ground in West Virginia and thus, ineffective as a tool for fighting the destruction of the university's academic mission. There may have been ways to make the report more engaging, to have reached a wider audience, or to have been cited more in media coverage. In the end, however, no amount of factual reporting can make up for a lack of faculty organization and solidarity, or for a public that doesn't support education.

Notes

1. See, e.g., Ryan Quinn, "WVU Professors Get Their Layoff Notices," *Inside Higher Education* October 17, 2023, accessed March 2025 at https://www.insidehighered.com/news/faculty-issues/tenure/2023/10/17/wvu-professors-get-their-layoff-notices.

2. The report can be read at https://wvufacts.wordpress.com/2023/05/24/the-wvu-budget-crisis/.

3. Mike Nolting, "WVU Senior Leadership Responds to Transformation Criticisms Days Ahead of BOG Vote," *WV Metro News*, September 12, 2023.

4. The statement is posted on WVU's faculty senate website as of March 2025: https://facultysenate.wvu.edu/resources/news/admin-feedback.

5. Nick Anderson, "WVU's Plans to Cut Foreign Languages, other Programs Draws Disbelief." *Washington Post*, August 18, 2023, https://www.washingtonpost.com/education/2023/08/18/west-virginia-university-academic-cuts/.

6. Liam Knox, "Slimming Down to Stay Afloat," *Inside Higher Education*, May 3, 2023, https://www.insidehighered.com/news/business/cost-cutting/2023/05/03/slimming-down-stay-afloat.

7. Anemona Hartocollis, "Slashing Its Budget, West Virginia University Asks, What Is Essential?," *New York Times*, September 18, 2023, https://www.nytimes.com/2023/08/18/us/west-virginia-university-budget-cuts-deficit.html.

8. Links are here as of March 2025: https://facultysenate.wvu.edu/minutes-agendas.

9. Dan Bauman, "Why Is West Virginia U. Making Sweeping Cuts?," *Chronicle of Higher Education*, August 11, 2023, https://www.chronicle.com/article/why-is-west-virginia-u-making-sweeping-cuts?

10. Melissa Korn and Kris Maher, "West Virginia University Banked on Growth. It Backfired." *Wall Street Journal*, August 28, 2023, https://www.wsj.com/us-news/education/west-virginia-university-banked-on-growth-it-backfired-16997d61.

4

Let the Record(ing) Show

Documenting the Voices of an Academy in Crisis

Sean Davis Lawrence

I was six months into my dream job when I found out the institutional bedrock beneath my new academic home, the land grant university I had joined bright-eyed out of grad school, was cracked. After ten frantic days of mad-dash writing while locked in my basement office—an annual holiday colloquially called "Spring Break"—I followed the stream of bleary students limping back onto campus from the previous week's hiatus. I had come out of my PhD one of the lucky ones. I had secured the coveted tenure-track job teaching my passion, the history of the environment, politics, and modern Europe. I was proud. I loved my work. I was thankful for kind and collaborative colleagues, and dedicated students. And I was entirely confident that West Virginia University, my university, would continue to do what public universities have done for decades: weather scattered political attacks against higher ed; take in meager-but-sufficient funding from our state legislature; support its faculty in producing high-caliber research across all kinds of disciplines, some esoteric, some monetizable, but all respected; and continue its mission of showing the young people of West Virginia that they will not be left behind and that high education is not just an elite privilege, but their right, and a place where they belong.

I had been on the job for scarcely seven months when I walked past a copy of the student newspaper, *Daily Athenaeum*, on the morning of

March 27, 2023. I blinked a few times and wondered aloud, *is that normal*? "WVU estimates $35 million budget deficit amid low enrollment, inflation" read the headline. Within two weeks, that deficit had been revised 30 percent upward, to $45 million. The university's existing blueprint for what had been euphemistically dubbed "Academic Transformation" accelerated to approach the speed of light. My department's search for a new tenure-track hire was canceled indefinitely. Layoffs were all but certain. Rumors haunted our offices that other departments faced much worse. In conspiratorial huddles in stairwells, outside classrooms, and over strong drinks at the local tavern, every conversation predictably turned to the budget and its portents. Talk started to spin like a tilt-a-whirl around and around the same questions: *What the hell happened? What happens now?*

Plans to eliminate the *entire* language department? Plans to weaken tenure protections? A new budget model designed to make departments compete against one another for a shrinking pot of money? Strip oversight of curriculum development from faculty? They want to cut the library resources *in half*? Surely these rumors couldn't be true. And if they were true, was *this* normal? I agonized. Could I do something? Should I do something? What does "do something," even mean, in this context? Should I resign in protest? Am I overdramatizing things? Don't all organizations face layoffs sometimes? *Is this normal*?

It was, in fact, not normal, though our predicament at WVU has been increasingly normalized across North American academia. Journalists from trade publications such as *Inside Higher Ed* and the *Chronicle of Higher Education* as well as major media outlets—the *New York Times*, the *Wall Street Journal*, the *Atlantic*, PBS, and dozens more—descended on our campus. The cuts animated podcast episodes and #WVUCuts started trending on the platform formerly known as Twitter. In my naivete, I thought all of this just happened organically. I had been a student until just six months prior, with the better part of a decade spent in silent archives rather than on the streets doing attention-grabbing public activism. I thought the national media had learned through the ether, by some ineffable sense of the world that journalists must have and historians do not, that something momentous was happening in our corner of the academic world. Only later did I get my arms around the fact that nothing in media happens except what people make happen; that my own colleagues and my own students had made *this* happen. They had made journalists, podcasters, and their acquaintances across the country aware of the drama at WVU. But at the time, this organizing was invisible to me. Whatever secret knowledge of how these things are done was hidden from me at the time. I felt debilitated and small. I wanted to do something, like those journalists who seemed to be getting the word out--what is a historian's role if not to publicize a record of events?

History in the Making: Uncertainty and the Drive to Document

The more I learned the more I realized how little I knew about the school I was a part of and the ways that narratives form and ossify. Among other things, the strange situation taught me an object lesson in how news media works relative to the plodding efforts of historians. The stories in these publications were well researched and well written, offering "both sides" of what was presented as a national debate about higher ed. Yet the information I was getting from conversations with faculty, staff, students, and administrators seemed so much more insightful, so much more important, so much more holistic than anything that even the best intentioned national journalist parachuting into West Virginia could hope to pick up while on assignment. The story of what really happened on our campus, why it happened, and to whom, would be in danger of disappearing once the national spotlight shifted elsewhere. What hit the pages of newspapers sometimes felt more like dueling propaganda efforts than an accurate and comprehensive record of the event.

I consoled myself that someone at the university was keeping a record of it all for posterity. We have people far more talented, experienced, and proficient than I at the work of real-time documentation. I learned so much contextualizing information about the school's situation, as did many of my colleagues did through the release of the anonymous *WVU Facts* blog. The *Daily Athenaeum* was on the beat in ways that continually floored me. The student journalists who staff it are sure bets for the Pulitzer later in life.

Despondent and straining to find something I had to offer, I mulled what, if anything, I could do. I have never been much given to the work of organizing and public activism, in part because, even as a historian who studies social change and mass movements, I never fully understood where to start, how the day to day of sustaining a movement of resistance actually happens. Still, as a somewhat flailing new member of a community in trouble, the toolkit I have at my disposal was that of a historian, so having not yet made the interpersonal connections that might have led me to become a foot soldier in someone else's mass movement, I landed on the idea of documenting the event as an oral history. I would approach the work of documenting as I do research, not as a tell-all or as a work of advocacy but as a labor of fact finding and of empathy, an opportunity to keep alive the words and experiences of those doing the raw, arduous work of sustaining a public outcry against the cuts at WVU. If nothing else, the end result could exist for posterity--perhaps in the university library somewhere. It would offer a chance for those who lost their jobs to remain, in some small way, a part of the WVU's history and fabric, and it would ensure that those who kept their jobs would not forget what had been lost.

A Primer on Documenting: Approaching Chairs and Deans

After a few conversations with fellow faculty members about my intentions, I approached my chair and explained my goal, although at that point it was still inchoate. At this point, I must note that how you alert your department chair will depend on your relationship with that person and the situation. In my case, I am fortunate to work under an exceptionally approachable and competent chairperson, whose main concern was that my documentary "side project" may distract from the all-important work of producing a book manuscript in pursuit of tenure. By being clear and open about my intentions and my chairperson's concerns, both my department and I were able to avoid uncomfortable questions from quizzical administrators as I went about my work. And the knowledge that my project was out in the open brought a certain confidence that proved vital to the task. Now, I was self-assured in having a camera in my office at all times for people to walk past and notice, in booking department rooms for interviews, and bouncing ideas off my colleagues openly and unapologetically.

I tried to think about the possibility that the record I was creating could be useful not just as evidence in support of a position I already held but also useful in the future to persuade individuals in power with whom I was not, in this particular crisis, ideologically aligned. Maintaining that balance would require that the documentary be as even-handed as possible, including the perspectives not only of students, faculty, and staff—who lost their jobs, opportunities, and, in some cases, their faith in our institution—but also ideally interviews with the people who made these decisions. My task in those interviews was not to convince administrators of the rightness of my own position but to listen, record, and glean understanding of a perspective that sometimes felt foreign to me.

I suggest conducting the work of recording out in the open, in the light of day. Bringing information to light, after all, was the entire purpose of recording in the first place. I made a deliberate choice not to, for example, contact potential interview subjects using an outside email address. I used my university email address and presented myself and my work not as an underground effort, but as a faculty member doing the work of a historian by creating an oral history. At a certain point, I was called into a meeting with our dean of personnel. I do not know whether my open and widely circulated emails asking for interviews from faculty who were being laid off prompted this meeting or whether they were simply checking in with a new hire. In any case, I made a point at that meeting of proactively bringing up the fact that I intended to continue a documentary project recording the process of what was then occurring at our school. To my relief, our dean expressed support for me and the project. Rarely have I been more grateful in an HR meeting.

Finding Subjects

The approach I took to documenting was basically twofold. First, I brought my camera with me as much as possible. This choice ensured that when something happened, it could be recorded on the spot. Of course, more often than not, carrying equipment was not always feasible. Luckily, today most of us wander around with powerful cameras embedded in the cell phones already in our pockets. I scheduled the interviews for about one hour apiece, though they usually went over. I reached out first to faculty I knew personally and concluded each interview by asking who else I should speak to. This approach planted a branching tree that allowed me to reach out to dozens of faculty whom I never would have known were involved in pushing back against the cuts at our university.

There is, of course, the issue of finding subjects who have something to say, knowledge to contribute, a unique perspective, who--and this part is rarer than you might think--are willing to allow that perspective to be recorded and shared publicly. In approaching your subjects, many will be discomfited at the prospect of saying on camera what they say in private. I made mistakes early on by reaching out in ways that were, in hindsight, much too cavalier. My overtures did not fully account for the tenuous employment situation that my colleagues--especially those classified as clinical or teaching faculty--had always faced. Given this precarity, many would-be documentarians try to keep their efforts secret, or at least to draw as little attention to their work as possible. There are clear benefits to this approach. It may inspire some degree of confidence in the subjects that you are seeking out and whose stories you are trying to capture if you approach the act of documenting quietly. It implicitly suggests that your work is an act of resistance, perhaps marking you as an ally, inspiring a degree of solidarity that can draw in the all-important act of establishing mutual trust with your interview subjects.

This knife cuts both ways. By being coy about your efforts to document events at your university, you may inspire distrust among those who are uncertain of your motives. These people will often be those who hold more power than you. Going about your work in secret also runs the risk of creating a situation in which you see yourself as a persecuted individual, regardless of whether your circumstances actually bear that out. I think this danger is real. If your goal in documenting is specifically to provide ammunition for frontline advocates, this goal will always involve highlighting certain perspectives and favoring certain narratives over others. As just as your cause may be, it is ultimately a philosophical decision to what extent you see your work of documenting and recording as an effort of advocacy versus an effort of historical record-keeping. While caricatures of cartoonishly cynical villains lying behind the immediate plight of our departments could be emotionally satisfying, these two-dimensional versions of events were rarely useful in understanding or communicating the actual dynamics that led to the decimation of so much of our university's institutional capacity.

I was surprised--though I should not have been--that so many of the people who multiple colleagues insisted I speak to were not venerable leaders of the faculty but rather fearless undergraduate students. Initially, I had planned on interviewing students but, teacher-brained as I had become, I expected few students to have much insight that couldn't be better gleaned from university employees. After a handful of student interviews, I was utterly disabused of my prejudice. Proportionally, more students than faculty were interested in speaking to me. Indeed, interviews conducted with undergraduates were some of the most enlightening, insightful, and fascinating that I undertook. Accordingly, a second piece of advice is this: Do not forget that students are the core of the institution you are charged with defending. They are an invaluable source of insight.

Structuring Interviews

My approach to the interviews was always the same: I scheduled for one hour and had a set of questions that followed the same pattern. I asked each person to explain who they were and their backgrounds, especially how they ended up at West Virginia University. Then I just asked them to narrate, from their perspective, the process of "Academic Transformation," leaving it to them to decide when that process began and what the major events along the road were. I concluded the interviews with a few questions relating to the future: first, what was next for the person, and then whether they had any advice either for advocates interested in organizing against attacks on academia or advice for any incoming administration at our university on how they could right the ship. This basic structure, because it was the same for each interview and because I did not steer questions specifically toward themes, topics, or events that I had preconceptions about, allowed me to both stay focused and also to get a much more holistic understanding of how events unfolded without foregrounding my own ideological commitments or the prisms through which I was predisposed to view the situation.

A Few Tips for the Uninitiated Videographer

I have no real background in journalism or filmmaking, so any reader with that experience can safely turn the page on this section. What anyone without this kind of background should take heart in is that you don't need to approach the task of documentation exactly as a journalist or professional filmmaker does. Whatever your discipline, you bring to it tools that can be usefully applied to the role of gadfly. For those tools you aren't preequipped with, I've assembled below a few scattered tips that I wish I had known before setting out.

- You may be the fly-on-the wall, but audio will be the fly in the ointment. Whenever possible, when conducting any sort of interview or recording a live moment, try to have at least two different devices recording audio simultaneously. If you have a way of visualizing the gain on your microphones, make sure you are prepared for substantial variance in the volume at which people speak. Blowing out the mic is never good.

- Try to vary the sets, settings, lighting, and composition, of your interviews. I took care not to record two interviews in exactly the same way. If I had no choice but to record an interview in the same room, I tried to find different angles, a different lighting setup, or a different lens or filter, such as a diffusion filter, to try to differentiate subjects from one another.
- As far as composition goes, some very basic things to keep in mind:
    - Keep the eye level of your subjects at approximately the middle of the frame tends to create a sense of empathy for the audience.
    - Positioning your camera at a higher or lower angle can create a sense of power (in the case of a lower angle) or lack thereof (if you place the camera at a higher angle).
    - Do not doubt that yours is a powerful story that may find sympathetic boosters within funding organizations. If your work of recording requires more resources than you have at your disposal, state humanities councils may be interested in your work, and they are a great first-line option if your work of documenting needs the helping hand of external funds.
    - Don't underestimate the power of B-roll. Make use of your equipment to document everyday aspects of your campus. These nonnarrative images are archives unto themselves. After all, it is the quotidian rhythms of your campus that its defenders are fighting for.
    - Finally, never forget that you are not alone. See if anyone else has been making recordings of their own and whether they will share footage with you. And better still, consider seeking out experienced filmmakers at your university or in your community for a more far-ranging collaboration.

Conclusion

In scholarship, as in art—and it seems, in documentary as well—work is never finished, only abandoned. As I write this, almost two years removed from that first dire warning of a budget shortfall, I continue to tinker with the film's edit and even to record interviews with a few individuals whose schedules have yet to align. So far, fifteen subjects have sat for these multi-hour interviews, many more than I expected at the outset. In the meantime, color grading, transitions, captions, repairing bad audio, and the many little flairs that make a thing one's own, all are small and very time consuming and are the stuff that make a filmic project worthwhile. And while there is never enough time found lurking in the corners of the day to make fast progress, the end is in sight for this project. The individual interviews will go to the West Virginia Regional History Center, as will a final, condensed version telling the story of Academic Transformation in the words of those who lived it. With a bit of luck, it may make the rounds at some local film festivals, and no doubt it will appear online. It will not make any money, nor would I want it to, since its content is derived from people who have had something important taken from them.

Nothing I've done since taking my dream job at WVU has left a deeper impression on me than conducting these interviews. As a new hire tossed into a wild circumstance, it is hard to imagine a better crash course in the ways of organizing a movement and in understanding the institutions and community of which I remain a proud part. The interviews I've now spent months watching and rewatching still move me. Some are full of anger, some despair, but there is so much hope in the willingness of these subjects to put much of their daily lives aside for months at a time in order to fight for something worthwhile. In sitting with their stories, I found my own footing, my own place, at a land grant university in the midst of great tension and great change. In documenting the voices of a community in crisis, I came to understand how fragile that community could be, how easily its pillars can be lost, and in grasping that fragility I found myself becoming fully part of it.

The dismantling of education happens in the dark. Documenting attacks on academia creates an archive for others in similar situations to use and plan from. But trying to build such an archive after the fact is too late. From brittle memories, events and details dissipate quickly. Documentation offers posterity a record of events as they unfold and may give defenders of academia and academic departments material evidence to bolster their case. It is also the first step in overcoming the grapevine effect wherein rumors swirl, and trying to nail down a clear set of facts about how, when, why, and whence departments are under threat can feel like pinning Jell-O to a corkboard. Shining a light on the process through which disciplines, departments, and individuals are marked for erasure is one measure that even those who are new, and themselves in the dark, can take in their defense.

5

Rednecks and Loud Voices

Building a Students' Union

Christian Adams and Winston Smith

West Virginia is a land steeped in the blood of class struggle. It's home to the largest labor uprising—and the largest armed uprising, period—in the US since the Civil War. Solidarity and fellowship are no strangers to our community, because as long as we have lived, the bulk of our economy has been driven by unionized business. To us, hell-raising is a natural extension of our identity. For many students, getting involved in the students' union is not just a choice they make for themselves–it is a concerted effort to carry the family torch.

A students' union is a union of students and student organizations fighting to consolidate and strategically direct student power. It is an organization capable of directing informal power and public opinion. Our Student Union was primarily created with these goals in mind:

- function as an auxiliary/support group for the Campus Workers Union;
- end single-issue organizing and unite various activist and advocacy groups under one banner to facilitate collaboration and cooperation; and
- connect and train aspiring organizers bolstering community-campus connections.

At WVU there was great need for a students' union. Organizing and advocacy across campus were dispersed into several small single-issue groups, with faculty and staff unionizing with AFT Academics, in response to mass layoffs and program dissolutions affecting everyone even remotely tied to campus. These cuts followed a budget shortfall, created by a top-heavy administration, poor financial planning, and rapid real estate development, while state funding and the pool of available students shrank. These factors led to the creation of the West Virginia United Students' Union. Without the development of the Union or the guiding hand of professional organizer Carl Shepard, we would have lacked proper support and people to rally behind. In the next few paragraphs we will articulate how to establish a students' union and effectively lead a debranding campaign. What we call "debranding" is uniquely effective at public universities because they have to answer to the public and their representatives.

What Is a Debranding Campaign?

A debranding campaign is a relatively recent development in the history of labor organizing, relying heavily on marketing and public relations skills. The fundamental goal of a debranding campaign is to damage the reputation of a corrupt institution (public or private) by weakening public trust in its leaders and exposing its corruption to a wide audience. Actions in a debranding campaign are intentionally high visibility and can include large-scale protests, interviews with journalists, organizing boycotts, creating infographics and other public-facing, engaging information such as press releases, essays, open letters, and petitions. The West Virginia United Student's Union is by no means the first to utilize a debranding campaign, but it exemplifies an effective one. One recent example is the Starbucks Workers Union's student campaign, seeking to pressure colleges into ditching their Starbucks franchises to punish Starbucks for their antiunion stance.

As part of our debranding campaign, we slowly escalated from emails to administration to open letters informing the public of the situation, collecting information, and developing infrastructure, all leading up to the announcement of our founding. Immediately, we tabled, drafted a petition, and spread flyers to recruit established organizations. From there we led protests at key points in our campaign in collaboration with

Campus Workers, to raise awareness of the issues, bolster our numbers, and connect with the press. At our walkout on August 21, 2023, our highest profile event of the year, journalists from across the state, and national papers such as the *New York Times* and the *Washington Post,* attended. In response, the WVU administration pushed back with their own PR campaign and disingenuous attempts at a dialogue, and ultimately increased our platform, garnering the attention of AP news, prospective politicians, and long-standing representatives of the West Virginia state government.

Organizing Fundamentals

As we saw at WVU, after adequately developing your students' union, your strategy will fundamentally change. While you can foment unrest, in the US it is not effective to rely solely on unrest to win victories. You must survive as the echo of unrest fades; you will need to exert institutional pressure and power, issuing press releases, advising on matters of policy, and ensuring that the people you represent have a seat at the table. The goal should be to hold those in power responsible and to win as many concessions as possible.

There are a few basic, low-speciality steps for organizing a students' union, and they are as follows:

1. Use existing social and activist networks to find a group that wants to build an engine for change.
2. Obtain and consolidate institutional information.
3. Identify key issues to organize around.
4. Recruit: AEIOU.
5. Agitate, Educate, Inoculate, Organize = Union, is a tried and true method.
6. Use your numbers to build your platform and your organizing capacity.
7. Repeat steps 2 through 6.

Cultural and strategic inspiration may be the bedrock of your movement. It will not always be the case that your community has a culture of resistance, but if it does, align yourself with it. It is in your best interest to tap into the hearts and minds of the people around you. The red bandanas we wore around our necks, as well as our red clothing, connected us to the 2018 teacher's strike and to the Redneck Army that fought during the Battle of Blair Mountain in 1921, which was the culmination of the Mine Wars and the largest labor uprising on US soil, which occurred in southern West Virginia. This image association enabled us to effectively connect with families of teachers, coal miners, and progressives across the state. As students, we find ourselves in a unique position; because we come from a diverse set of backgrounds, we are able to capture the attention and sympathy of a wide array of the population. This attention allows us to effectively avoid becoming pigeonholed or written off as youthful troublemakers.

Your students' union should champion not just students but also your community and its history. Developing community buy-in means building relationships with students, student organizations, reporters, and the local community. It can be wide in scope, but the goal is to develop your organization not as a club or a once-in-a lifetime event but to develop the image it has as an institution. To effectively build your image, you need to engage with what inspires people (e.g., their desire for justice).

We immediately started forming relationships with different progressive organizations. We connected with the Mountain Party, locals fighting against gentrification, the Mine War Museum, various unions with a presence in the state, and electoral movements from across the state. Many people from large movements and progressive organizations graduate to positions of community leadership. Therefore, you should make these connections and alliances where possible.

The primary difference between a raving madman and a genius to most people is how well they present themselves and their arguments. This fact goes double for your organization. If your message is not well and clearly communicated to the public, you are likely to be dismissed as political and ideological extremists. Therefore, your job is in part to formulate your ideas so that they are socially acceptable and commonsensical, lest you offend your audience. Beyond the rhetorical element, it is important for your organization to have an identifiable brand that projects power and is not confused easily with other organizations. Opportunistic individuals can and will co-opt what they want, whether they seek to use it for personal gain, to enrich their egos, or to pad their resume. Do not discourage these people from joining up, but do be wary of their ability to interfere. Fascist elements attempted to co-opt our messaging and imagery, people abused their power and role in our institution, and we've seen people with political ambitions embellish their role in our organization to win over respect from potential allies. Power of any kind attracts them like moths, and if left unchecked they will eat away at the fabric of your organization.

Ideally, the leaders of your organization should be on the same page ideologically, and the members should all be moving toward the same goals. Rhetorical consistency from leadership, members, allies, and the public is essential for cementing your narrative. Your union will undoubtedly be a coalition of people of all political persuasions, but this fact shouldn't affect the goal for the organization. Such differences, however, could spark internal debate on why the goal matters. To prevent these debates from splintering your group, ideological consensus among leadership is imperative.

Structuring the Students' Union

Organizing on a college campus around university issues offers unique benefits. First, college communities are close-knit. Most students live in close proximity to one another, interact with one another daily, and for some of the year, have significant amounts of free time when they can party—or, with the proper motivation, organize a students' union. Building a network of like-minded students and community members is much easier in this kind of environment than in others. Reaching out to advocacy groups on campus, and a campus workers union (if one exists on your campus), is a great way to start building a network of organizers. Locally owned off-campus places can serve as locations for meetings and events. Many third places are frequented by community members who don't attend the college but whose support is critical for building ties with the community.

Establishing meeting places is an important aspect of any organizing campaign, and the university setting makes this easy. There are three factors that make a good meeting place. First is accessibility–it should be easy for all the attendees to get to. Second is privacy–it should be free from distractions and prying eyes, especially if sensitive topics are being discussed. Third is utility–it should have everything you need to run the meeting efficiently. Places to sit, things to write on, and projectors are good for a standard informational meeting, but your specific goal may require different amenities. Empty classrooms and study rooms are ideal for meetings. If you have connections to local off-campus places, they may be willing to let you host meetings there. For working on more creative things, such as creating signs or banners, large green spaces have lots of flat space to lay down sheets or cardboard, which allows for safer spray-painting.

Spreading the word is essential if you want your campaign to gain traction. College campuses can make this work efficient. Spots with heavy foot traffic are well known to students, and the class schedule is predictable and reliable. University-provided printing is usually cheap, so flyers and posters can be created in bulk at little expense. Creating social media accounts for your campaign is easy, free, and a great way to spread information. News outlets can also spread the word for you. Your school paper will likely be glad to publish an interview with your organization, and if you make a big enough splash, local, state, and national news outlets may take notice. Establishing a conduit for official press releases will make it easier for more news outlets to publish your message.

All the benefits of college organizing are meaningless if you can't attract people to your movement. Building membership is crucial for forming and growing your organization. Involvement does not have to be formal or defined, but membership should be. For our organization, we created a membership application where a person could input their email and phone number, along with other information related to our specific students' union. We could manually approve members and add their information to a large spreadsheet. Being a formal member of our organization meant that you were on the spreadsheet. Of course, in reality, being a member is more than having your name on a list, as the level of involvement can vary dramatically from person to person. It is useful to divide members into distinct categories by their level of involvement with the organization.

Formal leaders are both the mouthpieces of your organization and, of course, the leaders. These are the people who head meetings, give speeches, and do interviews. Your organization is going to need a consistent narrative, and the leaders should be familiar with its intricacies. Making connections with organizers, news outlets, activists, and community members is their responsibility. Leaders ought to have defined roles, such as president, secretary, or treasurer. Lots of people will be involved with your organization, so you will have to keep tight control over who speaks for the students' union in an official capacity. The power to speak for the organization should be generally reserved for the leaders and extended only to others who are particularly familiar with the issues you are organizing around. Rank-and-file members are who really make the organization run, however. They staff events, print and hang flyers, spread the word, and engage in protests. In short, when the organization is doing something, they show up. It is important to keep in mind that being a leader does not put one above being a rank-and-file member; a leader ought to do anything a rank-and-file member is doing.

Beyond the official members of your union, the last two categories could more accurately be described as "allies" rather than "members." Allies are the people who agree with your organization and show support in small ways but are not directly involved. In contrast, attendees are the familiar faces you see at events and who interact with the organization online but who don't show up at meetings or discussions. This set is your most direct base of support, and getting feedback from the attendees is crucial to ensuring your campaign can adapt as the situation at your university is changing. "Slacktivists" are the people who share your organization's posts and articles about your organization online but don't attend events or engage politically offline. Despite the much lower level of involvement from these categories, they are still important to your organization. There won't be enough leaders and rank-and-file members to fill an administrators' meeting or a college green space. While slacktivism has a generally negative connotation, it spreads your message to people who wouldn't have otherwise heard it, and shows that your message has real traction and real community support.

Once you've built an audience, structuring your organization well is critical for ensuring efficient and effective organizing. The key is to find a balance between the benefits of a horizontal structure that allows anyone to get involved and to have a say, while still maintaining some formal leadership to keep the organization on track. The extremes of the balance could be called "under-structured" and "over-structured" respectively, and both will result in more stress, more burnout, and fewer results.

In an understructured organization, leadership is weak, and there may be few defined positions. Communication and actions become difficult to plan and are disorganized and/or ineffective. Workloads are dumped on only a few people, while others wait for something to do. In contrast, overstructurization delays work either bureaucratically, by making everyone follow arbitrary processes that add time and effort, or dictatorially, by forcing every decision through a single person or group. Additionally, people also have to learn the arbitrary rules, which is another barrier to entry. Some bureaucracy can be necessary for making big decisions for your organization, like spending your organization's money—but taking it too far is burdensome.

Taking Action

Once you've formed your students' union and have a few trusted members, it's time for action. There are many kinds of demonstrations or activities to choose from, but there are a few aspects all of them share. One is recruitment and fundraising: every demonstration is an opportunity to gain members and donations. This aspect doesn't have to be complicated: just passing around a link or QR code to a sign-up sheet or mobile payment app will suffice, as long as the link is properly explained. Another aspect is common colors. Picking a color for students to wear adds to the psychological effect of the demonstration, creating a greater sense of unity for the participant, and making your movement look stronger to the opposition. Finally, it never hurts to bring snacks.

After you're done planning, advertising your events is crucial to their success. Posts on your union's social media and in online community groups are an obvious start. Placing flyers on campus, preferably about a week in advance (or if you're trying to make it a surprise, only a day or two in advance), will get a lot more attendees than online posts. The key to an effective flyer is clarity and brevity. Our flyers were designed as such: WALKOUT in big red letters is so obvious people will read it without even realizing they're doing it. Underneath the title should be a short description of your cause with the date, time, and location in easy-to-read, bold text. Your union's social media accounts and a QR code to a sign-up sheet should be included.

When you're holding events, you need to raise funds to keep the movement going. Fundraising events at local third places is a fun way to get donations and increase the union's morale. Dinners, concerts, and karaoke or game nights, are just a few examples of simple activities that can be easy to set up in a sympathetic third place. Coffee shops, local venues, and a church were particularly sympathetic with our movement and helped a great deal with hosting events for us.

More than likely, your school administration will try to appear fair and democratic about their unfair and undemocratic practices. Any public town halls, open forums, or similar events they hold are opportunities for you to show up and build pressure. Getting as many of your members (wearing matching colors, of course) into the room to ask the tough questions and reinforce your narrative is the goal. These events will usually have reporters there, so memorable quotes made by your union's members with media training will have the opportunity to give more publicity to your union, keeping administration in the hot seat even if there are no upcoming public union events.

Our students' union's first demonstration was a large walkout. Outdoor rallies are highly visible, are a great opportunity to get your message out from the source, and are a great recruitment tool for your union. A walkout has the added bonus of being directly disruptive to the school's functioning for at least the duration of the event. High-traffic areas of campus are optimal spots to hold a rally. These spots are well known and easy to reach, so students don't have to go far out of their way to join in, and chances are, students who didn't know it was happening may join in while passing by. If there are multiple high-traffic areas to choose from, picking the one closest to the administrative offices is better. If the energy in the crowd is right, marching in front of the administrative offices will boost the morale of the ralliers and have the opposite effect on the administration. If there is an important public administrative vote or meeting, then that is often a great place for a rally. If it is a public meeting, maybe have a quiet, respectful rally; if it is a final vote, more volume may be warranted. If you are successful, ensure that your legacy of resistance is not forgotten.

Fighting for a better world isn't all about fighting, it's also about laying the foundation for future movements. Social change is iterative, so it is imperative to connect with historians, and journalists. Enshrine your mark on the walls of history, no matter how small, to someone; it will be a bastion of light in ceaseless night. As you connect with others, and as your movement grows, it, too, will become mythologized and embedded within the culture of your surroundings.

6

It Starts with a Visa

Supporting International Students

Emil Asanov

Context

Several essays in this volume focus on the recent crisis of "academic transformation" and program closures at West Virginia University (WVU), highlighting the experience of faculty, undergraduate students, and others during that time of upheaval and loss. One perspective that is missing from this list of contributors is that of international students, specifically, international graduate students. This chapter delves into the specific needs and challenges of international students through an individual case study: mine. International graduate students' experiences are of scholarly interest, but often ignored by much of the university community not directly engaged with international students. By including a personal story, I would like not only to add to the existing literature but also share my experience and offer tools that helped me navigate the challenges of applying for a visa and transferring schools, to offer insight to those in higher education who work with international students during this period of geopolitical crises and campus tensions.

I am an international graduate student pursuing a PhD degree in the US. I had to change institutions due to losing graduate funding. I first arrived in the US as an undergraduate exchange student on a J-1 visa to attend WVU during the 2018–2019 school year. I returned to the US in summer 2021 to complete an MA in Teaching English to Speakers of Other Languages (TESOL) at WVU. Having earned a master's degree, I stayed at WVU to do a PhD in Educational Theory and Practice in Fall 2022. However, I fell victim to WVU's devastating budget cuts[1], losing my graduate funding. I subsequently transferred to Florida State University (FSU), along with my PhD advisor, to once again have stable, consistent funding, for which I am eternally grateful to the FSU community and my advisor Dr. Amy S. Thompson. Despite the help and support I received, the experience was still devastating because I was in the process of earning a PhD degree from WVU, a school I fondly think of as "home" because it is where it all started for me in the US and because it is in West Virgina, my home in the US. However, the experience of being an international PhD transfer student grants me a unique perspective on graduate education and funding matters in the US.

Second, I am an international student from Russia. Whether undergraduate or graduate, international students and their experiences are always at least partially affected by geopolitical tensions. It is no secret that the current relationship between the US and Russia is poor. That status has already led to certain consequences for Russian students choosing to study in the US and American students wanting to study in Russia. A case in point is that to this day the US Embassy in Moscow does not accept applications for non-immigrant visas such as student visas. By the same token, a lot of study abroad programs that major U.S. universities have administered in Russia are now elsewhere in the Russian-speaking world.

There are 6.4 million international students across the world[2]. Per UNESCO'S definition, international students are "individuals who have physically crossed an international border between two countries with the objective to participate in educational activities in the country of destination, where the country of destination of a given student is different from their country of origin."[3] The United States hosts the most international students out of all countries in the world.[4] More specifically, as of 2023 there were a little over 1.5 million international students studying in the US.[5] Given that international students make up almost 5 percent of the total student population in post-secondary institutions across the US[6], it is no surprise that their experiences and their position in the education system have received significant attention in the scholarly community, as evidenced by published literature in journals such as *Journal of International Students* or *International Journal of Student Voice*.[7] Interestingly, the current research has primarily focused on the experiences of undergraduate students, all but ignoring graduate students.[8] That omission is surprising because, according to the 2023 IIE Open Door report, of the 1.5. million international students, 385, 097 were pursuing graduate degrees.[9] Furthermore, as Shyam Sharma observed, international students enrolled in US graduate programs "are viewed as 'top talent,' and they often feature in political debates and national policy discussions (such as in the many Congressional hearings in the past decade) as a valued asset."[10]

Often, these "valued assets" are left to fend for themselves. Although domestic and international students, undergraduate and graduate alike can experience "loneliness, homesickness, financial issues, stress, [threats to] socioemotional well-being, and loss of identity,"[11] it is nevertheless important to distinguish between their experiences. For example, Sharma notes that international graduate students are often assumed to be mature and independent[12] and thus find themselves *in media res*: "International students first encountering the US academe as graduate students don't have to take foundational courses, aren't exposed to the campus community as part of 'college experience, and aren't reached out for organized initiatives by various support units across campus."[13] Another example of this dichotomy is that international students often must develop at least minimal research skills. Because research and research publication standards vary from country to country, international graduate students in the US must familiarize themselves with—among other things—U.S. research standards such as IRB protocols, citation styles, and the specifics of writing research papers to succeed in their programs and afterward. Often, university libraries can serve as a forum where students can acquire research-specific skills that they are not exposed to in their classes. In fact, many universities already offer graduate-level workshops for students, both domestic and international. However, for international students to feel more comfortable using library resources, the libraries should implement programming that helps students adjust to university library systems, build relationships with library staff members and other library users, and learn about resources available to them because "when international students are aware of resources, they will often use and value them."[14]

Since international graduate students are under researched, it is important to share their experiences with faculty and staff not only to offer help to the international graduate students but also to understand why they need support. After all, "as faculty members, academic advisors, and student affairs professionals are on the front lines of creating, operating, and evaluating direct support for international graduate students, they hold significant support in contributing direct support for international graduate students."[15] I acknowledge that many international graduate students come to the US to study in graduate school of their own volition. However, that fact does not mean that they should not receive support or help from faculty, staff, and peers to succeed at their new home institutions. The presence of international graduate students on US campuses "not only broadens the educational experiences for domestic students but also strengthens the institution's global connections and reputation." Lastly, international graduate students can significantly contribute to the image of the US as a country leading in the number of international graduate students: According to the National Association of Foreign Student Advisors (NAFSA), attracting and supporting international students enrolled in graduate schools across the US shows that "the nation is committed to attracting talented individuals to study, conduct research, and teach at our institutions of higher education."[16] Lastly, international students significantly contribute to the US economy because "they bring huge financial benefits through the payment of international tuition and fees to their host institutions, as well as housing and other cost of living also paid to the institutions and local communities . . ."[17] For example, in 2023 international students contributed $40 billion to the US economy.[18]

Zhang and Morgan wrote that international graduate students should share their first-person accounts of different experiences, or else "it will be impossible to authentically recognize the challenges and subsequently address these areas."[19] I would thus like to use my own voice to contribute to the growing literature on international graduate students. Much of the literature, though it offers personal accounts, is primarily descriptive and rarely gives international students or their advisors alike any concrete suggestions on what the students should do in various situations. I have received immense support from the faculty and staff I have worked closely with. I realize, though, that my colleagues and I may have had all this support because we have been in multilingual, multicultural, and multinational units. Furthermore, I also realize that some of those people still may not understand all the nuances of being an international student because they are not one. Therefore, I offer my experiences as a case study for helping to understand how best to support students such as myself.

The Problem

The start of the process of becoming a US student requires a lot of paperwork. This account is not meant to serve as any legal or visa application advice because visa application rules change. I, however, hope it communicates how much work it is to apply for a visa. There are quite a few documents that you should have to apply for a visa: For example, some of the documents I had to present were an I-20 form, a form that confirms your university enrollment; form DS-160; and a receipt that shows you have paid your I-901 SEVIS fee, which is for a special record number assigned to you as a student. I had to apply for an F-1 visa. At first, my first visa application was delayed by the COVID-19 pandemic that caused many US Embassies and Consulates to shut down all over the world, including in Russia. Consequently, I started my MA program online, taking six credits in Fall 2020. I could not, however, start my graduate assistantship because it required me to be physically present in the United States. I was convinced that this online set-up would only last one semester, especially since some of my international classmates who also had to take classes online in Fall 2020 for the same reason started sharing that US Embassies and Consulates in their countries were gradually resuming their operations. That was, however, not the case with the US Embassy in Moscow. I ended up taking my second semester online. Then the situation was further exacerbated by worsening geopolitics and the US Embassy in Moscow decided not to accept applications for non-immigrant US visas such as student visas. Not being able to apply for a visa in my country of residence, I decided to make an appointment in Kazakhstan because at the time I could schedule a visa appointment in any third country. Most Russian citizens who were in line to receive student visas went to Kazakhstan at the time, including a colleague from WVU. I decided to get my visa in Kazakhstan, as well.

I had to wait 2.5 months just to be able to find an available date at the US Consulate in Almaty, Kazakhstan, in October 2021. That was not an option for me because I had to be in the United States in August to begin my third semester and to finally start my graduate assistantship. So, I had to come up with an alternative plan to accelerate the process.

My Solution

Having studied the visa application website, I realized that I could apply for an expedited appointment. Although I had tried applying for one in Moscow the year before, I did not have a scheduled appointment then. In Kazakhstan, I did, so requesting an expedited appointment was naturally the next step to take. You can request an expedited appointment when you must urgently travel to the US, which was true for me. To make my request more persuasive, I solicited letters of support from my department chair, graduate program director, and coordinator (see fig 1.). As a result, I was granted an expedited appointment, which allowed me to reschedule my appointment for a much earlier date. I am convinced to this day that if I had not received those letters of support, I would have stood no chance of receiving that appointment, especially as a nonresident applicant.

> I hope that you and yours are doing well.
>
> I am writing to you because ----- and I are desperate to ask a really huge favor of you. At the moment, no one can schedule a regular visa appointment at the Embassy in Moscow, and we are afraid that the situation will be the same all through the summer. However, we are looking at alternate ways to get our visas. For one thing, we are both thinking of applying for an emergency appointment that you can, however, apply for no earlier than 60 days before the start of the program, which would be June 19 in our case. It is an option, but last year I applied for one and the Embassy declined my request. For another, it is currently possible for Russian citizens to apply for US visas in Kazakhstan, and we are each planning a trip to Nur-Sultan to apply for a visa as long as there are slots available for non-residents.
>
> Either way, we were wondering if we could request a special letter from WVU explaining why it is so important that we come to the United States for Fall 2021. Given that the University is moving most of the classes in-person next semester (we read it in one of our recent university newsletters) and that you need TAs to teach Russian, we think that having a letter like that would be very helpful. It would be especially helpful when we apply for emergency appointments because embassy people require applicants to submit papers that prove that they have an emergency and so definitely need a visa.
>
> We are asking for this because it is now very hard to get any type of nonimmigrant visa. For that reason, we would really appreciate it if you could issue us a letter.
>
> Thank you, and please stay safe and well!
>
> All the best,
>
> Emil

My Take-Away

I share my experience in hopes that faculty and staff will remember it, especially when they are expecting a new graduate student coming from overseas who is struggling to get a US visa.

Faculty and staff can play a great role in helping international graduate students secure their visa appointments. For that reason, I would encourage faculty and staff to have templates for special letters that they can share with their incoming international graduate students to help them apply for an expedited appointment if need be. International students, on the other hand, can have a template for an email that they may send to university representatives, staff, and faculty should they need letters of support for visa purposes.

Conclusion

While I shared a story that may seem somewhat complicated, I primarily wanted to demonstrate that faculty, staff, and international graduate students should establish a rapport from the very beginning for faculty and staff to be able to provide support to graduate students, and for graduate students to be able to request and receive that support. Despite their presumed maturity and independence,[20] international graduate students greatly benefit from having a trusting, supportive relationship with the people around them, especially since they make such a significant contribution not only to the culture of US colleges, but also to the entire US society. By accommodating international students' needs, US universities ultimately accommodate theirs and those of the US and the global community.

Notes

1. "Student, faculty walk out in response to proposed program cuts." The DA. Last modified August 27, 2023. https://www.thedaonline.com/news/wvucuts/students-faculty-walk-out-in-response-to-proposed-program-cuts/article_3fdf1c16-4079-11ee-9311-ff329d00006d.html.

2. "International students," Migration Data Portal, accessed August 1, 2024, https://www.migrationdataportal.org/themes/international-students#definition.

3. "Internationally mobile students," UNESCO Institute for Statistics, accessed August 1, 2024, https://uis.unesco.org/en/glossary-term/internationally-mobile-students.

4. Migration Data Portal, "International students."

5. "International students," IIE Open Doors, accessed August 1, 2024, https://opendoorsdata.org/annual-release/international-students/.

6. Ibid.

7. Shyam Sharma, "Focusing on international graduate students," *Journal of International Students* 9, no. 3 (2019): 302, https://doi.org/10.32674/jis.v9i3.1276.

8. Mary Ann Bodine Al-Sharif, Mary Ann, Katie Koo, and Krishna Bista. "International Graduate Students: Unique Stories and Missing Voices in Higher Education," *New Directions for Teaching and Learning*, Early View (July, 2024): 2. https://doi.org/10.1002/tl.20616.

9. "International students," IIE Open Doors, accessed August 1, 2024, https://opendoorsdata.org/annual-release/international-students/.

10. Sharma, 302.

11. Al-Sharif, Koo, and Bista, 2.

12. Sharma, 302.

13. Sharma, 302.

14. Amanda B. Click, "International graduate students in the United States: Research processes and challenges," *Library Information & Science Research* 40, no. 2 (April 2018): 161, https://doi.org/10.1016/j.lisr.2018.05.004.

15. Koo, Katie, Krishna Bista, and Mary Ann Bodine Al-Sharif, ""From surviving to thriving" next steps for international graduate students: A call to action," *New Directions for Teaching and Learning*, Early View (August, 2024): 1, https://doi.org/10.1002/tl.20623.

16. The United States needs a coordinated national strategy for international education," NAFSA Association of International Education, accessed July 20, 2024. https://www.nafsa.org/issue-brief-united-states-needs-coordinated-national-strategy-international-education.

17. Kriti Gopal. "Hearing the voice of a graduate Indian international student in the United States: Why my voice matters," *New Directions for Teaching and Learning*, Early View (July, 2024): 6. doi: 10.1002/tl.20619.

18. "New NAFSA data reveal international student economic contributions continue to rebuild." NAFSA. Accessed July 25, 2024. https://www.nafsa.org/about/about-nafsa/new-nafsa-data-reveal-international-student-economic-contributions-continue#:~:text=Washington%2C%20November%2013%2C%202023%20%E2%80%93,by%20nearly%20%246.3%20billion%20(almost.

19. Bo Zhang, and K. Kayon Morgan. "Strangers in the North: Critical narratives on the postgraduation career transitions of international doctoral students," *New Directions for Teaching and Learning*, Early View (August 2024): 9. doi: 10.1002/tl.20622.

20. Sharma, 302.

Bibliography

Bodine Al-Sharif, Mary Ann, Katie Koo, and Krishna Bista. "International Graduate Students: Unique Stories and Missing Voices in Higher Education." *New Directions for Teaching and Learning*, Early View (July 2024): 1–9. https://doi.org/10.1002/tl.20616.

Click, Amanda B. "International graduate students in the United States: Research processes and challenges." *Library Information & Science Research*, *40*, no. 2 (April 2018): 153–162. https://doi.org/10.1016/j.lisr.2018.05.004.

Gopal, K. "Hearing the voice of a graduate Indian international student in the United States: Why my voice matters." *New Directions for Teaching and Learning*, Early View (July 2024): 1–10. doi: 10.1002/tl.20619.

IIE Open Doors. "International students." Accessed August 1, 2024, https://opendoorsdata.org/annual-release/international-students/.

Koo, Katie, Krishna Bista, and Mary Ann Bodine Al-Sharif. "'From Surviving to Thriving' next Steps for International Graduate Students: A Call to Action." *New Directions for Teaching and Learning*, (August 2024): 1–9. https://doi.org/10.1002/tl.20623.

Migration Data Portal. "International students." Accessed August 1, 2024. https://www.migrationdataportal.org/themes/international-students#definition.

NAFSA Association of International Education. "The United States needs a coordinated national strategy for international education." Accessed July 20, 2024. https://www.nafsa.org/issue-brief-united-states-needs-coordinated-national-strategy-international-education.

NAFSA. "New NAFSA data reveal international student economic contributions continue to rebuild." Accessed July 25, 2024. https://www.nafsa.org/about/about-nafsa/new-nafsa-data-reveal-international-student-economic-contributions-continue#:~:text=Washington%2C%20November%2013%2C%202023%20%E2%80%93,by%20nearly%20%246.3%20billion%2(almost.

Sharma, Shyam. 2024. "Focusing on International Graduate Students". *Journal of International Students* 9, no. 3 (August 2, 2019). https://doi.org/10.32674/jis.v9i3.1276.

The DA. "Student, faculty walk out in response to proposed program cuts." Last modified August 27, 2023. https://www.thedaonline.com/news/wvucuts/students-faculty-walk-out-in-response-to-proposed-program-cuts/article_3fdf1c16-4079-11ee-9311-ff329d00006d.html.

UNESCO Institute for Statistics. "Internationally mobile students." Accessed August 1, 2024. https://uis.unesco.org/en/glossary-term/internationally-mobile-students.

Zhang, B., and K. Kayon Morgan. "Strangers in the North: Critical narratives on the postgraduation career transitions of international doctoral students." *New Directions for Teaching and Learning*, Early View (August 2024): 1–10. doi: 10.1002/tl.20622.

7

If You Answer, They Will Call

Standing in the Media Spotlight

Lisa M. Di Bartolomeo

Usually, if faculty talk to reporters, it's because the reporters need our expertise for a story they're doing, or else something very, very bad has happened on our campus. If it's the former, we know what to say and how to say it; after all, that's a big part of what we do for a living. But if we're thrust into the media spotlight because of a campus crisis, many of us behave like the proverbial deer in the headlights. This essay draws on my recent adventures in media navigation to offer practical tips not only for your success but also for your own peace of mind.

In May 2023, my home unit, the Department of World Languages, Literatures, and Linguistics (WLLL) at West Virginia University (WVU), underwent extreme vetting as part of so-called Academic Transformation. My colleagues and I were told to offer a plan to trim the department and revise our programs to save them, and we collectively did that in good faith. Over the summer, as some of us built the case for our survival, others built public awareness to draw on extramural support to defend our department's very existence. Our solicitations drew thousands of responses, including emails from alumni, letters of support from most of our national professional organizations (including the Modern Languages Association, one of the biggest such groups in the country), and input from current students. We dutifully compiled these expressions of support and included them in our final "appeal" for clemency. That appeal was denied, and we have it on good authority that none of the letters in our report was even read—in fact, we were informed that including those letters was superfluous. Likewise, the hundreds of emails, letters, and phone calls that the president, provost, and board members received were unpersuasive. At the time, none of us even suspected how drastic the results would be—with the provost eventually recommending the complete dissolution of the department to the WVU Board of Governors. It was a bait-and-switch, matching our good faith effort with their bad-faith, predetermined outcome.[1]

Because the decision to terminate WLLL was so inconceivable (what state flagship land-grant R1 university eliminates its language and culture programs?), we received a great deal of media attention. At first that attention was mainly local. A colleague whose first language is not English asked me to substitute for her on a local radio show to discuss the proposed cuts; that was the initial connection with the media for me, though many other colleagues also were called on for media interviews.

Early on, when most of us thought there was a chance to save our programs, we focused on rebutting some of the factual inaccuracies in the consultants' and Provost's Office's initial report. For instance, they claimed that we cost the university money, when, in fact, we posted annual earnings of over $800,000 for WVU (numbers taken from the university's own filings). But it quickly became clear that fighting each factual inaccuracy wasn't going to be enough, not when the president held the biggest megaphone and was using it to defend his draconian cuts. We knew we needed to stretch beyond our local media markets to call out the lies and distortions. We needed to build our case broadly and persuasively.

I wish I could say that a few of us gathered together and planned out a media campaign, the way a political candidate might work with a team to develop their communication strategy. But our efforts were siloed and haphazard, and often each of us focused on our own programs rather than the threat facing our university as a whole. However, we quickly realized that it served none of us to advocate separately, and many of us quickly shifted from focusing on our home departments to folding in colleagues in other units whose jobs were also on the line. Many of us made a point to reference several of the threatened programs each time we talked with the press; for one, being more inclusive makes for a bigger story, with more people affected by the threatened cuts, and for another, it demonstrates that we were all concerned about the institution, in addition to our concerns over our own potential loss.

Over the next several months, from that fateful August 10, 2023, when my department learned we were recommended for elimination, through the dramatic protests and public comments at Board of Governors' meetings and elsewhere, to the final decisions on the cuts, to my department's last events, I worked to keep the spotlight on what was being lost to mismanagement and to a misguided idea of what the "future" of the land-grant university should be. Sometimes discussion with reporters centered on me cleaning out my office, sometimes on the final graduation of world languages' majors, but the continued coverage helped to keep our loss fresh in people's minds. On some level that continued coverage was helpful—just knowing that people still cared meant a lot to all of us who were losing our jobs and our programs; but on another level, it may have kept the wound open, preventing us from healing and moving on. I don't pretend to know the healthiest way to handle that part—the moving on—but if what I outline below can help you and your colleagues approach a looming disaster with more strategy and foresight than we had at WVU, I'd consider that a small victory.

The following is a far from comprehensive list of some practices and strategies that helped me, or else actions I wish I'd taken or hadn't taken. Each of these lessons was hard learned, and I'd rather save others the painful learning process if I can. Consider these "dos" and "don'ts" as a starting point for a discussion with your colleagues.

1. Don't burn any bridges. I put this rule first because it was the hardest one for me. I had to constantly remind myself not to paint my face blue, yell, and attack like William Wallace, because I felt so righteously angry and deeply wounded. When your campus is in crisis, it's critical to center your concern for the students and for the institution and avoid any personal or ad hominem attacks. Even if you're convinced that a specific person has put your campus in crisis, strive to decenter that person; instead, refer to "leadership decisions," focus on misguided interpretations, cite incorrect datasets. I realize that using such passive and vague constructions not only goes against precepts of good writing but also against the fire in your belly over the injustices you're suffering. But staying above the fray protects the needs of students and the institution. You may say things now, in the depth of your despair and the heat of the moment, that you'll regret later. Protect yourself before you wreck yourself.

2. Do be yourself. If you're angry, you can share your anger, but without bitterness or rancor. If you're sad and get choked up as you're talking to a reporter, that's fine. We're all human beings, and facing a campus crisis is often existential, threatening our careers, not to mention our healthcare and income. Showing your feelings shows the human costs of your campus leadership's decisions and missteps; we are all part of the fallout, and our emotional expressions also make for a compelling story. But also remember the next step.

3. Do center students, not yourself. For the broader audience, the student experience of the crisis is the most interesting and critical; your emotional state or worry about your personal future isn't. If you focus on you, you risk convincing your audience that you're only interested in helping yourself. You need to demonstrate that your central focus is on what the students will lose, what the community will lose, what your state or region will lose. You won't win people over by whining about how hard it will be to publish with an increased teaching load. You must pitch your appeal broadly, and make it about what students will lose as a result of a particular set of cuts; what the institution will suffer in terms of reputation and recruiting talented faculty, staff, and students; and what your community will lose in terms of vibrant citizens, local engagement, and practical concerns such as real estate, income taxes, and decreased demand for goods and services. Remember that when the public consumes your discussions with reporters and they hear the word "students," they think of their children, their grandchildren, nieces, nephews, and neighbors. The less you center yourself in the narrative, the more likely you are to appeal to your audience. At WVU and other land-grant institutions, the students we serve often come from backgrounds and experiences lacking in international focus or learning, so when my colleagues from WLLL spoke to the media about "academic decimation" as we came to call it, we worked to center our students, current and future, and what they were losing in terms of access to the world through language and culture education. If we had rent our garments and wept about our own travails, we certainly would have been correct; however, we would also have appeared as self-centered crybabies rather than as educators genuinely distraught over what generations of students in West Virginia and beyond were losing as WVU axed WLLL.

4. Do appeal to alumni and your community. Most of us don't keep a database of our alumni or how to contact them, and that's one vital action each of us can take, regardless of the health of our institution, just in case. Having that information available will ensure a rapid response when you need one, rather than a last-minute flailing in a moment of calamity. Failing that kind of record-keeping, reach out via social media; many of us stay in touch with former students via social media, or we can attract their attention with a post. Once you have a cause to rally them behind, set them loose—on a letter-writing campaign focused on influencing your institution's leadership, on public rallies and protests, on community-based events such as benefit concerts and vigils, etc. At WVU, my colleagues across the institution and I worked to attract notice, and often one of our posts went viral enough that even national reporters noticed and contacted us. Maybe because WVU was an extreme example of cuts to academic programs, we looked novel, and because we are such an economic engine for our state, the effects were clearly dire for the broader public of West Virginia. Reaching out to our community accompanied the push to bring in alumni, and social media also helped reach our friends, neighbors, and concerned community members. Everyone in Morgantown quickly understood that losing over three hundred faculty and staff members—plus their families and partners—would be a huge blow to the town. When we organized a rally concert to raise awareness, we had no trouble getting an iconic local venue to offer its space, or local bands to offer their talents, to bring attention to what was facing WVU.[2] Town and gown relations differ from place to place, but WVU and Morgantown are inextricably intertwined, and attentive local folks knew what the cuts would mean to real estate prices, the local census count and schools, patronage of local businesses, and more. The clearer you can be about the local fallout of a campus crisis, the more allies you can activate.

5. Don't use academic jargon or rely on your audience to be familiar with academia. No one wants to hear about the fine distinctions of your research, and no one wants to hear from someone who seems to be condescending to mere mortals. Speak to the media not like an academic but like a normal person; avoid highfalutin phrases and GRE vocabulary words. Your goal is to communicate with and convince the ordinary and attuned public, and you can't do that if they don't understand what you're saying. I'm not advocating that you pander, but do your best to communicate clearly. Ideally, your go-to media person will already be able to "code switch" in this way without sounding artificial.

6. Do prepare. Think about what you might be asked ahead of time, do some research into other examples you can offer, and think about your strategy for dealing with the interviewer. This kind of preparation is your bread and butter, after all—you know how to back up your assertions with facts and bring receipts. Make your training work for you here. If another institution has faced a similar crisis and reacted differently than your campus did, bring that model into the conversation. Offering counterexamples and other solutions is an important way to fight the prevailing narrative promulgated by your campus leadership. It's too easy for them to sound authoritative—after all, they have the most impressive titles and the swankiest offices in the nicest, most historic buildings on your campus. And they're paid a lot of money to manage the place. Everything you can do to undermine that authority, to challenge their numbers, to offer alternative solutions not only shows that you're reasonable and open to cooperation to solve the problems but also that the company line is flawed. In financial crises, bring numbers on how much administrators are paid or on how their ranks have swelled in recent years while students keep getting gouged with rising tuition, and faculty and staff face stagnant wages and benefits. In ideological crises, point to your leaders' mistakes alongside the ways other leaders elsewhere made different, more successful choices. It always pays to offer a counterpoint solution because central administrators will push the necessity of their proposed cuts and claim that these cuts are happening everywhere in academe when they are not.

7. Don't hog the spotlight. Consider your allies, and whom to hand the mic to, whether that's students, alumni, faculty or staff colleagues, or community members. Even if you're the one the reporters keep calling, you need to bring in other voices. Those other voices should help make your point, and you should think about who they are, what unit or constituency they represent, and how effectively they communicate. You may have a colleague who knows the institution's budget inside and out but who has trouble articulating that in an interview; consider connecting that person with print media reporters so that their strengths shine. You may know of a student who has a particularly poignant story, but be sensitive to that student and check with them before you unleash the media on them. Yours should not be the only voice, but you and your colleagues will want to consider carefully who best represents your concerns and who is most agile in discussing them.

8. Do stick to your message. It helps to have on hand, or in your head, a set of talking points or key issues that you always want to hit. Message discipline can help prevent your campus's key concerns from getting lost in the noise. However, in addition to hammering those points home every time, mix things up with the reporter so that you're not simply recycling the same old lines, and so that the reporter's preconceived ideas about the cuts are challenged; this approach will provide the public with fresh information. Find a new angle on the story; for instance, when we discussed the RIFs at WVU, one variation on the story of the people being fired was the way WVU chose to RIF one partner in a couple while retaining the other partner—and they did so to numerous couples. In the same unit, a husband was RIFd but a wife was not, and this appalling narrative was one we could point to not only to demonstrate the cruelty inherent in the RIFs but also the inevitable knock-on effects: namely, that the remaining partner would likely leave as soon as they could both find other jobs, or else families would be split up. Finding new angles to explore with a reporter offers them a reason to keep talking to you, and leads into the next point. . . .

9. Don't let the attention die down. Eventually, reporters, and their audience, will tire of your story, no matter how dramatic and life-altering it is for you and your colleagues, and then move on to the next shiny object. But by constantly offering new ways to look at the situation—new people's voices to hear, new permutations and effects—you can help keep the press cycle from moving on from your campus's crisis too soon. In fact, you can consider ways to keep them coming back by considering those downstream effects and helping to craft a hook—then working with a reporter or an outlet you've developed a relationship with.

10. Do think local *and* national (or international). For maximum attention and exposure, you need a good mix of local (campus, town, state, region) and national or international attention. It helps if your story is particularly shocking and egregious, as was ours at WVU; we were a perfect "canary in a coalmine" of what is coming for other campuses. But if only West Virginia media had noticed "academic transformation," our programs would likely have died in obscurity. Because we caught the attention of national professional organizations and national outlets such as the *New York Times* and *The Atlantic* as well the *Chronicle of Higher Education* and *Inside Higher Ed*, we were able to turn up the heat enough, we believe, to save a faculty line here or there.

These ten recommendations are neither exhaustive nor authoritative, but they may offer a helpful guide if you find your campus besieged by consultants or undermined by poor leadership and financial mismanagement. I didn't address the cost of speaking out; I don't presume to know anyone's tolerance for risk other than my own. In the end, I decided that I would speak out in a professional way that reflected my sincere beliefs and my genuine love for my institution, but I recognize that not everyone will make that choice. Consider what you have to lose beyond what you're already losing and negotiate that fine line.

Finally, maybe my list is less convincing because, well, we lost; WVU cut many programs and classes as well as many jobs. But we didn't lose because we didn't fight, and I would rather help arm more fighters than to quietly nurse my wounds.

Notes

1. See my essay, https://thepointmag.com/forms-of-life/zeroed-out/.
2. Shout out to the good folks at 123 Pleasant Street.

Part 2

Fighting Fiscal and Political Interference

Any book that seeks to capture an ongoing crisis, such as the ones now facing higher education, runs the risk of losing salience over the course of writing, revising, and publishing, simply because no book can possibly keep up with the onslaught of challenges facing higher education, and, indeed, our nation and world. Some consistent themes, however, have emerged within the turbulence: Right-wing efforts to suppress curricula and crush shared governance, and the continuing mania for austerity and retrenchment, to name the leading examples. The essays in this section focus on fighting fiscal and political interference, from curricula to institutions, from ideologies of austerity to "culture wars." Sadly, the threats to DEIJ work and free speech have been boosted by the current Trump administration and many state and local politicians; things are getting much worse, not better. In that spirit, the chapters in this section offer some help in guiding your own efforts to preserve academic freedom and commitment to core liberal values. Similarly, as you perhaps sit across the table from outside consultants, we have some advice for how best to handle those campus interlopers, as well as some inspiration for how to stay focused on what higher education can and should mean for us all.

8

A Plague of Consultants

Fighting the New Epidemic in Higher Education

KEVIN M. GANNON

The epidemic usually starts quietly, its first symptoms manifested in an email to the entire campus community, with a grave yet cordial beginning: "Dear colleagues, as you are likely aware, our institution faces significant financial headwinds in the near future." This grim acknowledgment is often followed with a breezy statement that reads less like firm resolve than it does whistling past the graveyard: perhaps something like "despite these headwinds, I remain confident in the resilience and resourcefulness of our community." But then the hammer drops: "The educational needs of today's students have changed; we can no longer continue with business as usual. To meet our challenges head-on, we will begin a thorough review of academic programs, with the goal of aligning our offerings with student demand." And if you're really unlucky, your administrators have decided the "bold leadership" and "readiness to make tough decisions" they're purportedly known for—the qualities used rationalize their large salaries during easier times—are actually insufficient to "meet our challenges head-on," so it's time to bring in reinforcements: "To assist us in this complex process, we have entered a strategic partnership with [insert consultancy here], and look forward to their expert guidance as we navigate these tough waters."[1] Once a certain breed of higher-ed consultants gets involved, it's over. There's only one possible outcome in this scenario: programs will be cut, people (except for administrators) will lose their jobs, students will suffer, and the institution will exit this process far poorer (literally and figuratively) than it was at the beginning. To use this chapter's metaphor, the patient will either die or linger indefinitely in an anemic, debilitated state. This may seem an excessively harsh indictment, but it comes from empirical evidence that exists across higher education, where a small army of consultants has wreaked havoc on the operations, morale, sustainability, and missions of a rapidly increasing number of US colleges and universities.

Knowing what will happen without having strategies for when it does, however, is a recipe for hopelessness and resignation. Moreover, if program cuts are on the table, it likely means your campus has already found itself in difficult times—fiscal and otherwise—and hopelessness and resignation already have a tangible presence. In this climate, a campus communication along the lines of the example above can serve to accelerate the already precipitous decline in morale, leading to enervation and a sense of powerlessness, even paralysis. When educational consultants arrive on the scene, then, many faculty and staff may well be already detached from anything outside their classroom or office walls, and those who remain engaged in campus affairs are likely to be well on the way to burnout. But as other chapters in this volume demonstrate, detachment and disconnection only ease the march of the consultant army across your campus and into your academic portfolios and governance structures. While there may be no definitive way to stop a campus administration bent upon bringing consultants to campus, there are plenty of things we can do to make that process more transparent than is usually the case and raise collective awareness of the actual stakes involved. Most importantly, however, we at least have the ability—and I would argue, the obligation—to not let the consultant cycle pass quietly: we can force both campus leaders and their consultant allies to listen to specific questions and challenge them to produce the "data" by which they say all their decisions are made. They may refuse, but they'll have to do so publicly. This behavior, of course, is not the action of a group confident their agenda is one which would find consent from the campus community in a full and fair hearing. What follows, then, are some specific questions and strategies we can use to challenge the specific proposals—and the particular higher-ed worldview they emerge from—employed by these consultants and their administrative enablers.

What are the specific qualifications of the individual consultants, as well as of the firm in general, who have been contracted to work with the institution?

Many prominent consultancies working in the higher-ed space are not firms that specialize in our particular sphere. For example, First Tryon Advisors, the firm retained by the administration of UNC-Asheville, recommended the university eliminate fourteen programs and their faculty (for context, that's roughly 40 percent of the university's departments, and a swath of liberal arts programs at the institution that's officially designated as North Carolina's "public liberal arts university").[2] But First Tryon is not a higher education consultancy, nor does a search of its clients and previous work turn up much in the way of education, save for a handful of private and charter schools. Their website gives prominence to their work in financial markets and derivatives ("our team has significant experience structuring, implementing and monitoring transactions involving a variety of derivative products including interest rate swaps, caps, collars and options"), but one has to click through a few levels to get to any mention of education.[3] Even the firm's tagline—"simplifying public finance"—reveals where both its priorities and experience reside.

McKinsey and Company, to cite a more (in)famous example, works across an array of industries, and even though they employ consultants who work exclusively in higher ed, their modus operandi for every sector is to recommend draconian cost-cutting measures and boost the immediate financial outlook to produce flashy short-term gains—with dire implications for long-term stability.[4] This singular focus on budget-slashing (particularly labor costs) means McKinsey consultants are usually making a post hoc case; the "solution" is already decided upon, and facts and data are carefully selected to tell a story that only has one possible ending. This tendency may explain why McKinsey's reports on the higher-ed sector are no more than a mix of generic cost-cutting recommendations and business-speak bromides disguised as expert insight. Thus, we get gems of wisdom such as "it's easier to change the course of history, than it is to change the history course," and—*stop the presses!*—"Remote and online learning are here to stay."[5]

The intent, though, is not to offer nuanced analysis so much as it is to sell a particular solution, so any "data-driven" insights must point in that direction only. It's no surprise this report—representative of the genre—is riddled with injunctions to cut costs: supposedly obsolete programs and thus redundant personnel, student services, even facilities (you don't need buildings for online learning!). There is literally nothing about student success, effective teaching and learning, or anything that might touch on the actual mission of a college or university. The fact that the two lead authors of the report possess degrees and pre-McKinsey experience in economics and law—and not education of any sort—may have something to do with that.

Even consultancies that specialize in higher education embody these problems. Several partners in the rpkGROUP (the firm partially responsible for West Virginia University's "academic transformation") have higher-ed experience, but it's almost exclusively in the chief financial officer and business operations areas. A thorough (albeit unscientific) search of the rpk website and associated LinkedIn profiles reveals a wealth of what one might call "higher education-adjacent" experience: other consultancies, nonprofits, think tanks, and lobbying organizations.[6] But one does *not* encounter, at least so far as I could find, any of their consultants with actual classroom or student affairs experience. This exclusive emphasis on the administrative and financial operations sides of the house shows up in all of the work these consultancies—rpkGroup or otherwise—do. Their solutions to campus crises always involve cutting: costs, programs, staff, facilities. They are the embodiment of Abraham Maslow's observation that if the only tool one has is a hammer, one tends to see every problem as a nail.

Faculty and staff (and students) at affected institutions, then, need to do their research as early as possible. When the first suggestion of outside consultants is broached, begin investigating the possible firm(s). The questions to pose (formally, and ideally through established bodies such as the faculty senate and student government) should include:

- What are the general qualifications of this firm? Do they specialize in higher education? If not, why are we contracting with a firm that advises primarily corporate clients, not nonprofit or educational institutions? Is our college/university the same thing as a private corporation?
- What are the qualifications and experiences of the individual consultants who will work with our campus? If they are being asked to look at the offerings in our academic portfolio, what

is their experience and expertise in curriculum design and pedagogy? Have any of them ever built curricula or academic programs before?

- What added value does this consultancy bring to campus that makes it a preferable choice over the in-house expertise our institution already employs?

Any preliminary press release or public communication issued by the administration needs to be met with a counterpart from this perspective, posing those same questions, as soon as possible. Again, using extant bodies of representation and governance is important; these communications need to be collectively framed in order to carry sufficient weight in the public eye.

What institutions has this consultancy advised before they came to us? What were the recommendations they made, and what were the outcomes for those previous clients?

One of the primary ways in which higher-ed consultancies market themselves is through extensive client lists, as if to say, "We've worked with all *these* colleges and universities, so you can trust us and our experience." But what recommendations did they make to those clients, and did those strategies ultimately accomplish their intended goal of restoring financial stability to the particular school? The answers, put bluntly, are "cut programs and staff," and "not really." The rpkGROUP is a good case study here, as they are not only associated with the most notorious implementation of the cut-your-way-to-stability strategy, but their extensive client list offers a range of data to analyze. One of rpk's most recent clients is, of course, West Virginia University, and as several chapters in this volume lay out in devastating detail, what their consultants delivered were one-size-fits-all recommendations based on both faulty premises and bad data, thus creating the conditions for a disastrous implementation. Within the first year of WVU's launch of E. Gordon Gee's vaunted "academic transformation" (which rpkGROUP helped shape), Gee's handpicked vice president of strategy left his role for a nebulous "advisory" position in the administration but has now returned to the private sector, the provost abruptly retired shortly after the 2024–25 academic year started, the chief marketing and engagement officer resigned and took another job, Gee himself announced he would be retiring as president and returning to the faculty in 2025, and many faculty who didn't get fired have either voluntarily retired or left for other jobs, creating large holes in several academic departments.[7] The sheer scale of this turnover, compressed into such a short period, is not a marker of a healthy university; org-chart carnage like this never accompanies the successful implementation of a strategic program.

Similar stories emerge from another recent rpkGROUP client, the University of North Carolina-Greensboro, whose administrators announced in early 2024 that twenty academic programs would be cut, kicking off a process of program review that most faculty members criticized as arbitrary, informed by bad data, and lacking in transparency. One professor pointed out that the administration had not demonstrated how the cuts were actually going to save the type of money necessary to offset the university's enrollment decline; faculty members argued the programs targeted for closure actually paid for themselves budgetarily, and that number of majors was a far less accurate measure of impact than total number of FTEs ("full-time enrolled") taught per term.[8]

Other faculty pointed to the vague (and ever-changing) rubrics used to review academic programs for future viability. The Anthropology Department, for example, was scored at "meets expectations" (the second-highest criteria on the rubric) but ended up a victim of the cuts nonetheless. One of its members summed things up: "People are now just really angry and really distrustful of the administration. We needed more of an idea where we were going, to start off with. We needed more real input about what the process would be. And then we just needed the process, as we decided upon, to operate fairly, which it did not."[9] This troubling recent trend of rpkGROUP clients self-immolating reveals the following questions you should demand your campus administrators answer should they employ consultants to address financial difficulties:

- What institutions have been clients of this consultancy over the last ten years? How healthy is their fiscal status now? What have their enrollment trends looked like since?
- Are there any members of senior leadership who were in place during the period they worked with consultants still at the institution? If some or all departed, why?
- Is there a uniformity to the consultant's recommendations? In other words, are they Maslow's Hammer? Is "cut programs and staff" their only solution to fiscal problems?

- What specific metrics will be used to determine program viability? If it's "number of majors," why has that been chosen over the number of FTEs served per term?

Are these consultants here to recommend a decision that's already been made? Are program and staffing cuts the only available option? Will those cuts actually fix the enrollment declines responsible for our financial downturn?

Borrowing from the neoliberal logic of corporate capitalism, with its fetish for "efficiencies" as the driver of vaguely defined "growth," many college and university administrators (especially those who come from the corporate sphere) are unable to resist the Jack Welch–style logic of cutting your way to profit despite the disastrous long-term outcomes that strategy inevitably produces.[10] This logic puts them in ideological sympathy with the higher-ed consultants they bring in to address financial precarity. Indeed, the two groups overlap and are drawn largely from the same narrow demographics—and sometimes the same pool of people. From their blinkered perspective, the case for slashing expenditures and going after the lowest-hanging fruit appears incontrovertible: cut academic programs and their staff, usually majors "no one wants any more" (almost always in arts and sciences, *never* in the business school). Using misleading metrics (why we always see "number of majors" trotted out as a surrogate for a program's impact and enrollment) and market-driven rhetoric, consultants will thus make what most upper-level administrators already see as eminently reasonable—perhaps the *only* reasonable—recommendations.

Are academic program and staffing cuts the only option? Of course not. One could argue it would be easier to trim administrative positions and salaries, or athletic programs, and more quickly deliver the desired fiscal results. As Christopher Newfield, among others, has pointed out, universities cut programs in the name of fiscal austerity, yet the programs cut are almost all revenue-neutral, or enroll enough students in their courses on a term-to-term basis that they bring in revenue beyond the amount of funds they're budgeted (including salaries and benefits). In other words, they are a net gain for the institution. The programs most expensive to maintain—where the per-student cost can be more than double that of most arts and sciences courses—are the same ones administrators and consultants hold up as avatars of "revenue-generating" majors: various engineering fields (factoring in the cost of faculty salaries, labs, and equipment, as well as support staff); business, particularly finance, programs (where faculty salaries are often markedly higher than in other units in order to compete with private industry); and data analytics programs (that can require additional computing infrastructure and involve similar types of salary competition as business).[11]

Yet when one peruses various lists of academic programs being cut at places such as WVU, or UNC-Greensboro, or UNC-Asheville, or any of the other institutions in these rapidly swelling ranks, it's clear something besides cost/revenue measures are driving the consultancies' metrics and thus administrators' ultimate decisions, even though those decisions are purportedly being made to meet an immediate financial crisis. Facing a budget shortfall of several million dollars (in the case of somewhere like WVU, a deficit caused by rampant overspending on buildings and administrative perks), and deciding to eliminate—for example—language, physics, mathematics, history, and/or philosophy programs, is analogous to buying a Maserati, realizing the monthly payments are way beyond your means, and deciding you'll cancel your Netflix subscription to bridge the fiscal gap. Are consultants' recommendations for your institutions based on similarly dubious logic? Here are some further questions to probe the matter:

- How will cutting programs actually address enrollment shortfalls—especially programs that serve large numbers of non-major students through institution-wide initiatives such as general education curricula? What is the plan for when (not if) students encounter barriers (lack of available sections for prerequisites, for example) caused by program cuts?
- How does this solution—cutting academic programs and staff—*specifically and incontrovertibly* advance the institutional mission?
- Aren't program cuts simply the equivalent of a "Queen Sacrifice" in chess: a profoundly risky strategy, born out of desperation, that rarely if ever prevents one from losing?[12]
- What actual, concrete examples can the consultancies provide of institutions that cut their way to enrollment growth and robust financial health?

It's highly unlikely that pushing these questions and demanding answers from administrators will stop higher-ed consultants from doing what they do, as they have done so effectively over and over again. But there's something to be said for making the people responsible for decisions actually defend them publicly, and having to do so in settings that aren't filled with yes-men who are literally paid to go along with them. All too often, program cuts and other disastrous consultant recommendations are framed passively: "The market has made it impossible for us to continue offering these courses," as if some big, nebulous, impersonal force was responsible. Or they're presented via circular logic: cutting courses and staffing in a particular area, only to exclaim "our students just aren't taking [insert subject here] courses!" *Don't blame us, blame the market.* There's plenty of blame to go around, for sure, but it falls on actual people. Administrators and consultants shouldn't be allowed to impose their draconian austerity measures unopposed. Effective advocacy and use of shared-governance institutions, demanding light and transparency (especially where university spending is concerned), public communication and competing press releases, self-education on consultancies and the ideological frameworks that produce their recommendations—these may not save your programs, but they can be part of a larger regimen of inoculation. This type of regimen, made widespread and comprehensive in its application, is the best course available to us to prevent this plague of consultants: particularly virulent when it preys on hosts—already exhibiting symptoms of institutional precarity and fears of financial doom—from laying waste to the people and programs which make higher education go.

Notes

1. For some reason, these types of administrative communications tend to rely heavily on nautical navigation metaphors.

2. Addison Wright, "Presentation Obtained by Watchdog shows 14 UNCA academic programs highlighted for potential reductions, elimination," *Asheville Watchdog*, June 7, 2024. Available at https://avlwatchdog.org/presentation-obtained-by-watchdog-shows-14-unca-academic-programs-highlighted-for-potential-reductions-elimination/.

3. See https://www.firsttryon.com/.

4. See the thorough exposé of McKinsey's activities over recent decades by two *New York Times* reporters in Walt Bogdanich and Michael Forsythe, *When McKinsey Comes to Town: The Hidden Influence of the World's Most Powerful Consulting Firm* (New York: Random House, 2023).

5. André Dua, Jonathan Law, Ted Rounsaville, and Nadia Viswanath, "Reimagining Higher Education in the United States," *McKinsey & Co.* website,

October 26, 2020, https://www.mckinsey.com/industries/public-sector/our-insights/reimagining-higher-education-in-the-united-states.

6. See the descriptions available at https://rpkgroup.com/.

7. Ryan Quinn, "One Year After Massive Cuts, West Virginia is Still Bleeding Faculty, Administrators," *Inside Higher Ed*, September 9, 2024, https://www.insidehighered.com/news/faculty-issues/tenure/2024/09/09/year-after-cuts-wv-still-bleeding-faculty-administrators.

8. " 'It's inescapable:' UNCG tenure-track professor worries whether her job will survive cuts." WUNC, Feb. 20, 2024. Available at https://www.wunc.org/education/2024-02-20/unc-greensboro-uncg-program-cuts-professor-job. For a thorough dissection of the "number of majors" versus "full-time enrollees" metrics, with a convincing argument that the former is used primarily because it obfuscates the actual costs of instruction and makes it easier to rationalize draconian budget cuts, see Christopher Newfield, *The Great Mistake: How We Wrecked Public Universities and How We Can Fix Them* (Johns Hopkins University Press, 2016), and *Unmaking the Public University: The Forty-Year Assault on the Middle Class* (Harvard University Press, 2008), 142–207.

9. Sonel Cutler, "UNC-Greensboro Reckons With the Fallout of Painful Academic Cuts," *The Chronicle of Higher Education*, February 9, 2024, https://www.chronicle.com/article/unc-greensboro-reckons-with-the-fallout-of-painful-academic-cuts.

10. "Jack Welch's Legacy Looks Very Different Than it Did 20 Years Ago," *The Week*, March 2, 2020. Available at https://theweek.com/articles/899343/jack-welchs-legacy-looks-different-than-did-20-years-ago; David Gelles, *The Man Who Broke Capitalism: How Jack Welch Gutted the Heartland and Crushed the Soul of Corporate America—and How to Undo His Legacy* (New York: Simon & Schuster, 2022).

11. Newfield, *The Great Mistake*; Fidel J. Tavárez, "Mispricing Tuition," *Inside Higher Ed*, Nov. 16, 2022; "The Costs of Program Delivery: What the Research Shows," *Stamats*. Available at https://www.stamats.com/insights/costs-program-delivery-what-research-shows/; you can access comparative salary data at the College and University Professional Association for Human Resources (CUPA-HR) website: https://www.cupahr.org/surveys/cupa-hr-signature-surveys/.

12. I am indebted to Bryan Alexander for this framing. See his numerous expositions and examples of this institutional move at https://bryanalexander.org/tag/queensacrifice/.

9

Teaching a University Budget Crisis as Activism

William Caraher

This chapter offers a case study of classroom based activism as a response to a campus crisis. The case study is from the University of North Dakota (UND), a mid-sized, public university which from 2016 to 2018 labored under a painful series of budget cuts triggered by state financial shortfalls. These cuts extended across campus, and the termination of the university's prominent women's hockey program (Cimini 2017) and successful music therapy degree made national headlines (Associated Press 2016). The negative publicity generated by these cuts bewildered and angered students and faculty alike. The naming of an unpopular figure, Mark Kennedy, as university president further stoked a sense of outrage on a campus (Jacobs 2018). At the same time, a failed effort at program prioritization, the implementation of a seemingly complex new MIRA-type budgeting process (Model for Incentive-based Resource Allocation), and the growing reach of an increasingly bureaucratized administration also contributed to a feeling of helplessness in the face of university processes and decision-making. Much of the frustration derived from not understanding the complex mechanisms through which budgetary decisions occurred. While this complexity was a byproduct of twenty-first-century methods to professionalize the modern university, faculty and students worried that it encroached on the shared governance of the institution.

In response to this growing sense of crisis, I taught a class on the University of North Dakota budget. The class was offered as an honors section of our department's venerable History of North Dakota class and taught at the intermediate level. It was open to both honors and nonhonors students and quickly enrolled close to its twenty-student cap. This chapter describes and assesses this class as a response to the campus crisis.

Teaching as Activism and the Twenty-First-Century University Campus

Recent scholarship related to teaching as activism is as broad and complex as the social problems that it seeks to resolve (Ozaki and Parson 2020, 2021). Despite its abundance, I was largely unaware of this important work when I proposed the class on the budget. Instead, I took at my point of reference the "teach-in" movement of the 1960s and 1970s that emerged in response to the Vietnam war and Ira Shor's work on empowerment in the college classroom from the 1990s. These dated landmarks still offer a useful lens through which to appreciate the potential of teaching (and learning) as the foundation for social and institutional change.

The origins of the "teach-in" movement came as a response to the US bombing of North Vietnam in 1965 (Rothman 1972; Sahlins 2009). They argued that the approach forged a compromise between calls for a teaching strike and calls for a form of protest that would be more in keeping with the educational mission, resources, and the "special competency" available at the university. The first teach-in at Michigan offered a way for faculty and students to engage with "a clear factual and moral protest against the Vietnam War" (Rothman 1972). While unapologetically top-down in its approach, it nevertheless recognized the key role of universities as places to educate as well as to organize and support students (and the university community more broadly) confronting a crisis. The subsequent adoption of the teach-in as a response to crises—from episodes of racist hate crimes on campus to growing concerns about the environment—reveals the persistent potential of the teach-in as a tool to produce better educated activists and larger social change.

While each generation produces a new canon of literature on student empowerment, my efforts found inspiration in Ira Shor's classic work *Empowering Education* (1992). He began his work with an anecdote about the first day of a new semester teaching "English One" at a New York public college. The students were surly and unresponsive until Shor asked them bluntly what was going on. At that point, the class became surly and *responsive* and explained that they were angry about the English writing test required for all first-year students. The class went on to explain to Shor that they felt the test to be unfair. Shor leveraged their frustration both to build an empathetic relationship with the students and to encourage them to channel their anger into the goals of the course. He admitted that despite the students' ability to articulate their views, they stopped short of wanting to become activists themselves and did little, in the end, to change the character of the required English writing exam. What Shor recognized, however, is that giving students space and time to voice their anger and frustration started a process where they worked together to articulate their concerns. He was also giving students the critical tools to express their ideas in more compelling ways.

To inform the discussion of the contemporary budget the class turned to Christopher Newfield's recent work for a detailed analysis of the historical and contemporary perspectives on the changing financial and economic landscape of American higher education (Newfield 2016). He acknowledged that even mid-sized college campuses were complex institutions and argued that the growing complexity of the contemporary public college campus is a symptom of the increasing privatization of public universities. For Newfield, this privatization involves the shift from collaborative to transactional modes of interaction across the institution. The financialization of interactions across the institution, for example, reconfigures curriculum from a collaborative responsibility to produce prepared and well-rounded students, to a competition for resources across campus. While advocates of this kind of competition imagine it as a way to produce efficiencies through a "marketplace of ideas," instead it has intensified commitments to the professionalized standards of expertise and competence that often produce "silos" across institutions and hinder collaboration and cooperation. The logic of competition-born efficiency extends throughout our institutions not only fortifying claims to discreet professional competences but also creating barriers to "shared governance." For students and faculty, these barriers can often mean that we are on the outside of a byzantine bureaucracy looking in even as the fate of programs, departments, and services crucial for our own expectations hangs in the balance. It is unsurprising that during these times of crisis the bureaucracy itself becomes the object of vitriol as faculty and students from across the ideological spectrum attack the lack of transparency, "administrative bloat," and levels of compensation as the cause rather than the symptom of the changing financial environment facing twenty-first-century universities.

Teaching the UND Budget Crisis

These works informed how I used teaching as a response to the heightened experience of certain structural inequalities which came about as a result of the 2016–2018 budget crisis at UND. Consistent with the teach-in movement, the crisis inspired me to prepare students to become more informed participants in the campus community. Participants in Vietnam era teach-ins, however, described their efforts as largely a top-down phenomenon. The courses described below draw on more contemporary approaches to student empowerment as articulated in Ira Shor's work, which recognized in the classroom a space where structural inequality could be identified, questioned, and overcome.

As with many crises, a proximate encounter with the budget cuts inspired the response. In the spring of 2017, we received news that our department's long-standing and successful graduate programs in history would lose funding. When this news came out, the last class of funded graduate students in history was enrolled in a graduate historiography and methods class typical to most graduate programs. Though I tried to continue the class as a traditional history reading seminar, these events quickly overtook this possibility. The students were understandably upset about the news and pushed me to pivot the class to discuss the conditions both locally and nationally that allowed this change to happen. As in the experience of the students in Shor's freshman composition class, the news distressed, distracted, and angered the students even though the department assured them that their funding would continue. This assurance did little to elevate the mood of the class nor did my rather facile efforts to explain the calculus that led to the budget cuts. As our conversation continued during class and afterward, the students' frustration turned to a desire to engage, to decry, and to lash out at the perceived injustice.

Following Shor's inducement, the class abandoned the plan for traditional papers, which asked the students to consider how the readings of the class shaped (or would shape) their practice of history, and pivoted to writing a series of essays on the value of history for the institution, our community, and the world. The class critiqued, edited, and compiled their essays together in a short open-access digital book titled, *Defending History: the Graduates' Manifesto*.[1] The book consisted of chapters that situated the study of history in the history of higher education in the US (and at UND) and considered the role that the university played in the life of the community, the nation, and diverse "imagined communities."

The book was raw and immediate and carried traces of the frantic feeling the loss of funding imparted in the class. The students circulated this book via email, social media, and my blog as a statement to anyone who might be interested.

My experience in this class made clear to me that students not only saw themselves as deeply invested in the institution but also wanted their voices to be heard by the administration and the community. In response to this desire, I worked with Joe Kalka, a student from this graduate seminar and another graduate student, Andrew Larson, to develop an undergraduate class focused on the university budget over the course of an independent study in the fall of 2017. We read classic works on the history of universities and colleges in the United States and sampled recent scholarly and professional works that dealt with the growing sense of crisis across higher education. These readings both informed Andrew Larson's DA project "Not Your Advisor's Doctorate: The Doctor of Arts and The Modernization of Higher Education 1945–1970" and helped us prepare readings for the undergraduate class (Larson 2020). The results were two documents: one was a short history of American higher education written by Larson, and the other was a "Document Reader" on higher education and budgets compiled by Kalka. A version of the former ultimately became part of the Larson's DA project and the latter was a rough and ready document designed to give students access to a sample of public documents related to budget cuts both at UND and across the US. We used the Internet Archive's "Wayback Machine" to create archival links to the various documents lest they succumb to the internet's ephemeral character or be hidden behind firewalls. Both Kalka and Larson continued to participate in the planning and development of the course and injected a sense of urgent frustration manifested in the graduate seminar into the planning for the undergraduate course.

Our work in the graduate historiography seminar and the subsequent reading course helped develop the four goals for the undergraduate course on the budget:

1. To become more familiar with the complexities of the modern university and UND, in particular.
2. To encourage critical thinking about the institutional structure of higher education in the US in a historical context and local context.

3. To understand the relationship between the institutional organization and the purpose of the university.

4. To produce a short guide to the UND budget for students that allows them to be more critical consumers and participants in university life.

The undergraduate course centered on three main sources: one was Larson's and Kalka's readers described above. The second was a series of readings in Christopher Newfield's *The Great Mistake: How We Wrecked Public Universities and How We Can Fix Them* (2016) and David Labaree's *A Perfect Mess: The Unlikely Ascendency of American Higher Education* (2017). Both texts seek to situate the changing nature of American higher education in its historical context. Complementing these readings, the third source was visits from many of the key stakeholders in the budget crisis: a member of the state legislature (and the higher education committee), a vice chancellor of the statewide university system, the provost of the university, the head of the university's alumni foundation, our college dean, an assistant coach of an impacted sports team, and a panel of department chairs. Each offered perspectives on the institution, from the mechanisms and formulae present at the state level for funding institutions to the way in which funding is incentivized and distributed within the university, to the challenge of raising donor funds and the impact of budget cuts on instruction and coaching.

The students largely led these conversations especially as they became more comfortable in the class (and when the interlocutors were particularly engaging or forthcoming). At the same time, the students began to bring together the framework for a guide—of sorts—to the budget crisis. Following Shor's instinct to activate the feeling of confusion and anger in his first-year writing class, the budget class took these feelings as its point of departure. Thus our work initially focused on the decision to cut the UND Women's hockey team and the successful music therapy program. The resulting book titled: *Hawks, Hockey, and the Budget at the University of North Dakota* featured four chapters, an introduction, a preface, and a glossary of key terms.[2] Each chapter included a case study relevant to the situation in North Dakota and a reflection on the broader situation in American higher education. This approach not only paralleled the organization of the class, but the students also reckoned that it would help readers connect the crisis at UND to larger national trends in higher education. Each chapter was reviewed and edited by the class, and then I typeset them all into a PDF digital book. The conversations among the students were vigorous, respectful, and ideologically diverse. The book embodies much of what occurred in the classroom.

Once the book was complete we circulated it to the various stakeholders and encouraged the students to circulate it in their social digital and analog networks. It remains unclear whether the book had an impact beyond the classroom, but as an object of student engagement, the experience of writing, reviewing, and editing helped the students to refine their understanding of local and national trends, articulate the various positions encountered in the class, and offer critique. In this way, the book represents evidence for the successful accomplishment of the course goals.

Conclusion

The students in this course channeled their frustrations surrounding the UND budget into academically and intellectually productive activities. The class itself and the publication of the book created opportunities for students to develop a more sophisticated and nuanced understanding of the budget and bridge the knowledge and professional gap between students, faculty, and the administration. The impact of the course beyond the semester remains unclear. Administrators who received copies of the students' work were not particularly inclined to engage with it. One expressed some disappointment in the students' conclusions, but did not explain why. Faculty who received copies of the book generally viewed them as tokens or even novelties rather than significant intellectual interventions in an ongoing campus crisis. While students planned to circulate the book among their own social networks, these routes remained largely closed off to me as a faculty member. In some ways, the challenges facing the circulation of this book were unsurprising. On our campus, student activism is rare. Moreover, faculty (and student) workloads ensure that outrage often offers a more convenient outlet than the kind of understanding needed to bridge the divide between professional administrators and the faculty rank and file in a productive way (cf. Zerr and Gjellstad 2018). That said, interventions like these classes may offer faculty and students firmer ground from which to critique administrative processes and the structures that produce them.

As I write this conclusion, campus protests over the Israeli invasion of Gaza have turned violent, evoking the fraught campus politics that inspired the teach-in movement and a generation of campus activists. Amid this crisis, splits across the campus community have taxed our collective capacity for empathy and understanding. Divisions forged by a half-century of professionalization, specialization, and competition on campuses have compromised our ability to respond to campus crises by assuming adversarial or, at the very least, incommensurate perspectives across the institution. I grounded my contribution to this volume in the assumption that these divisions require subversive practices that will allow students and faculty to critique and even participate more thoughtfully in the decision-making process. Perhaps this hoped-for outcome misses the mark (see also Caraher 2023). Maybe creating spaces for cross-campus dialogue during crises is more important for creating institutional (or even community wide) reserves of empathy and compassion during fraught times. In the end, despite the anxiety that our budget crisis created among students and faculty alike, the stakes were comparatively low. The current campus violence, however, reminds us that the next crisis may not be low stakes. Understanding the diverse positions and responsibilities across campus and recognizing the potential of teaching as a space for cross-campus dialogue may help us develop alternatives to violence when the next crisis occurs.

Finally, this paper is dedicated to the memory of Provost Tom DiLorenzo who was shot and killed shortly after retiring from UND. As provost, he not only visited patiently with students in this class but also consistently supported my interest in the processes and structures that supported and produced the university budget.

Notes

1. You can download a copy of this book here: https://web.archive.org/web/20240518122657/https://mediterraneanworld.wordpress.com/wp-content/uploads/2017/05/dfhistory_v1_1.pdf.

2. You can download a copy of this book here: https://web.archive.org/web/20240429203045/https://mediterraneanworld.wordpress.com/wp-content/uploads/2024/04/budgetbook2018.pdf.

Bibliography

Associated Press. "Students Protest Decision to Suspend Music Therapy Program." *Huron Daily Tribune*. March 15, 2016. https://www.michigansthumb.com/news/article/Students-protest-decision-to-suspend-music-7274117.php.

Associated Press. "University of North Dakota students protest decision to suspend music therapy program." *The Stockton Record*. March 16, 2016. https://www.recordnet.com/story/entertainment/music/2016/03/16/university-north-dakota-students-protest/32387505007/.

Caraher, William. "Documenting Wesley College: A Mildly Anarchist Teaching Encounter." In *Teaching and Learning the Archaeology of the Contemporary Era*, edited by G. Moshenska, 41–60. London: Bloomsbury, 2023.

Gjellstad, M., and R. Zerr. "Faculty Navigating the Age of Austerity: Affirming Roles and Renewing Alliances." *NDQ* 85, no. 1–4 (2018): 162–82.

Jacobs, Mike. "Can This Presidency Be Saved?" *Grand Forks Herald*. April 17, 2018. https://grandforksherald.com/opinion/mike-jacobs-can-this-presidency-be-saved.

Labaree, David. *A Perfect Mess: The Unlikely Ascendency of American Higher Education*. Chicago: University of Chicago Press, 2017.

Larson, A. "Not Your Advisor's Doctorate: The Doctor Of Arts And The Modernization Of Higher Education 1945–1970." PhD diss., University of North Dakota, 2020.

Newfield, C. *The Great Mistake: How We Wrecked Public Universities and How We Can Fix Them*. Baltimore: Johns Hopkins University Press, 2016.

Parsons, L. and C. Ozaki. *Teaching and Learning for Social Justice and Equity in Higher Education*. Vol. 1. Cham, Switzerland: Springer, 2020.

Parsons, L., and C. Ozaki. *Teaching and Learning for Social Justice and Equity in Higher Education*. Vol. 2. Cham, Switzerland: Springer, 2021.

Rothman, Jack. "The Radical Liberal Strategy in Action: Arnold Kaufman and the First Teach-in." *Social Theory and Practice* 2, no. 1 (1972): 33–45.

Sahlins, Marshall. "The Teach-ins: Anti-war Protest in the Old Stoned Age." *Anthropology Today* 25, no. 1 (2009): 3–5.

Shor, Ira. *Empowering Education: Critical Teaching for Social Change*. Chicago: University of Chicago Press, 1992.

10

The Solutions Project

Liberatory Student-Centered Strategies from a College in Crisis

Meaghan Davis, Kathleen Gray, and Sara Rzeszutek

Our campus crisis burned slowly before it exploded.[1] Cash-strapped and seeking creative solutions, our small, private, urban, commuter college moved to a new location, only to find that this maneuver was not the financial cure we hoped for, as the New York City real estate market was thrown into flux by the COVID-19 pandemic. Increasing financial pressures and a rapid transition of executive leadership led to a laserlike focus on balancing the budget through spending cuts. In March 2023, the college terminated support staff, including a large number of student-facing employees. Two weeks later, the college eliminated its NCAA Division I athletics program. These changes threatened undergraduate retention rates. Uncertain of the college's future, many more long-serving staff and administrators left. The remaining employees worked tirelessly to continue to provide a quality experience for our diverse student body, yet the need for innovative, sustainable solutions that go beyond budget cuts remained clear.

Although our campus relocation was unique, our larger financial and enrollment troubles were not. Across higher education, colleges are grappling with ways to stay open, secure, and relevant in the face of diminishing public confidence in the value of a college degree, an impending enrollment cliff that will result in fewer college students, and a political climate hostile to areas of higher education that are not obviously career-oriented and those that focus on diversity, equity, and inclusion.[2] For institutions serving historically excluded student populations such as first-generation, low-income students of color, these trends threaten our financial viability and our ability to provide the extensive academic, social, and financial support needed to make good on higher education's promise of social mobility.

As our crisis loomed, several academic leaders worked behind the scenes, collaborating with faculty, staff, and students to build a stronger infrastructure for navigating what might come. We discovered that faculty, staff, and administrators at struggling colleges can implement scalable, iterative, long-term solutions that can weather fiscal crises. We can sustain a consistent and liberatory experience for students while reducing cost by leveraging existing investments in student leadership development and integrating the work of faculty, staff, and students in a comprehensive liberatory model that prioritizes strengthening students' ability to navigate complex institutions, self-advocate, and become the architects of their own learning.

Our proposed Solutions Project will allow faculty, staff, and administrators to keep their focus on student needs while leadership pursues efforts to address financial shortfalls. A campus in crisis should lean into the liberatory potential of higher education, focus on equity and inclusion, and emphasize the needs of its most vulnerable students. The most transformative solutions and strategies live in these efforts. The strategy we developed included six ingredients for effective higher education solutions: center student needs; be anchored in liberatory goals; focus on students' skill development; draw from research- and evidence-based practices; develop a roadmap to scale it out to all our students; and ensure financial sustainability.

With these goals in mind, we reimagined four evidence-based, high-impact initiatives: First Year Seminar, peer leadership, learning communities, and new student orientation.[3] Our commitment to embodying a liberatory lens and praxis while strategically layering these initiatives is what sets our model apart, opening a pathway from proven practices to new possibilities.

We define a liberatory approach as one that is brave enough to struggle with awakening, mending, and transforming ourselves, our systems, and our institutions—while stepping away from existing hierarchies of power to shape with our students a new vision for the world they will inherit. We emphasized liberation itself as an outcome of higher education, bringing intention to cocreating experiences and communities designed for power to be shared. Inspired by our overarching strategy, we co-created transformational, student-centered, joyful, and critical educational experiences for our diverse student body.

Our dreaming and scheming about solutions for our students led to an exceptional pilot project beginning with the creation of a new Office of the First Year Experience. Building this new office provided an opportunity for us to reposition existing initiatives such as the First Year Seminar and a peer leadership development program. Our first-year experience is part of the college's general education program, making it inherently inclusive and scalable, and as a launchpad for students, it heavily influences institutional culture, making it an essential ingredient in our new layered approach to scalable student support. The first-year experience had four primary student learning outcomes:

- integrating the student experience across academic, co-curricular, and social spaces;
- developing strong college-level student success skills, specifically focusing on communication;
- building competencies in self-care, self-advocacy, and self-awareness; and
- establishing community, connection, and a sense of belonging.

With these goals in mind, we reimagined and redesigned the First Year Seminar course model and curriculum to more seamlessly connect it to the new student orientation programming and onboarding processes. We also added First Year Learning Communities (discussed in more detail below) and aligned the outcomes and structure of our peer leadership programming through the creation of a new Peer Leadership Academy (PLA) and an Orientation Leadership program.

The extraordinary impact of the FYE office in just two short years has been profound. It challenged our campus culture to prioritize student retention and amplify student agency across multiple touchpoints in the first year. At the height of the pandemic, our First Year Seminar course saw DFW grade rates as high as 36%. In the first year of this new model, despite the challenges that accompanied moving to a new building, including ongoing space and technology problems and complications with on-boarding logistics, those rates dropped to 20 percent. By fall 2024, DFW rates were just 8.5 percent, far surpassing the goals set when the redesign was first proposed.

The primary vehicle for this success was the repositioning, facilitation, and assessment of our peer leadership development efforts. We created a Peer Leadership Academy (PLA), where our student peer leaders could be trained for the remarkable work they do for the FYE. The PLA embodies a unique model that is steeped in liberatory practice and specifically focuses on personal and leadership development, co-creating liberatory structures and culture, and sharing and challenging power within the institution and beyond. Our model is an alternative to the sometimes-exploitative way student employees or leaders are used to fill in gaps but do not necessarily benefit from the work they do. In crises, colleges often rely even more on student employees and student leaders to serve the institution, but meeting students' needs and contributing to their growth are set aside. This model of peer leadership is designed for students to lead and grow with one another, centering student needs over institutional needs. This model shows, though, that when student needs are prioritized, institutional needs are also met.

The PLA has two main goals: the success of first-year students and the growth of the student leaders who guide them. Within our model, peer leaders are instrumental in educating and culture-creating with and for first-year students. Their rigorous training equips them with strong skills and challenges them to grow their empathy and confidence. They develop advanced communication and facilitation skills, deepen critical thinking and problem-solving skills, and engage in introspection and decision-making. Peer leaders learn about themselves and their position in the world, connect with their bravery and power, embark on a journey of unlearning, and move beyond themselves.[4]

Peer leadership development and peer education must provide peer leaders and first-year students with dynamic, real-world opportunities for growth and application of what they are learning. The PLA plays a major role in the execution of first-year experience courses, providing independent instruction in small-group recitation sections. Peer leaders work together to provide individualized and comprehensive student support and to implement campus-wide initiatives including Title IX education, community service, and more. In addition, the team holds weekly leadership development programming, self-assessment, and one-on-one mentorship to ensure they are prepared to lead with confidence, integrity, and expertise. Peer leaders also create equity-driven projects that offer sustainable solutions to gaps in the student experience. The year-long PLA journey concludes with a student-led conference called "Students Today, Leaders Forever," at which the peer leaders present their projects and tell leadership stories in breakout sessions.

Building on the success of the PLA, we rebuilt the FYE course within our General Education Program, using faculty and student feedback as well as research on FYE best practices. This involved redesigning course goals, student learning outcomes, assignments and assessments, service learning projects, lesson plans, and other instructional materials. We prioritized connection and preparation for first-year students through a large group, high-energy, and student-centered lecture paired with a small, intimate, peer-led recitation component. Additionally, we embedded co-curricular badges directly into the FYE assignments to introduce first-year students to service-oriented leadership, global citizenship, diversity, equity, inclusion, and professional development opportunities across campus. In the first year, 90 percent of first-year students participated in co-curricular badging. Testifying to the efficacy of these changes, a student survey, administered to first-year students through their first year experience course during the final third of their first semester, demonstrated that nearly all students agreed that FYE is relevant to their needs and a space in which they learn essential skills.

Continuing our commitment to layer student experiences in a coherent institution-wide model, we collaborated with faculty to create, implement, and assess first-year student learning communities (LC). LCs integrate and deepen content knowledge, develop essential college-level success skills, build and hone self-care, self-advocacy, and personal growth, generate connections, and foster community and belonging. Learning communities are made up of a small cohort of students linked together through shared academic courses within the General Education Program. One of the courses in every LC is FYE, and every LC has a designated peer leader assigned to support a cohort of fifteen to twenty first-year students. We partnered with our Center for Advancement of Faculty Excellence to provide professional development and community for FYE and LC instructors. The student survey administered to first-year students through their first-year experience course during the final third of their first semester showed that as a result of this work, over 90 percent of LC and FYE students agreed that their experience was engaging and led them to develop a strong sense of belonging.

To support student enrollment and onboarding, FYE grew to include New Student Orientation. We restructured and expanded New Student Orientation and trained student orientation leaders. Instead of taking a deficit perspective of students' college readiness, we intentionally created spaces and activities that enabled students to deploy their existing strengths and skills to complete onboarding tasks in community with each other. This significantly increased student engagement in the orientation process and helped them achieve critical onboarding benchmarks, such as setting up their college email, checking their financial aid status, and reviewing their courses in the scheduling and learning management systems. Developing specific competencies and completing necessary steps to begin their college careers prepared students for success from the time they arrived on campus.

Taken together, the changes to the First Year Seminar, PLA, LCs, and orientation put students at the center as learners and leaders in a comprehensive first-year experience. Importantly, integrating these elements required a deep understanding of and engagement with everyday life at the college, which was more available to faculty, students, and staff than senior leadership. Crisis requires that cabinet-level leaders focus more acutely on financial maneuvering, the concerns of the Board of Trustees, external stakeholder engagement, and compliance issues. These areas of focus distance them from everyday strategic planning with faculty and staff who have essential information and skills that could be mobilized as a part of the crisis response. Similarly, students' perspectives and their role in shaping the institution are often overlooked. The frequent result is financial cuts that neglect to consider a cohesive plan for how the college community will sustain student learning with a bare-bones budget. In these cases, it becomes urgent that student support staff, sub-cabinet leadership, and faculty collaborate to center students, attend to questions of scale and sustainability, and ensure a healthy organizational culture persists through the crisis. By bringing faculty, students, and staff together in planning and implementing this work, we learned that focusing on a liberatory peer education paradigm enables a larger mission-driven, resilient, and cost-effective infrastructure that can withstand institutional turmoil.

The success of our layered and liberatory approach to FYE is proof of concept for a larger model that we call the Solutions Project: an approach to peer education that layers student support and high-impact learning practices into a multiyear credited experience prioritizing student agency. The Solutions Project begins with our credited student-led First Year Seminar course, followed by a second-year project-based credited learning experience, and then a third-year credited leadership development program. In this model, third-year student leaders facilitate the first two years of the program. This structure creates a low leader-to-learner ratio and eliminates the potential cost of additional staffing. It also ensures all students are actively engaged in co-creating the conditions for student success. As they transition from learner to leader, students master the academic, professional, and interpersonal skills needed for their upper-level coursework, internships, and postgraduate plans while developing, practicing, and celebrating their agency in their own learning.

In the first year, the Solutions Project draws on our existing model to emphasize connection and preparation. In large lecture sections of one to two hundred, new students are welcomed to college and develop their collective cohort identity. New students meet faculty and staff from across campus, reflect on the value of college and their future goals, and learn how to access essential college services. In small recitations, peer leaders guide new students in developing foundational skills. Together, learners and leaders strengthen their essential college-level success skills, build self-care and self-advocacy skills, and foster community, connection, and belonging.

In the second year, the Solutions Project emphasizes project-based learning. Students serve in credited project-based learning incubators where they apply the skills and knowledge from their general education and major courses to solving real-world problems at the college. Project-based learning courses retain a liberal arts focus by teaching skills such as cross-cultural communication, self-advocacy, identity development, ethical decision making, and critical analysis of systems while building students' confidence and critical thinking skills. The project-based learning incubators can align with existing student pathways. For example, students in a Marketing and Communications Incubator could work on creative ways to promote summer orientation events to new students while students in a Social Entrepreneur Incubator could work on plans to launch a college resource pantry. In each incubator, students are encouraged to share in the process of building and improving the institution, developing a sense of ownership in the college's success, and learning that they have the collective ability to shape the things that affect their lives.

In the third year, the Solutions Project offers a credited leadership development program. Peer leaders immediately apply what they learn by facilitating First Year Experience and project-based learning incubators. This is particularly meaningful for students who are not yet getting professional and experiential learning opportunities in clinicals, student teaching, internships, or study abroad programs. As leaders, students take ownership of the Solutions Project model, which makes their learning more relevant and applied.

Peer education, project-based learning, and leadership development are proven high-impact practices in higher education, but few institutions combine them in intersecting credited courses that ensure the participation of every student.[5] The Solutions Project has the power to create institutional resiliency by improving student support ratios while decreasing cost. It does so by redeploying the time and money that both students and the institution already invest in elective and general education credits and FYE programs. Dedicated Solutions Project faculty oversee the learning of leaders, who in turn oversee the learning of project-based learners and new students, which significantly amplifies the impact of each credit of faculty load. By ensuring low leader-to-learner ratios, training leaders to provide holistic student support, and emphasizing student agency and skill development, the Solutions Project also decreases the need for extra-curricular student support initiatives, thus enabling institutions to avoid the expense of additional staff, space, and supplies. Finally, the Solutions Project resolves the tensions between career-focused education and liberal arts education by weaving them together and demonstrating how higher education enables a depth and breadth of skill development that goes beyond discipline-specific learning.

Our experience through a campus crisis forced us to think differently about how to prepare for and navigate the worst. Too often, particularly during crises, institutions get away with underserving students, especially those who have been historically excluded from, or marginalized within, higher education. Because the most vulnerable students are already accustomed to not getting what they deserve from institutions both within and beyond their education, colleges have come to expect that paring down the student experience will go unnoticed or uncriticized. In a crisis, it seems easy for the mission and the corresponding goals to devolve into simply "keeping the door open." The Solutions Project does the opposite at a low cost and offers nimble, adaptable, and creative ways to develop and strengthen student support. Efforts to mitigate a crisis can emphasize equitable, supportive, mission-focused educational excellence, even during periods of financial austerity. We learned that it is important to take risks to build what is possible and to embrace liberatory leadership with a clear vision.

While no campus wishes for a crisis, it is possible to find within it an opportunity to reimagine a new model of higher education that produces agile, creative, and passionate leaders who can build an equitable world. Staff, faculty, and academic affairs administrators know how to mobilize existing infrastructures and create new ones that can weather crises and improve student experiences, if given the space to do so. The Solutions Project, building on the success of our reimagined FYE and PLA programs, offers a scalable, iterative approach that doubles down on liberatory student success even when finances are tight. In doing so, it reimagines what higher education can provide to students, helping them develop into strong, collaborative, empathetic citizens who know how to solve problems, innovate, navigate challenges, and forge a better path for those who will come after them.

Notes

1. The Solutions Project was inspired by the work the authors did at one institution. We have now taken that work to other institutions, where we apply these concepts and continue to collaborate on ways to problem solve in higher education. Because this chapter emphasizes our ongoing work and seeks to share these ideas with other higher education change-makers, not to represent the institution where it originated, we have chosen not to name the institution.

2. Michael Brenan, "Americans' Confidence in Higher Education Down Sharply," Gallup.com, February 7, 2024, https://news.gallup.com/poll/508352/americans-confidence-higher-education-down-sharply.aspx.

3. AAC&U, "High-Impact Practices," AAC&U, 2024, https://www.aacu.org/trending-topics/high-impact.

4. meaghan davis, "Cocreating Liberatory Spaces in Higher Education" (EdD diss., New England College, 2024) ProQuest (31241569).

5. J. Zilvinskis et al., *Delivering on the Promise of High-Impact Practices: Research and Models for Achieving Equity, Fidelity, Impact, and Scale* (London: Routledge, Taylor & Francis Group, 2023).

Bibliography

AAC&U. "High-Impact Practices." AAC&U, 2024. https://www.aacu.org/trending-topics/high-impact.

Brenan, Michael. "Americans' Confidence in Higher Education Down Sharply." Gallup.com, February 7, 2024. https://news.gallup.com/poll/508352/americans-confidence-higher-education-down-sharply.aspx.

Davis, Meaghan. "Cocreating Liberatory Spaces in Higher Education." PhD diss., New England College, 2024. ProQuest (31241569).

Zilvinskis, John, Kinzie, Jillian Daday, Jerry, O'Donnell, Ken, and Vande Zande, Carleen, eds. *Delivering on the Promise of High-Impact Practices: Research and Models for Achieving Equity, Fidelity, Impact, and Scale*. Routledge, Taylor & Francis Group, 2023.

11

Understanding Campus Free-Speech Controversies

Law, Power, Solidarity

Andy J. Carr

For decades, America's college campuses have been recurring subjects of intense public discourse. From battles over racial integration and Vietnam War protests to more-recent scrutiny of curricular decisions, salient political debates have been waged on and about our higher education institutions. But among the most common, frequently recurring topics of concern are those falling under the broad label of "campus free speech" issues. Unfortunately, both many campus insiders and members of the general public have internalized a mythical view of free speech and, in doing so, failed to appreciate how claims about controversies are weaponized and escalate. This chapter thus provides a corrective to long-standing mythologizing of speech and specific suggestions for protecting campus communities from bad-faith campaigns.

Below, I briefly summarize relevant legal rules concerning on-campus speech and synthesize warning signs of crises likelier to escalate. Next, I show how present-day disputes fit longer historical patterns of speech-related backlash, identifying repeated discursive hallmarks and tactics of reactionary actors. Finally, I conclude with reflections on the political economy of these on-campus crises, including their unevenly distributed risks—financial, physical safety, and otherwise—and on the prospects for solidaristic action.[1]

Legal Frameworks and On-Campus Speech

No single essay could provide a comprehensive overview of free expression under the First Amendment.[2] Still, the US Supreme Court offers some ground rules that, taken together, gesture toward a consensus favoring "absolutist" free speech.[3] Two leading principles underlie this consensus: (1) the First Amendment is "anti-censorial," commanding government to uphold "strict . . . neutrality between topics and ideas"[4]; and (2) the outer bounds of free speech are defined in the negative, by *exceptions* from narrow speech "categories . . . that are either unprotected or subject to lesser degrees of protection."[5]

Traditionally, "lesser" or lower-value speech categories include those related to commercial transactions or conveyed via "expressive conduct," as well as sexual expression.[6] Exception categories have expanded to include incitement to violence,[7] threats,[8] terrorism-linked speech,[9] and criminal conspiracies[10]—infrequent situations but ones where, most agree, speech should yield to overriding safety concerns. Put simply, the absolutist consensus holds that the government cannot prohibit speech based on its content or the speaker's viewpoint. Government *may* impose reasonable "time, place, and manner" (TPM) restrictions, such as requiring protest permits, to maintain public order,[11] but if speech neither violates reasonable TPM restraints nor fits an exception category, it is inviolable.

That's the theory, anyway. Critical scholars have highlighted many inconsistencies, with permitting approvals and reviewing courts' decisions complicating absolutist axioms.[12] Moreover, legal and societal changes in recent decades transformed the nation's free speech environments. Money surging into politics (as "speech" itself[13]), changing control over loci of speech (e.g., digital media and platforms' dominance[14]), expanding government capacity for surveilling speech[15]—all momentous changes, accompanied by increasingly connected speech debates and partisan-ideological conflicts.

Seemingly fundamental distinctions in law—public versus private actors, for instance—are slippery. Private institutions, including private colleges and universities, generally should have wider leeway to restrain speech than public ones. Freedom of speech is freedom from state interference, after all, so one should expect most controversies to arise at public institutions. Insofar as the state is uninvolved in speech-restrictive actions, on-campus speech is a private institution's domain.

Recent speech-related controversies belie this theoretically sharp "public–private" distinction. Consider the congressional hearings launched in late 2023, ostensibly bringing in elite universities' presidents to address concerns regarding on-campus antisemitism. These spectacles embodied what Amy Kapczynski labeled then the "rightwing outrage machine." This machine is "asymmetric and selective," but systematic: media select targets for electeds to attack, amplifying attention and caricatures of academia's "radicalism" while granting media hysteria their official imprimatur.[16]

These narrative-building campaigns often succeed: Penn's president resigned December 9, 2023, days after testifying; by January 2, 2024, Harvard's president had followed. The latter, Claudine Gay, faced further allegations of plagiarism in her dissertation and later writings. But as Adria R. Walker noted, the maelstrom was a campaign by "activists" less concerned with Harvard's viewpoint diversity or academic rigor than "oppos[ing] diversity, equity and inclusion [DEI] initiatives." Gay herself bluntly characterized the "frightening" campaign as being "subjected to personal attacks and threats fueled by racial animus."[17] Not only did public–private distinctions collapse during that episode—much less during the spectacle of 2024's student encampments[18]—but such dynamics also underscore how bad-faith actors effectively mobilize around "speech" claims.

A Political Economy of Pretextual "Speech" Claims

Despite breathless news coverage, the foregoing were merely the latest in a long line of cases. Placing them in context elucidates long-routinized strategies of isolating targets to chill disfavored ideas. As far back as the 1960s, the politics of on-campus speaker controversies ring familiar. In March 1961, for instance, politicians and activists spoke out against plans for Frank Wilkinson to deliver a speech at the University of California at Berkeley. The speech was to take place shortly after the US Supreme Court had upheld his contempt-of-Congress conviction for refusing to testify before the House Un-American Activities Committee, an all-but-forgotten event today, but fiercely contested at the time.[19]

Just two years later, op-eds denounced San Diego State College for barring a planned speech at that campus. The speaker was Robert Welch, then-leader of the conspiratorial, far-right John Birch Society. One Pasadena Independent editorial writer assured readers they had "no use" for Welch or his organization but implored readers to see that "the free exchange of ideas, even objectionable ones, is essential to . . . democratic society," principles contravened by the college's decision to exclude Welch.[20] The absolutist view of free speech in the editorial could be pasted into any number of more-recent letters decrying on-campus censoriousness. But when read alongside Wilkinson's case at Berkeley, these cases also belie at least a hint of the "rightwing outrage machine" dynamic Kapczynski described, with asymmetric, partisan-aligned selective offense.

However familiar those early cases may seem, this is not to say contemporary controversies—or the threats and selection of targets they involve—are identical to those of the 1960s. Two 2017 incidents emphasize the point. The first brings us back to Berkeley, where clashes between protesters and police became touchstones for those decrying Berkeley's alleged hostility to free speech. But precipitating events deserve attention. As Judith Butler explained, escalating calls to cancel a campus talk—far-right provocateur Milo Yiannopoulos—were never about his "conservative ideas." Rather, many students and faculty objected to patterns of conduct: in prior events, Yiannopoulos "brought cameras into his lecture hall [and] projected images of members of his audience . . . to shame and berate," as well as purposefully "incite harassment" against selected targets. During the 2016–17 academic year, Yiannopoulos unleashed those tactics against University of Wisconsin-Milwaukee student-protester Adelaide Kramer, a "trans student [there] who found her image projected . . . during the event" and faced torrents of invective long after.[21] Like the 2023–24 campaigns against elite university presidents, rightwing media got to work, obfuscating organized harassment while generally vilifying students.[22]

UWM was hardly unprecedented. Just months earlier at DePaul University, Yiannopoulos deliberately goaded protesters, many Black and brown faculty or students, and generated intended results. After "paint[ing] people of color as criminals and sex objects," protesters "stormed the stage, taking the microphone," prompting on-campus groups who'd invited Yiannopoulos to claim "they were being silenced."[23] DePaul's leaders promptly apologized, emphasizing "freedom of speech" commitments, but fallout intensified anyway: "Hysteria over collegiate oversensitivity eclipsed the grave impact of [the talk], which set off a firestorm of racial hate." That "firestorm" included overtly racist incidents such as "nooses strewn around campus," anti-Mexican statements "painted . . . outside the school's quad," and death threats against one former professor who "resigned in protest over Yiannopoulos' speech."[24] Inciting actors harass targets, pivot to "crying persecution," then become a "conservative cause célèbre."[25] Rinse and repeat.

A second case is seldom remembered as a "speech" controversy at all: August 2017's Unite the Right (UTR) in Charlottesville, Virginia. As journalist P. E. Moskowitz observed in *The Case Against Free Speech*, UTR initially was advertised as a "free speech rally," obfuscatory language still appearing in criminal defendants' efforts to evade civil liability[26] stemming from the murder of UTR counterprotester Heather Heyer.[27] Having witnessed UTR, Moskowitz provides a clear-eyed perspective on the broader political economy of speech in two ways. First, free-speech debates in the US are really debates about where "we put those lines [separating] speech and acceptable action, acceptable action and violence"[28]—choices not based on reasoned analysis but rather on our changing preferences about what speech we like or abhor.[29] The US has never had entirely unrestrained speech, after all, nor is there compelling evidence that US laws are less restrictive than in other high-income liberal democracies. Second, on-campus and online speech are shaped by financial interests ranging from individual billionaires—such as Robert Mercer, one-time Yiannopoulos benefactor, or universities' most-influential donors[30]—to conglomerates consolidating local news sources, exemplified by Sinclair Broadcast Group.[31]

The vast majority of us do not work at Harvard or elite public flagships such as Berkeley or UVA. Nor can we rely on media allies and deep-pocketed donors when facing job-threatening harassment campaigns. For most, resources are depleted, faculty governance is specious, and adjunctification leaves widening swaths of academia atomized and exposed. Yet anyone in our communities can be targeted by sometimes-violent factions claiming the "free speech" mantle, backed by those hoping to control academic institutions or personally embracing extremist politics.[32] And with new state laws targeting protesters, schools, or both, the machine's monitoring power only grows.[33]

Toward Solidaristic Action

Two lessons merit emphasis. First, working at private institutions—whether parochial or elite and globally recognized—confers no protection from organized campaigns. The corollary is that politicization of these crises is unavoidable, both for institutions and for all of us individually. Even if remaining "apolitical" is desirable normatively, that's not how these dynamics work. Second, given the illustrations above, assessing risk demands awareness of context-contingent factors and the national speech ecosystem. Anticipating when nascent crises might spiral entails knowing the identities, media-generating capacities, and financial supports of key actors: speakers, targets, administrators, media.

It's complex terrain, but navigable. The question remains: How can we counter reactionary campaigns *without* jeopardizing on-campus speech and academic freedom? Two possibilities seem promising, one already apparent: organizing to expand union-backed protections. Waves of on-campus unionization votes and strikes indicate some momentum toward revitalizing union power exists—explicit contract provisions covering speech and academic freedom included.[34]

"Momentum," though, is relative. Union density remains at historic lows; right-to-work laws and antagonistic state leaders are genuine obstacles. Yet a second, related possibility pertains regardless of union-based organizing capacity—less-formal, but more-widespread organizing based on shared principles and mutual defense. The moment demands solidaristic action.

Nathan DuFord defines solidaristic action as "under[taking] coordinated efforts to work together to achieve political goals, based on shared values or aims, through the agitation of conflict."[35] Managing campus speech crises—and resisting reactionaries' interference—requires abandoning conflict-averse postures, our perceived political "neutrality." Deliberation and compromising with interlocutors are laudable normative commitments at times, but in these contexts they constitute unilateral surrender. You don't get to choose whether you want to "engage in politics." There's no opting out. Thus, acting politically, engaging in oppositional, perhaps combative ways, may be imperative—including willingness to challenge extant hierarchies. As the congressional hearings showed, placating niceties accomplish little; at worst, they can exacerbate threats to on-campus speech environments.

But solidaristic action, DuFord adds, involves accepting the *internally* conflictual nature of solidarity. Contestation intrinsically arises even among those sharing commitments to "democratic life," nationally or on campus.[36] That doesn't mean becoming quarrelsome "debate me!" types, but rather facing "substantive" conflicts head on—those "generated in the course of advancing a constitutive aim,"[37] such as preserving protest rights, academic freedom, and much more. Solidaristic action is an "ongoing project," one developed through mutually defined "common interest and coordinated action" and eschewing individualism, competition, or conformity."[38]

Who might contribute to these positive, communal forms of solidaristic action? How can mobilizing even begin?

Since solidaristic action is an evolving dynamic, forecasting foreseeable trajectories a priori is impossible. Still, potential confidants are identifiable—anyone who shares the pro-democratic values underlying expressive liberty and academic inquiry, who accepts the ways "dynamic" solidarity can be personally transformative.[39] Solidaristic action means a socially "thick" solidarity, a "lived practice" or "ethic," DuFord explains, combining social with political, *democratic* action.[40] Our communities can be democratic, vibrant speech environments—if we make them.

Notes

1. Nathan R. DuFord, *Solidarity in Conflict: A Democratic Theory* (Stanford, CA: Stanford University Press, 2022) ["*Solidarity*"].

2. For one recent, book-length examination of the First Amendment and free speech, see Ashutosh Bhagwat, *Our Democratic First Amendment* (Cambridge: Cambridge University Press, 2020). For a critical perspective on conventional speech doctrine, see David Kairys, "Freedom of Speech," in *The Politics of Law: A Progressive Critique*, ed. David Kairys, 3rd ed. (New York: Basic Books, 1998), 190–215.

3. Zachary S. Price, "Our Imperiled Absolutist First Amendment," *University of Pennsylvania Journal of Constitutional Law* 20, no. 4 (2018): 821.

4. Ibid., 822–23.

5. Ibid., 823.

6. See, e.g., Virginia State Board of Pharmacy v. Virginia Citizens Consumer Council, Inc., 425 U.S. 748 (1976); Central Hudson Gas & Electric Corp. v. Public Service Commission of New York, 447 U.S. 557 (1980). For a case on "expressive" physical actions—namely, flag-burning—see Texas v. Johnson, 491 U.S. 397 (1989). And for discussion of "lower value" sexual expression, see City of Erie v. Pap's A.M., 529 U.S. 277 (2000).

7. Brandenburg v. Ohio, 395 U.S. 444 (1969) (per curiam).

8. Virginia v. Black, 538 U.S. 343 (2003) (articulating the "true threats" doctrine).

9. Holder v. Humanitarian Law Project, 561 U.S. 1 (2010) (holding speech or advocacy may constitute forbidden forms of "material support" for designated terrorist organizations).

10. See, for example, United States v. Hassan, 742 F.3d 104 (4th Cir. 2014).

11. "TPM" regulations encompass not just protest permitting, but also (potentially) approval for marching routes or venues. Regardless, TPM restrictions must use the least-restrictive means possible and be applied in content-neutral ways. Watchtower Bible & Tract Society of New York v. Village of Stratton, 536 U.S. 150 (2002).

12. See, for example, Toni M. Massaro and Helen Norton, "Free Speech and Democracy: A Primer for Twenty-First Century Reformers," *U.C. Davis Law Review* 54, no. 3 (2021): 1667–70.

13. Citizens United v. Federal Election Commission, 558 U.S. 310 (2010).

14. For a wide-ranging overview of how free speech, communications law, technology, and online platform governance intersect, see Kate Klonick, "The New Governors: The People, Rules, and Processes Governing Online Speech," *Harvard Law Review* 131, no. 6 (2018): 1598–1670.

15. For early reflections on these concerns and corporate actors' growing surveillance capacities, see A. Michael Froomkin, "The Death of Privacy," *Stanford Law Review* 52, no. 5 (2000): 1461–1544.

16. Amy Kapczynski, "The Real Lessons We Should Draw from Claudine Gay's Resignation," LPE Project Blog, January 8, 2024, https://lpeproject.org/blog/the-real-lessons-we-should-draw-from-claudine-gays-resignation/.

17. Adria R. Walker, "Harvard President Resigns Amid Claims of Plagiarism and Antisemitism Backlash," *The Guardian*, https://www.theguardian.com/education/2024/jan/02/harvard-president-claudine-gay-resigns.

18. The latter context is more alarming after the June 2024 arrest of four Northwestern University educators for "obstructing police" during the same protest wave. Per Josh Honn—a librarian among those arrested—the charges "stem from the first day of the encampment . . . when faculty members and other staff formed a defensive line between student[s] and campus police." Lisa Kurian Philip, "Northwestern Police Arrest Four Educators, Months after Pro-Palestinian Encampment," WBEZ (Chicago), July 18, 2024, https://www.wbez.org/education/2024/07/18/northwestern-police-arrest-four-educators-months-after-pro-palestinian-encampment.

19. Wilkinson v. United States, 365 U.S. 399, 401 (1961). Wilkinson "unlawfully refused to answer a question pertinent to [investigations of] the House Committee on Un-American Activities" in 1958. Ibid., 400–01. For an op-ed calling on Berkeley to exclude Wilkinson, see, e.g., "Cancel Wilkinson's UC Talk–Mulford," San Francisco Examiner, March 21, 1961, at p. 9.

20. Editorial, "Free Speech on the Campus," Pasadena Independent, March 28, 1963, at p. 10.

21. Judith Butler, "Limits on Free Speech?" Academe Blog, December 7, 2017, https://academeblog.org/2017/12/07/free-expression-or-harassment/.

22. Diana Tourjée, "Trans Student Harassed by Milo Yiannopoulos Speaks Out," *Vice News*, January 3, 2017. In the UWM case, harassment-inciting speakers and far-right media personalities obfuscating incitement really were one and

the same: Yiannopoulos wrote for Breitbart at the time, an outlet that repeatedly condemned ostensibly anti-"free speech" UWM. Karen Herzog, "Breitbart Writer Targets Transgender UWM Student," *Milwaukee Journal Sentinel*, December 14, 2016, https://www.jsonline.com/story/news/education/2016/12/14/breitbart-writer-targets-transgender-uwm-student/95420206/.

23. Nico Lang, "Trolling in the Name of 'Free Speech': How Milo Yiannopoulos Built an Empire Off Violent Harassment," *Salon*, December 19, 2016, https://www.salon.com/2016/12/19/trolling-in-the-name-of-free-speech-how-milo-yiannopoulos-built-an-empire-off-violent-harassment/.

24. Ibid.

25. Ibid. For his part, Yiannopoulos fell out among the US right-wing ecosystem shortly after the UWM controversy because of resurfaced comments in which he defended pedophilia as potentially "hugely positive experiences." In early 2017, he resigned from Breitbart, lost a $250,000 book deal and the support of "billionaire backer" Robert Mercer, and soon became embroiled in largely unfavorable lawsuits. Emily Sakzewski, "Patreon Bans Controversial (and Broke) Far-Right Activist Milo Yiannopoulos from Fundraising," ABC News (Australia), December 7, 2018, https://www.abc.net.au/news/2018-12-07/patreon-bans-controversial-far-right-activist-milo-yiannopoulos/10595788. That is not to say Yiannopoulos exited public life: since failing to revive his "free speech" celebrity in Australia, he has worked for US Rep. Marjorie Taylor Greene (R-GA) and rapper Kanye West's brief 2024 presidential campaign. Mark Savage, "Kanye West Announces 2024 Presidential Bid," BBC News, November 25, 2022, https://www.bbc.com/news/entertainment-arts-63754702.amp.

26. See Sines v. Kessler, 324 F. Supp. 3d 765 (W.D. Va. 2018).

27. P.E. Moskowitz, *The Case Against Free Speech: The First Amendment, Fascism, and the Future of Dissent* (New York: Hatchette, 2019), chap. 1.

28. Ibid., 11.

29. Ibid., chap. 5.

30. Sakzewski, "Patreon Bans"; Moskowitz, *Against Free Speech*, chap. 6. For recent analysis of billionaire donors' efforts to monopolize university policy writ large—including Bill Ackman's involvement in Claudine Gay's ouster—see Reeves Wiedeman, "Raging Bill," *New York Magazine*, February 12, 2024, https://nymag.com/intelligencer/article/bill-ackman-war-harvard-mit-dei-claudine-gay.html.

31. See, for example, Gregory J. Martin and Joshua McCrain, "Local News and National Politics," *American Political Science Review* 113, no. 2 (2019): 372–84.

32. On the importance of financial backing to those evading erstwhile "cancellation," see, for example, Katelyn Burns, "Ezra Miller Proves You're Only as 'Canceled' as the Rich Person in Your Corner," MSNBC, June 17, 2023, https://www.msnbc.com/opinion/msnbc-opinion/ezra-miller-flash-reviews-cancel-culture-rcna89741.

33. For a paradigmatic case of state hostility to academia and academic freedom—Florida—see *Preliminary Report of the Special Committee on Academic*

Freedom and Florida, Association of University Professors (AAUP), May 24, 2023, https://www.aaup.org/file/Preliminary_Report_Florida.pdf, 11–15. Nationwide, the International Center for Not-for-Profit Law (ICNL) reports at least 305 anti-protest bills have been proposed since January 2017; 49 were enacted, some enhancing penalties for protesters who block access to oil and gas facilities or public roads, or who damage monuments ("acts of terrorism," under Arkansas law), others criminalizing masking at protests (North Carolina) or granting civil immunity to drivers who injure (*e.g.*, Iowa) and even kill (*e.g.*, Louisiana) protesters. "U.S. Protest Law Tracker," ICNL, last accessed July 24, 2024, https://www.icnl.org/usprotestlawtracker/?location=&status=enacted&issue=&date=&type=legislative#. North Carolina's law criminalizing protests "willfully imped[ing] traffic" includes mask-wearing as an aggravating factor that may trigger harsher penalties, its "sponsor [citing] recent protests on college campuses against Israeli's military campaign in Gaza, where some protesters have worn masks," among their justifications. Ibid.

34. See, for example, *Collective Bargaining Agreement Between The New School and SENS-UAW, Local 7902 (2023–2026)*, The New School Labor Relations Office, July 25, 2024, Appendix A; *Collective Bargaining Agreement Between The New School and ACT-UAW, Local 7902 (2022–2027)*, The New School Labor Relations Office, July 25, 2024, Art. VIII, Appendix A. Both are available at https://www.newschool.edu/human-resources/labor-relations/.

35. DuFord, *Solidarity*, 1.

36. Ibid., 2.

37. Ibid., 15.

38. Ibid., 11, 14, 43–45. DuFord deems the latter, individualistic type "antisocial solidarity," where groups' memberships are "exclusive and exclusionary," and whose aims are "domination or oppression." Ibid., 81, 84–86.

39. Ibid., 30. While these prerequisites dovetail with leading justificatory theories of free speech—which emphasize pro-democracy features and the "marketplace of ideas" metaphor—DuFord argues solidaristic practices, unlike prevailing speech theories, do not presume "consensus" will be reached. Ibid., 35.

40. Ibid., 48–49.

12

Teaching "Divisive Concepts"

The Destructive Impacts of a University Culture of Censorship

Christine Zabala-Eisshofer and
Lindsay Stallones Marshall

University culture has never been perfect in its embrace of diversity and social justice. However, in recent years Republicans have enacted legislation aiming to prevent universities from teaching about diversity in any capacity. This chapter focuses on the political and organizational landscape of the University of Oklahoma, following a 2021 legislative change that banned required courses on "divisive concepts." Christine and Lindsay taught "Gateway to Belonging at OU" at the University of Oklahoma as it transitioned from being a required diversity course to an optional course on belonging. In providing a personal history of teaching the pilot semesters of Gateway, we begin by tracing the creation and adaptation of the course over time by analyzing news articles, social media, and university websites. Then, we discuss our experiences teaching the course, focusing on the impact on our well-being and pedagogy. Finally, we conclude with recommendations for university administrators and teachers to be successful within this uncertain landscape. Gateway was created in response to student protests advocating for a better campus climate, but the University of Oklahoma failed to meet its commitment to students and instead eroded campus support and loss of goodwill. We write this analysis from the perspective of two faculty members hired to teach this once-required once-diversity course in an ultimately unsupportive environment.

Context

The University of Oklahoma began as a segregated institution in a sundown town. The university has a legacy of racism that students, faculty, and community members have regularly manifested. Throughout OU's history it is student activism that has forced a reluctant administration to make changes that expand belonging at the university. From George McLauren and Ada Lois Sipuel Fisher's lawsuits that forced OU to desegregate, to student groups such as OU Unheard's successful demands for a university response to racist actions in the OU community, progress toward a more diverse and inclusive campus community at OU has nearly always come from student action in the face of administrative reluctance to pursue structural change. In 2019, OU's Black Student Association announced the creation of the Black Emergency Response Team (BERT) to organize a response to "any racial incidents in the future and play a strategic role in making the University of Oklahoma a more inclusive environment" following several high-profile incidents of students wearing blackface and using anti-Black slurs on campus.[1] BERT organized actions and petitioned OU administration in September 2019 when another blackface incident occurred,[2] and again in February 2020 when two different professors used anti-Black slurs during class. When OU administrators failed to respond to BERT petitions, BERT organized a sit-in and hunger strike. Among the group's demands, which the university adopted, was a mandatory semester-long diversity class for all incoming OU students.[3]

From its beginning, the purpose of the mandatory course was diversity, equity, and inclusion (DEI). The July 2020 Board of Regents meeting minutes reported a desire to include a mandatory DEI course by Fall 2021.[4] Top university administrators repeatedly emphasized OU's commitment to DEI goals and highlighted their prominent place in the university's new strategic plan, *Lead On, University*.[5] Administrators also linked the new proposed course to BERT's demands. In an *OU Daily* retrospective on the sit-in published in February 2021, one administrator presented the Gateway course as a companion to the mandatory online DEI training required of all students, faculty, and staff at the time. Another administrator stated,

"We anticipate that this course will provide an introduction and pathway to the many, primarily upper-level courses . . . that focus on particular aspects of diversity, equity, and inclusion."[6] When another OU student's racist social media posts came to light in April 2021, the university's official response linked the upcoming course as a remedy for the incident: "According to the student, those photos originate . . . prior to attending OU or receiving any diversity, equity, and inclusion training or education. This harmful event is a prime example of why training and education are so important for students to receive in their first year of college."[7]

While OU made these steps toward an inclusive campus, the Oklahoma state legislature scrambled to prohibit them. In February 2021, House Republicans introduced HB 1775, its text lifted from the Heritage Foundation's model bill. While the purpose of the bill was ostensibly to prevent instruction or training that would cause "any individual to feel discomfort, guilt, anguish, or any other form of psychological distress on account of his or her race or sex," bill sponsor and Norman Representative Rob Standridge wrote on Facebook, "These cowardly, racist radical [white] leftists are unbelievably willing to sacrifice the opportunities and prosperity of their own children and grandchildren based solely on the color of their skin."[8] When Governor Stitt signed the bill into law on May 7, 2021, President Harroz wrote to the university community explaining that despite the fact that the training did not violate the law as written, the once-mandatory DEI training for students was now voluntary. In the same letter he touted the Gateway class as a supplement to that training and announced that the course would now be one of three possible courses to fulfill the new general education requirement. As such, the Gateway course, intended to "help develop our students into people who know how to understand others not like themselves" was not in violation of the new law.[9] Around the same time, the requirement name was changed from "Diversity, Equity, and Inclusion" to "First-Year Experience," of which the three new courses would be a part.[10]

The hiring process was in motion, a director selected, and faculty candidates applying to a job posting for candidates with "demonstrated knowledge of and commitment to diversity, equity, and inclusion education and best practices in cultural competency."[11] Candidates invited for interviews in May 2021 were given a course description that stated, "You [students] will increase your understandings of the structure of opportunity and inequity, of power and privilege that have shaped the communities and identities of your classmates."[12] Those hired as Gateway faculty arrived on campus in August 2021 prepared to teach a course aligned with DEI principles with the purpose of inspiring OU students "to engage fully in the on-going task of creating an inclusive community here on our campus and wherever your path takes you after you leave,"[13] assured by campus leaders that HB 1775 did not prohibit them from doing so. In short, Gateway to Belonging was designed as a diversity, equity, and inclusion class, was added as an option to the required general education curriculum in response to student action against patterns of racism on OU's campus and did not violate HB 1775 in its content or status as a required course.

Failure of Implementation

Once the course began, the university fell silent. The public shift in tone around the course was mirrored by our experience teaching the course. As tensions began to mount over the political climate in the state, the institutional support turned reactive. Higher education scholars have warned of the chilling effect of anti-DEI legislation, which we felt at our institution as well.[14] Once the course began, administrators began to distance the course from DEI language and goals, citing the influence of HB 1775. This distancing negatively impacted our ability to teach in three specific ways. The climate surrounding the course compromised our ability to build relationships with students in the classroom. We adhere to a critical pedagogy predicated on mutual respect and love for students. However, the political ecosystem prepared students to be oppositional, even before students knew what the course would be about. Institutional actors and faculty onboarding did not dispel this expectation and ultimately encouraged an adversarial climate with students. We were cautioned to view students as potential spies who could report our activities to parents or news sources, and to operate as if we were being recorded.

The vagueness around the purpose of the course and the language of belonging made achieving course outcomes difficult. Illustratively, the First-Year Experience website does not define belonging.[15] The switch from the language of "diversity" to that of "belonging" had a profound impact on our experience teaching the course. "Belonging" is a neutral category that can easily be applied to "all" students. With this rhetoric, addressing harmful or derogatory student behavior or ideas became almost impossible as "all" students in the class needed to feel like they belonged. Other scholars have noted how an emphasis on "all" students tends to mean "traditional white students with citizenship,"[16] and our experience was no exception. As we see in the publicity around the course, Gateway was initially proposed as a response to the BERT sit-in, but course content about the history of Gateway in the class itself intentionally refuted this history. Administration mirrored this shift, and we found that articulating the purpose or outcomes of the course in a meaningful way was virtually impossible.

Finally, the content of the course was significantly softened between the interview process and the course rollout. While we (among others) advocated for discussions of privilege, cultural appropriation, and institutional racism, including any DEI content was a struggle. In internal communications with faculty, HB 1775 was blamed. However, the implication that the university had to roll back the course and its content is a fiction, and the university went significantly beyond what was required to comply with the letter of the law.[17] The university made the course optional, guaranteeing that it did not fall under the purview of this legislation. Additionally, none of the proposed DEI topics compelled students to believe that people of color are superior to white people or that white students should feel guilty for past and present inequalities. Even if the course were required, the actual language of the law never applied to the proposed content.

Recommendations

In writing this chapter, we do not aim to lay blame on individuals. There are many educators and administrators at OU who are fighting to improve the campus climate for all students. The failure is systemic. Based on our own experiences, we would offer the following recommendations for university communities looking to respond to anti-DEI legislation in a way that supports marginalized students and faculty.

For administrators:

- Remain consistent about messaging to the public and students. We can see from public media coverage that the university was extremely vocal about how the course would address campus climate issues, but after the launch of the course, university press coverage of the course stopped. This cessation left significant confusion around the goals of the course and why students were required to take it.

- Avoid making decisions based on fear of how students might respond. Universities should not take action that makes it easier for legislators to end DEI programming or offices. Universities should respond only to what laws require if they do not feel comfortable challenging legislation directly.
- Provide support for faculty through professional development, clear direction, and coherent messaging about course goals and objectives. Many universities are now using the language of "belonging" as a politically palatable stand-in for diversity language. However, belonging as a concept can be defined in many ways, leaving faculty and students open to confusion about the actual goals of such initiatives.
- Create course objectives and assignments based on available multicultural education literature and pedagogical best practices. There is a significant amount of literature on diversity coursework which should be leveraged, and faculty experts in these fields should have a central role in the curriculum design process.
- Many faculty who apply for these DEI-oriented positions and find themselves in antagonistic situations risk not only their current employment but also their professional reputations by continuing to teach restricted courses. If possible, an avenue toward protecting that reputation can be found in publication, service, or teaching outside the diversity course.
- Student evaluations in these environments may not actually reflect faculty's pedagogical skill, and when used for evaluative purposes student feedback should be adjusted or interpreted with caution. It is equally important for administrators and supervisors of faculty teaching these courses to understand the research on the non-linear nature of student learning in these courses. Universities should have a framework for analyzing and responding to student discomfort necessary to process the content in these courses.

The above suggestions will make it easier for faculty to teach diversity content amidst the ongoing legislative crisis. However, we are also aware that individual faculty members may have little to no input into the university-wide response to state-level legislation that restricts spending on DEI. In the absence of administrative support, we also provide suggestions for faculty members who may be teaching similar courses with little to no university backing.

- Some approaches to creating a space to have classroom conversations when institutional support is minimal, absent, or even antagonistic include strategic adherence to the letter of the restrictive law, rooting inquiry in historical or otherwise distanced scenarios and allowing students to draw conclusions about their implications, or adjusting classroom engagement in ways that offer students multiple avenues for anonymized or individualized engagement with course topics and questions. For example, while we were not allowed to require our students to complete any assignments that included personal reflection, we could provide students space in class to individually reflect on their personal relationship to the material.
- Despite widespread concern that students would react with hostility toward the content, we found that students were much more likely to disengage from the material as a result of its lack of critical reflection. Of course, our positionality as white women teaching this course may have driven some of these attitudes, as faculty of color who teach similar content have noted that student resistance to the material may have more to do with faculty identity than the material itself.[18] We would encourage faculty to think about not only how the presence of critical pedagogies might lead to student resistance, but also how the lack of these kinds of strategies might also lead to student disengagement.
- When the institution makes it impossible for faculty to create the supportive classroom space that enables conversations about difficult topics among students, faculty often need to design pedagogical strategies that allow students to engage and ask questions directly to the professor. However, this approach creates a significant burden on faculty, especially faculty who share marginalized identities being discussed in the class.

- Faculty need to develop strategies for self-preservation under these circumstances, often outside the institution itself. We would also encourage those faculty whose positionality affords them more privilege in academic spaces to leverage that privilege in support of their colleagues.
- We want to affirm that the choice to respond to attacks on classroom instruction with minimal engagement (such as disengaging from difficult subjects when faculty cannot guarantee their own or student safety in those conversations) is valid and, unfortunately for our students, often the only option available to contingent or otherwise precarious faculty members.

Conclusion

As of this writing, Gateway to Belonging no longer exists. While no press releases were made, the class navigation tool shows no courses titled "Gateway to Belonging" offered in Fall 2024.[19] Instead, the university offers Gateway-titled courses designed to introduce students to disciplinary methodologies in various colleges. OU's decision to abandon the diversity course it promised in response to BERT's sit-in is a missed opportunity that falls fully in line with the university's historical role as an institutional obstacle to inclusivity in the OU community.

Reflecting on the university's response to racist incidents on campus just before the sit-in, BERT leaders expressed disappointment but not surprise that the institution was reluctant to make significant changes. One student leader observed, "If it [the university's promised diversity initiative] doesn't help the university's bottom line it might as well disappear."[20] Just a few years later, despite public commitments from top administrators and even a place in the institution's much-heralded strategic plan, that's exactly what happened.

Notes

1. Nick Hazelrigg, OU Black Student Association Announces Creation of Emergency Response Team Following Recent Racist Incidents," *OU Daily* January 24, 2019. https://www.oudaily.com/news/ou-black-student-association-

announces-creation-of-emergency-response-team-following-recent-racist-incidents/article_990ef3d8-2008-11e9-8209-5f966b416cb0.html.

2. Scott Kirker, "Interim OU President Joseph Harroz Condemns Racism Following Blackface Incident," *OU Daily*, September 22, 2019. https://www.oudaily.com/news/interim-ou-president-joseph-harroz-condemns-racism-following-blackface-incident/article_25cd38c0-ddaa-11e9-99c0-83b74663f39e.html.

3. KOCO Staff, "OU Officials Release Statement After Sit-In Following Professors' Use of Racial Slur in Class," *KOCO News 5*, Feb. 26, 2020. https://www.koco.com/article/ou-officials-release-statement-after-sit-in-following-professors-use-of-racial-slur-in-class/31125529.

4. Minutes of a Special Meeting, The University of Oklahoma Board of Regents, July 27–28, 2020. https://hdl.handle.net/11244/330086.

5. "Lead On, University. The University of Oklahoma Norman Campus Strategic Plan," April 9, 2024. https://www.ou.edu/leadon.

6. Blake Douglas, "BERT Sit-In One Year Later: What Has Changed at OU?," *OU Daily*, February 25, 2021. https://www.oudaily.com/news/bert-sit-in-one-year-later-what-has-changed-at-ou/article_66ed6f78-7782-11eb-bd0c-c30cc89c001a.html.

7. Blake Douglas, "As OU Freshman's Racist Social Media Posts from High School Emerge, University Reiterates Need for New Diversity Course," *OU Daily*, April 14, 2021. https://www.oudaily.com/news/as-ou-freshman-s-racist-social-media-posts-from-high-school-emerge-university-reiterates-need/article_c147cb7e-9d4f-11eb-ba1c-6b7bea5573a9.html.

8. Reese Gorma, "Standridge Advocates for Anti-Diversity Training Bill," *The Norman Transcript*, April 25, 2021, https://www.normantranscript.com/news/standridge-advocates-for-anti-diversity-training-bill/article_764e3d9a-a53a-11eb-8e4d-23faed6c9855.html.

9. Harroz email to OU Community, May 7, 2021.

10. Minutes of an Organizational Meeting, The University of Oklahoma Board of Regents, May 27–28, 2021. https://shareok.org/handle/11244/330729.

11. "Ranked Renewable Term Faculty Position, General Education Course "Gateway to Belonging" posted to Interfolio on March 16, 2021.

12. Draft course description attached to email from Lori Snyder to Lindsay Marshall, 20 May 2021.

13. Draft course description, ibid.

14. NASPA, "Student Affairs Perspectives on Anti-Critical Race Theory State Policies and National Narratives." NASPA Issue Brief. 2023.

15. "First Year Experience," *Dodge Family College of Arts and Sciences*, University of Oklahoma, accessed June 28, 2024, https://www.ou.edu/cas/fye.

16. Liliana E. Castrellón, " 'As Soon as They Hear "Undocumented," They Stop Advising': Theorizing a (Sub)Conscious Evasion of Responsibility from Institutional Agents to Undocumented Students." *Educational Studies* 57, no. 3 (2021): 269–86.

17. A similar charge was leveled at OU regarding its response to COVID-19 state legislation. See Jillian Taylor, "'It's Just Not Willing to Lead On': OU Law Faculty Call University to Fight Senate Bill 658, Executive Order," *OU Daily* August 19, 2021. https://www.oudaily.com/news/it-s-just-not-willing-to-lead-on-ou-law-faculty-call-university-to-fight/article_151a626e-0102-11ec-b41f-87970b0685f6.html.

18. Scheuths et al., "Passionate Pedagogy and Emotional Labor: Students' Responses to Learning Diversity from Diverse Instructors," *International Journal of Qualitative Studies in Education* 26, no. 10 (2013): 1259–76.

19. "Fall 2024 Semester," *ClassNav*, The University of Oklahoma, accessed June 28, 2024. https://classnav.ou.edu/#semester/202410.

20. "Words Matter: Race and Racism at the University of Oklahoma" On Our Campus, podcast, February 17, 2020, https://podcasts.apple.com/us/podcast/words-matter-race-and-racism-at-the-university-of-oklahoma/id1496625965?i=1000465886530.

13

SB 202

Opposing Anti-DEI Legislation at an R2 in Indiana

Camille Engle, Sheron Fraser-Burgess,
Jennifer Grouling, and Matthew R. Hotham

Jonathan Friedman's "Goodbye, Red Scare; Hello Ed Scare" draws stark parallels between the Red Scare and conflicts over K–12 education that followed Black Lives Matter protests and George Floyd's murder (Friedman 2022). Two years later, this backlash came to higher education in Indiana with Public Law 113 (State Bill 202). This legislation used boilerplate wording from the American Legislative Exchange Council (ALEC), echoing similar legislation in other red states (Mabry 2016). The law radically alters academic labor by scrutinizing university teaching and mentorship on the grounds of "intellectual diversity," a term taken from David Horowitz's "Academic Bill of Rights." It also creates a system for employees and students to inform on non-compliant or potentially noncompliant faculty. According to Senator Deery, one of the bill's coauthors, the discomfort expressed by conservative students illustrated in a state-wide Gallup survey warranted this reform (*IGA Education Committee* 2024). It is noteworthy that we could not verify the claims Deery made about this Gallup survey since the numbers he cited do not match the published data and may be based on unpublished survey data specific to Purdue or on cross-tabs not published in the public report (ICHE 2023). This bill exemplifies a larger conservative effort to transform higher education.

Political actors who distrust these institutions' capacity for self-governance will now monitor professors. Academic integrity and expertise have been exchanged for brute neutrality or "both sides-ism." It's unclear what ideas will be considered neutral or how well-accepted ideas must be for them to meet curricular standards. Legislators will hash out the higher education scope of this law messily affecting academic careers and student learning. The law questions whether the tenure process is sufficient to assess a professor's expertise. It replaces years of graduate study, a rigorous hiring process, a seven-year-long probationary period, and yearly continuing review by colleagues with a to-be-determined department or college assessment. Rather than evaluating faculty based on teaching ability, publication record, or service to the university, trustees will have the final say as to whether faculty have exhibited sufficient political non-neutrality.

As Ball State University (BSU) community members, we believe the citizens of Indiana deserve better from their lawmakers. A serious commitment to democracy should foster pathways to protect higher education as a public good and spaces that promote freedom of thought, critical thinking, and respect for differences that advance an egalitarian society. With this in mind, we gathered our forces to fight this bill. In this chapter, we share our experiences and strategies for resisting this bill at an R2 institution, including perspectives from both faculty and students.

The Ball State Context and Non-R1 Experience

BSU's advocacy chapter of the American Association of University Professors (AAUP) was reinvigorated in 2020 and was growing its membership when SB 202, now Public Law 113, was advanced in the Indiana legislature. The three faculty authors of this article are members of the AAUP, which was aware of several educational bills working their way through the Indiana Senate. Dr. Sheron Fraser-Burgess informed the AAUP that SB 202 was moving quickly through the Senate and would soon pass on to the Indiana House of Representatives. In a meeting between the BSU administration and the Black Faculty Association she learned that our administration would not be opposing the bill. We had a small, but active group of participants that quickly jumped into action, realizing the urgency of the situation.

A part of our early work was reaching out to other state AAUP organizations. Building statewide resistance, however, took time. Meanwhile, our AAUP chapter remained busy. By the first statewide meeting of AAUP chapters, by drafting an opposition statement, sending letters to potential allies, proposing a resolution before Faculty Council, and had held a campus teach-in. While we found our colleagues across the state invaluable allies, we also discovered that our advocacy at an R2 university took different forms and faced different challenges than at the flagship universities in the state. This journey of resistance has brought us closer together, fostering a sense of unity and collaboration in our shared purpose.

Challenges in Getting Press Coverage

Although the law would impact all state universities, the press presented the bill as a contest between the two flagships: the more conservative-leaning Purdue and the more liberal-leaning Indiana University (IU). National AAUP advocates suggested we write op-eds and push a press-heavy strategy. The *Muncie Star Press*, with only one local reporter, did not respond, and neither did multiple statewide and national publications. Meanwhile, IU and Purdue faculty were frequently quoted and published. Ball State faculty only recognized when they expressed the conservative side of the issue, such as business professor Michael Hicks (Hicks 2024). Thus, we found that our "press" strategy needed to focus more on social media. Our AAUP chapter maintained a strong and frequent presence on Twitter (X) and Facebook, allowing us to reach community members, likeminded organizations, and even students. Several national organizations told us they learned about or tracked SB 202 developments through our tweets.

Differences in Focus

The tenor of discussion at Ball State also varied from other AAUP organizations. Immediately we saw the discourse at the state level focus on protecting tenure. While this was certainly important, Ball State's large teaching faculty typically has a 4-4 teaching load. Tenure-track faculty teach a 3-3 course load, with teaching assistants for a few faculty. While this leaves less time for advocacy, it allows for deeper connections with our students. Furthermore, our university serves many first-generation diverse students and is purported to value "inclusive excellence." Many faculty members were trained to provide culturally responsive pedagogy and engage in hiring practices valuing faculty and promoting diversity, equity, and inclusion. The bill posed a threat to these efforts, and we responded not only as scholars but as teachers worried about our students.

Student Outreach

One of our first actions, then, became outreach to student organizations that might be impacted by SB 202. Although this bill does not ban DEI initiatives, it does require a yearly account of money spent on DEI as part of the process for requesting university funding from the legislature. We fear this will have a chilling effect on services for our multicultural and LGBTQIA+ students. We also worry that the bill will limit what views students hear and are permitted to express in the classroom as faculty on campus will alter their lesson plans out of fear of being fired for teaching, commenting on, or even intervening in student discussions about "controversial" topics.

It was our duty to warn students of these threats to their education through a teach-in. At this event, the provost claimed that we had not properly understood the bill and that it posed no threat to students or faculty at Ball State. The students strongly challenged these claims, calling out Ball State for recruiting students of color while not fighting this bill. In addition, ten undergraduates testified the following day at the House Education Committee, nine of them from BSU. Students brought a fire to both the teach-in and to the House testimony that was visibly absent from other universities. Furthermore, students took deep offense to Representative Jake Teshka's statement that "we've seen a lot of students here today and I'm just wondering if this is faculty driven" followed by an attempt to get a student to name faculty who had attended the teach-in (*IGA Education Committee* 2024). The implication that students were so easily led by faculty as to need government protection angered them. As the weeks continued, students turned out to support faculty, hold rallies, and posted signs on campus. The supportive relationship between faculty and students made our more teaching-focused university stand out among state efforts to resist the bill.

Student Perspectives and Actions

Camille Engle was one student who became particularly engaged in activism surrounding SB 202. In this section she shares her experience as a member of a student organization who assumed the call to action.

As a secondary education major who chose BSU for its teaching program, I was appalled by the BSU administration's failure to defend educators' and students' rights against the overreach of the Indiana General Assembly (IGA). In spirit, the bill was an extension of the far-right Christian nationalist movement to control spaces of public education, and other students needed to know what was happening to their education.

After some initial planning, a student organization, the Honors Organization for Promoting Equity (HOPE), began advertising the AAUP teach-in on social media. At the teach-in, any faith I had in the university's administration died watching the provost attempt to defend an indefensible bill. After learning about the opportunity to testify before the House Education Committee, the next day, nine BSU students signed up. While most Republicans on the education committee chose to ignore their constituents, the students were not done.

HOPE continued to make flyers to raise awareness about SB 202. The AAUP offered us fliers, but we declined them to make the point that our professors were not guiding our opposition but that our voices must be listened to as our own. We wrote a petition opposing SB 202 that included a list of recommended actions for the BSU administration. We organized an on-campus protest as a coalition of seven student organizations. Seeing students show up on a freezing February afternoon to sign our petition and hold posters was encouraging. Two student news organizations stopped by, providing on-campus publicity (Ground 2024).

We collected more signatures than expected but our petition led to an unproductive email thread with BSU President Mearns, who clarified that students would have no role in SB 202 implementation and interpretation. His discomfort having an open dialogue with students showed in removing the other student organizations CCed on the email, replacing them with administrators and General Counsel. Our exchange continued, but he consistently accused students of misunderstanding the bill and refused to meaningfully engage with our requests for more information and a seat at the table.

As an activist, educator, and student, I learned much by losing this fight. University administrators and legislators do not expect students to represent their interests, but by doing so we proved that we do not need the sort of paternalism that bills like this foster. Furthermore, in a deeply problematic trend toward corporatizing institutions of higher education, students are consumers. Yet we can exploit this: they cannot ignore us entirely if we complain loud enough and hold our money as ransom. If students make it clear that ethical and equitable practices and values are a guiding factor in where they choose to go to college, the business of higher education must meet consumer demand. My fellow students worry about how SB 202 will impact their education and wonder if they need to transfer to a private school or a different state. Ball State will lose business because of SB 202.

Finally, and what started all of this for me, is the necessity of establishing relationships with faculty. Despite what the IGA claims, faculty are not the ones suppressing student voices. By lifting each other up, our shared protests are only made louder.

Strategies for Fighting Similar Bills in Your State

Build Relationships and Networks

Bills like SB 202 can move quickly. Faculty and students need to be prepared and aware before a bill gets proposed. Assess the insider vs. outsider relationships among faculty governance, administration, and campus faculty activists. "Insiders" have cultivated relationships with administrators, who will collaborate with them off the record. One salient question is whether administrator allies are truly coconspirators for academic freedom and social justice. Activists typically have been loud and proud in resisting institutional policies and speaking truth to power. Administration views them as troublemakers, leaving them marginalized in official settings. A truly democratic institution is responsible for listening to these voices. By bringing together students, community members, staff, and administrators at various levels within the university, and faculty members of all statuses to our teach-in, we attempted to give both activists and insiders epistemic weight and consideration. Preparing starts with a strong group of faculty activists, organized before the crisis strikes. The AAUP is an ideal, but not the only, locus for such activism. It is helpful if some members of this group occupy service roles across the university. Our AAUP chapter had members on numerous committees, subcommittees, taskforces, and on Faculty Council. This allowed us to gather information quickly, learn how various levels of the administration were grappling with the bill, assess potential allies and pressure points, and ask tough questions at multiple steps.

Don't just focus on the impact of legislation on tenure-track faculty, and don't underestimate student allies. While our active AAUP chapter and robust university service allowed us to become aware of and quickly mobilize to oppose SB 202, one of the clearest differences between Ball State's opposition to the bill was our student engagement. We were the only university with multiple undergraduates testifying before the House Education Committee. We were the only university to hold a teach-in before the bill's passage to inform students about its impact. Students pushed back against the provost's talking points, which put him off balance and caused him to briefly backtrack on his support for the bill. Student support buoyed our spirits, kept the pressure on the administration when our energy flagged, and provided an additional and more acute point of pressure on the administration.

Start building community allies as well. Build relationships now with your senators and representatives. Call them, send them notes, speak with their legislative assistants. Be cognizant of the background, districts, and voting history of the House and Senate Education Committee members. Republicans in districts with a university might be more amenable to your arguments than those without a university. Learn about the process by which legislators propose, amend, and pass bills in the legislature. It is helpful to have someone with legal training to help you interpret the bill. This could be a faculty member or a friendly legislator's legal team. Small missteps in understanding the content of the bill or the legislative process will be latched on to by legislators and university administrators to discredit faculty criticism, so it's important to be accurate as well as timely when critiquing the bill.

Through getting to know our representatives, we learned that faculty opposition was of no consequence to Ball State's administration and the state legislature. We, therefore, pivoted to inform people whose voices did matter to them. We contacted alumni groups to inform them of the bill's provision disenfranchising alumni in selecting board members. Alumni pressure resulted in its removal from the bill's last version. We drafted letter templates to state representatives that focused on how SB 202 contradicted the conservative values of small government and free speech, circulating them among students, parents, alumni, and local political organizations. Over the course of fighting the bill, we built relationships with statewide and national organizations that have continued to bear fruit. Once the bill passed, we brought a panel of experts from national organizations, including the ACLU and PEN America, to speak about the dangers of SB 202 in the context of similar laws in Florida and Texas.

Keep Making Plans

In addition to building relationships, it may be necessary to support rigorous evidence-gathering and research. K–12 teachers' unions often have dedicated legislation watchers you can work with. Your university has legislative liaisons, but, notably, they advocate for the university as an institution and business and not specifically for faculty or academic freedom. Once the legislature passes and implements a bill, you may need to gather information on its impact for use in future legal cases. Our AAUP chapter, for example, is collecting data on faculty self-censorship in response to SB 202.

There should also be a pipeline through which accurate information is consistently and regularly disseminated. A hastily assembled statewide AAUP WhatsApp group proved unwieldy and was occasionally a source of misinformation and panic. Our BSU AAUP chapter's Slack proved a more effective means of organizing resistance, with channels dedicated to specific topics and tasks: some only open to AAUP leadership and some that included broader audiences.

Lastly, develop a public communication plan. This should include op-eds when possible but also social media. Having a preexisting social media presence is important for gaining traction when you most need it, so be sure to maintain an active social media presence before a crisis strikes. You will also need an on-campus communication strategy. Often, the university will bar you from using their email servers, printers, and bulletin boards to communicate. It is important to have other means of keeping faculty, staff, and students informed. Collect noninstitutional email addresses for all your members. Set up a means of rapid communication via Slack or another non-university platform. The administration will use university email and official meetings to communicate their position on such legislation with faculty and students, so it is important to have a preestablished means of responding in kind.

Conclusion

Due to our size, status, and context, bills like SB 202 impact Ball State differently from larger universities, requiring different strategies and responses. While much attention was focused on IU and Purdue, Ball State students and faculty were able to mobilize in impressive numbers, using a host of strategies to challenge the bill. While this was a loss, our activism slowed the bill's progress, helped to get some problematic elements of the bill stripped from the last version, and let our administration know that we were paying attention. For other faculty at nonflagship public universities, these strategies might also be useful.

Bibliography

Friedman, Jonathan. 2022. "Goodbye Red Scare, Hello Ed Scare." *Inside Higher Ed*, February 23, 2022. https://www.insidehighered.com/views/2022/02/24/higher-ed-must-act-against-educational-gag-orders-opinion.

Ground, Olivia. 2024. "Students and Faculty Grow Concerned about Senate Bill 202 and the Potential Changes in the Tenure Track." *Students and Faculty Grow Concerned about Senate Bill 202 and the Potential Changes in the Tenure Track*, February 29, 2024. https://www.ballstatedaily.com/article/2024/02/students-and-faculty-grow-concerned-about-senate-bill-202-and-the-potential-changes-in-the-tenure-track.

Hicks, Michael. 2024. "Deep Ideological Chasm behind SB 202 Will Remain." *Muncie Star Press*, March 17, 2024. https://www.thestarpress.com/story/opinion/columnists/2024/03/17/sb-202s-challenge-to-critical-theory-doesnt-come-from-right-wing-conspiracy/72991997007/.

Indiana Commission for Higher Education (ICHE). "Indiana Campus Free Speech Report 2023." 2023. https://www.in.gov/che/files/Campus-Free-Speech-Report.pdf.

Indiana General Assembly Education Committee Meeting - Weds, Feb. 14 - 10:30 AM. 4:27:10-4:36:42. 2024. https://iga.in.gov/session/2024/video/committee_education_0400.

Mabry, Brittany Lauren. 2016. "The Influence and Impact of the American Legislative Exchange Council (ALEC)." George Washington University.

Part 3

Building Communities of Care

When faced with a crisis, it helps to have built or be building a resilient community, as many of the essays in this section demonstrate. With campus-wide cultures and habits of care, rooted in values as well as in centers of teaching and learning and other sites of faculty confluence and interaction, we can help our students and our colleagues, as well as our institutions, handle crises. By emphasizing the values inherent in any thoughtful and committed pedagogy, these essays offer ways to build the muscle memory needed to support a campus in crisis, to use the work we all do in teaching to enable coping, for individuals as well as for the community as a whole. And, even when the worst happens and your campus is shuttered, those connections can help us all deal with the grief that accompanies such loss, and, perhaps, to lead to some healing.

14

Starting Good Things

Generative Pedagogy and the Art of Creating Community on Campus

Luke Waltzer

The university is vital to efforts to enact more just futures. That much of the instability facing public higher education has been instigated by actors outside of the university is evidence of how important our institutions are as ballast against the crescendoing impacts of neoliberalism and right-wing revanchism. Universities are not only sites for new knowledge to emerge but also house institutional spaces where it has long been possible to establish relationships, ways of being, and communities of practice that resist, interrupt, and provide alternatives to dehumanizing social systems. Attacks on academic freedom, new state and federal directives outlawing inclusive practices, programs, and curricula, and the regular subjugation of institutional priorities to market logics have diminished the capacity of universities to operate as sites of possibility. Yet much of the university's value remains in the collective thinking and dreaming about freedom that it can spark, even as this work happens amidst increasingly precarious conditions. If our institutions are to be worth saving, their potential for establishing communities of practice that prioritize justice and well-being must be preserved.[1]

Good things don't just start on their own in universities, however. They're produced by the labor and relationships at the heart of our institutions: the teaching, learning, and research that faculty and students do, and the service and leadership of staff and administrators. Higher education pedagogy, then, is more than the work we do in the classroom with students. It is also the foundation for how we understand the university and move through it as workers. A generative, radical pedagogy of freedom challenges or resists systems and decisions—such as the uncritical acceptance of grades and weed-out courses, the prioritization of the endowment over community relationships, or the diversion of vital resources to flashy new programs—that are not primarily concerned with the goals of learners or the communities that support the institution. Recent scholarship from critical university studies, Black studies, feminist and critical pedagogy, the digital humanities, and the scholarship of teaching and learning offers values, models, and specific strategies for doing the work of the university in principled, democratic, nonhierarchical, generative, and community-affirming ways.

Foundations: Critical Scholarship, the University, and Freedom Dreams

Scholars working within the field of critical university studies have detailed the political economy of higher education, tracing the emergence and evolution of the consumer model of the academy, and exposing the various pressures upon institutions that have produced the current intertwined crises of student debt, austerity-driven budget regimes, and the outsourcing of curricular decision making to unaccountable third parties. This scholarship has shown us how the modern American university has been shaped in service of capital, and how power as exercised through budgets, political pressure, and administrative priority setting has consistently placed inquiry and community in the back seat.[2] The crises facing higher education are both structural and ideological, and an awareness of this history is necessary to intervene in the university's trajectory.

Scholars at the intersection of critical university studies and Black, race, and ethnic studies have also taught us about the university's historical complicity with racism, exclusion, exploitation, dispossession, and carcerality. Fred Moten and Stefano Harvey's work on the "undercommons" rejects the structures of the university and the forms of knowledge it produces. They argue that the university turns "insurgents into state agents" through professionalization, and advocate for the subversion of institutions from inside: they urge us to be "in" and not "of" the university.[3] Yet without the university, a vibrant undercommons is difficult to imagine. Harvey, Moten, and others do affirm that the university remains a place of refuge for the subaltern, which is an invitation to use the institutions as a launching pad in the pursuit of broader freedoms.

One needn't believe that the university is irredeemable to be drawn to the possibilities for freedom that percolate in the undercommons. Fugitivity—the enlightened stance Moten and Harvey promote, which Jarvis Givens has defined as "a social and rhetorical frame by which we might interpret black Americans' pursuit to enact humanizing and affirming practices of teaching and learning"[4]—offers an orientation to the university that is in service of communal, liberatory goals rather than elite social reproduction. Givens focuses on the hunger for education at the center of the Black freedom struggle, reminding us that pedagogical conditions need not ultimately be constrained by the intent of institutions. Rather, the conditions of learning should be determined by the goals of teachers, students, and the communities of which they are a part. There's risk involved in efforts to liberate university resources for "non-institutional" goals, but many histories show us it is possible.

Since the 1960s Black feminist teacher/activists/organizers and critical pedagogues have adapted to the university strategies that enact liberatory praxis even within dehumanizing systemic constraints, such as curricula that don't represent the histories of students or academic policies that are punitive rather than affirming. Danica Savonick's *Open Admissions: The Poetics and Pedagogy of Toni Cade Bambara, June Jordan, Audre Lorde, and Adrienne Rich in the Era of Free College* explores what this looked like in the 1970s at the City University of New York, when Black and Brown students flowed into the university, changing the composition of the student body.[5] The teaching methods of these "teacher-poets" interrogated power, welcomed different modes of expression, engaged with local communities, and promoted collectivism. Chy Sprauve has traced how the care work of civil rights movement-era organizers and educators like Ella Baker and Septima Clark resonates today in the field of Writing Studies. Sprauve details how the questions asked in the Mississippi Freedom Schools in the 1960s about receptivity, reflection, ritual, and craft have utility in justice-oriented college teaching today.[6] Like Paolo Freire, bell hooks, and other critical educators, these scholars and the activist/educators they study understand the boundaries between universities and contemporaneous social movements as porous. Ideas and critiques that emerge from literacy and arts movements, prison abolition efforts, and political and labor organizing find their way into the university. So too do pedagogies that resist or reject the constraints the university imposes upon learning and community formation.

Scholars in the digital humanities (DH) have also resisted circumscribed ways of being in the university. DH has fostered projects that are more collaborative than competitive, integrate labor from different domains inside and beyond the university, and develop knowledge with and for various publics. This conceptualization of DH work as a communal good has a wider political utility. As Jessica Marie Johnson told Melissa Dinsman, "The digital—doing digital work—has created and facilitated insurgent and maroon knowledge creation within the ivory tower. . . . DH has offered people the means and opportunity to create new communities. And this type of community building should not be overlooked; it has literally saved lives."[7]

DH projects are often designed with a spirit of generosity, with and for communities that have historically been excluded from, exploited by, or invisible to the university. One example is the work of the Center for Black Digital Research at Pennsylvania State University. Among their projects is "Douglass Day," a distributed, community-based transcription project facilitated every year on Frederick Douglass's birthday. It features an "Organizing Kit" that provides detailed guidance to any local organization or institution that wants to join the celebration and preserve Black history in their own communities. The kit includes outreach and promotional copy, design templates, tips on finding and setting up space for events, curricula for the integration of projects into classrooms at varying levels, and more.[8] Undergirding the labor, care, and organizing acumen of Douglass Day is a vision of the university as a crucial node in the American social fabric, as well as a sense of pedagogical obligation to share institutional resources and practical expertise with various publics. The university, as Kathleen Fitzpatrick notes, isn't just a source of wisdom, though; it requires engagement and support of those publics to navigate the "panoply of crises" it faces. Doing so effectively requires " 'generous thinking,' a mode of engagement that emphasizes listening over speaking, community over individualism, collaboration over competition, and lingering with the ideas that are in front of us."[9]

A spirit of generosity also runs through recent publications in the scholarship of teaching and learning, focused specifically on college-level pedagogy. Over the past decade the Teaching and Learning in Higher Education series published by the West Virginia University Press released more than fifteen titles on topics such as the science and emotion of learning, ungrading, reading in the digital age, teaching as a radical act of hope, and more.[10] Each book weds original research and theoretical sophistication with practical guidance that educators can begin implementing immediately in the classroom. This work and others like it have been a tremendous resource for those of us who support teachers on our own campuses, allowing us to focus our energy on the important labor of distilling expert guidance for our specific contexts.[11]

Principled Action: Building the Community We Desire

The scholarship cited above shares a vision of the university as a site where transformative community and thinking are a social and collective process produced by the commitments and labor of students, faculty, and staff inside the university. Like most other scholars, I have learned about academic administration, fundraising, mentorship, and leadership entirely on the job. But I've been guided by the values, commitments, and methods of scholars and activists like the ones referenced above who have taught me how to hold space for meaningful work and community to emerge. They've shown me how to take into my teaching, mentorship, and collaborations a responsiveness to context, a clear sense of my goals and an openness to the goals of others, the belief that there is usually more than one correct answer to a question, the understanding that learning is enriched by multiple forms of knowledge, a commitment to care for the well-being of others, and a desire to share what we produce openly. These approaches have helped my colleagues and me navigate a series of traumatic disruptions over the past decade at the City University of New York. Together we've worked through artificial scarcity and recurrent and chaotic budget cuts, drastic changes in leadership and institutional priorities, drastic shifts in federal policy that put funding at risk and expose undocumented and other non-American students to potential deportation, COVID and its accompanying social, political, and mental health disruptions, student protests against racist state violence and the war in Gaza, and much more. Only some of those moments produced "campus crises," but they each in their own way created crisis conditions for members of the community.

We must continue to address the large systems and resist the forces that undermine higher education. We are better positioned to do so if we see our work as part of a community whose commitments and practices enact the visions we have for more just institutions, and if our labor opens up space for new ideas to emerge. This is not just a set of values to be proclaimed but rather offers strategies and methods for doing the day-to-day work of the university in ways that affirm its potential to start good things. Below are some suggestions for how to build and tend to resilient community within the university. This guidance is intended mostly for those in leadership positions, though it assumes that everyone in a community should play a role in determining how engagement happens. Ultimately, taken together, it demonstrates that a generative pedagogy is both a commitment and a set of practices that can be learned.

Meetings and Collaboration

The distinct value of meeting is the opportunity to tap into the collective wisdom and knowledge of those assembled in ways that generate intellectual or programmatic momentum. Meetings, like class sessions, should have a clear purpose and intent, with expectations that everyone will have opportunities to contribute. The facilitator should open and hold space for inclusion, sense-making, and sharing. A goal is for participants to leave feeling empowered and more able to fulfill their role within the collective trajectory of the program, initiative, or course. Tools for meaningful meetings include co-written agendas, rotating facilitation roles, cumulative and collaborative note-taking, freewriting for reflection or to prepare to share thoughts, entry and exit tickets, and "taking stack" to ensure all have a chance to speak.

If you can feed people, do. Food is a universal expression of care.

Sharing Credit

Individualistic ways of being, which are reinforced by the incentive structures of the university, treat credit as currency. But credit is not zero sum, and sharing it generously is an honest representation that our work is the product of the communities of knowledge from which it emerges. Credit is a way to acknowledge and express appreciation for labor, though it is distinct from and not a substitute for compensation. Credit can be shared privately and publicly, in ways large and small, through citation and regular acts of acknowledgment, in classes, meetings, and public and semipublic statements. When acknowledgment comes your way, think about whose labor made your work possible and share. No conference happens without staff to set up and break down rooms: thank them. Think also about which groups and social identities are underrepresented in the acknowledgment that happens at your institution or in your field, and make efforts to share credit in a way that may redress prior injustices.

Awareness of Affect

Feelings are important and complex and inform how community takes shape. In many academic spaces, expressions of emotion are discouraged. Crisis, however, produces and intensifies emotion, as do the bonds of community. Our work will be stronger and more honest if we acknowledge this. Leaders should be attentive to the affect of individuals, and to collective feelings as well, and find a balance between acknowledging what's in the air while maintaining a focus on the community's agreed-upon goals. This is especially important and challenging during moments of acute crisis. Verbalizing an observation about the mood of the group or the room can invite members of the community to share feelings that the collective may acknowledge and affirm, though facilitators may want to avoid being drawn into dialogue about individual feelings in group settings. If leaders are in a position to offer additional support, they may choose to follow up privately to connect those in need with resources. Individual check-ins, naming and acknowledging troubling events and contexts, and holding a nonjudgmental space for others to work through difficult emotions are valuable strategies for sustaining community, even amidst tension and disagreement.

Playfulness and Joy

People are not drawn to work in the university for material rewards or stability so much as for the opportunities it offers to explore our passions, commitments, and curiosities. Much of the work of the university is a privilege, and there's great joy to be had. What's the point in not sharing our excitement? Playfulness, art-making, music, and laughter are all social expressions that remind us that the work we do within the university is an extension of our humanity. Welcoming this orientation at opportune moments can deepen the connection to the work for members of the community, reminding us that in the university we may have more control over how to be in relationship with one another than we might in other spaces. Start classes with music; devote meeting time to making art; when appropriate, be silly and laugh. The work's seriousness will still shine through.

Grace

Most college courses are taught by adjuncts, and part-time workers are responsible for increasing amounts of labor at the university. Students live complex lives, balancing work and caregiving responsibilities with their pursuit of a degree. All of this is to say that, for those of us who are in stable, full-time appointments, there is a good chance that a significant percentage of the folks we manage, teach, or collaborate with do not have the same level of security or autonomy. Inevitably, folks will fall short of their commitments. Fulfilling commitments is important, and there are times when there should be consequences for failure. But really think about the cost and benefit of consequences for both the individual and the collective. Responding with understanding, flexibility, and care can bind community closer together. Ultimately, the onus is on those who have the privilege of security to lift others up whenever possible.

The methods humbly offered here become more complicated and challenging in specific contexts. They, alone, do not consolidate the power ultimately necessary to protect or change the university. But, for me at least, they are an expression of how I want to *be* in my work, and a reminder that the values that get us through crisis are the very same values around which an institution that fully lives up to its promise might be built.

Notes

1. This essay is indebted to the scholars I've been fortunate to collaborate and learn with at the City University of New York. Their work has buoyed and propelled my own. Thanks to Stephen Brier and Matthew Gold for their feedback on this draft, and to Kevin M. Gannon and Lisa M. Di Bartolomeo for their stewardship of this volume.

2. See Christopher Newfield, *The Great Mistake: How We Wrecked Public Universities and How We Can Fix Them* (Baltimore: Johns Hopkins University

Press, 2016); Stephen Brier and Michael Fabricant, *Austerity Blues: Fighting for the Soul of Public Higher Education* (Baltimore: Johns Hopkins University Press, 2016); Tressie McMillan Cottom, *Lower Ed: The Troubling Rise of For-Profit Colleges in the New Economy* (New York: The New Press, 2018); Marc Bousquet and Cary Nelson, *How the University Works: Higher Education and the Low-Wage Nation* (New York: NYU Press, 2008); Stanley Aronowitz, *The Knowledge Factory: Dismantling the Corporate University and Creating True Higher Learning* (Boston: Beacon Press, 2001); Ariana González Stokas, *Reparative Universities* (Baltimore: Johns Hopkins University Press, 2023).

3. Stefano Harney and Fred Moten, *The Undercommons: Fugitive Planning & Black Study* (Wivenhoe/New York/Port Watson: Minor Compositions, 2013), 23.

4. Jarvis R. Givens, *Fugitive Pedagogy: Carter G. Woodson and the Art of Black Teaching* (Cambridge, MA: Harvard University Press, 2021), 11.

5. Danica Savonick, *Open Admissions: The Poetics and Pedagogy of Toni Cade Bambara, June Jordan, Audre Lorde, and Adrienne Rich in the Era of Free College* (Durham, NC: Duke University Press, 2024).

6. Chy Sprauve, "Recognition as a Pedagogical Formation: Re-Tracing Black Rhetors' Care-Work in the Field of Writing Studies," *Dissertations, Theses, and Capstone Projects*, June 1, 2022, https://academicworks.cuny.edu/gc_etds/4790.

7. Melissa Dinsman, "The Digital in the Humanities: An Interview with Jessica Marie Johnson | Los Angeles Review of Books." https://lareviewofbooks.org/article/digital-humanities-interview-jessica-marie-johnson/.

8. "Organizing Kit 2024—Douglass Day," https://douglassday.org/kit-2024/.

9. Kathleen Fitzpatrick, *Generous Thinking* (Baltimore: Johns Hopkins University Press, 2019), 4.

10. "Teaching and Learning in Higher Education | West Virginia University Press," https://wvupressonline.com/series/teaching_learning_higher_education.

11. The series has been put on hiatus as part of WVU's "Academic Transformation." See Derek Krissoff, "Lessons about Publishing from West Virginia," Substack newsletter, *Book Work* (blog), October 20, 2023, https://derekkrissoff.substack.com/p/lessons-about-publishing-from-west and Lisa M. Corrigan, "The Evisceration of a Public University," *The Nation*, August 16, 2023, https://www.thenation.com/article/society/wvu-cuts-higher-education/.

15

Radical Empathy and Radical Hope

A Guide to Teaching, Learning, and Caring in Times of Crisis

Brian Smentkowski

Content Note: This chapter discusses homicide and the associated trauma and aftereffects on a university campus community.

Introduction and Overview

On November 13, 2022, four University of Idaho students—Madison Mogen, Kaylee Goncalves, Xana Kernodle, and Ethan Chapin—were tragically killed in a home on the southern border of campus. At the time, like most other colleges and universities, we were struggling to return to "normal" after COVID-19. Like many Centers for Teaching and Learning (CTLs), ours facilitated the transition to and from online instruction. We mapped user experiences, identified technology deserts, and invented digital oases to support student engagement. At the same time, we realized the motivating impact of our students—of *their* lives and *their* experiences—and the trust invested in us to develop and reinforce a bond that would transcend the pandemic and reflect our commitment to learn*ing*, learn*ers*, and one another. The tragic events of November 13, however, were different: they were not part of a global pandemic; they were specific to our community. There was no vaccine, only trauma. The complex union of grief, fear, urgency, vulnerability, and uncertainty was paralyzing. Despite the lessons learned from Covid, there was a gap in our knowledge of how to handle a crisis of this magnitude as it unfolded in real time.

Scholars like Therese Huston and Michele DiPietro, Nancy Chick, and Derek Bruff have provided outstanding resources for teaching and learning *after* a crisis, but what we needed, and therefore generated, was a framework for teaching, learning, and caring *during* a crisis.[1] The difference may seem small, but it is important. On the same day of the Idaho murders, there was a mass shooting at the University of Virginia. Three people were killed, and two others were injured. The first shots were reportedly fired at 10:15 p.m., and by 11:24 a.m. the next day, a suspect was in custody. At the U of I, the person accused of fatally stabbing four students to death was arrested on December 30, 2022. For forty-seven days, the academic community experienced multiple waves and layers of trauma, each with its own set of distinguishing characteristics, and each meriting meaningful engagement. The immediate ask of our center was to help our faculty support one another, to communicate effectively with their students, and to learn and apply strategies to teach mindfully, respectfully, and supportively.

This chapter presents a toolkit and a framework for teaching and learning in times of crisis. It builds on the core skills and values of the educational development field and presents strategies we can apply within and across different populations, contexts, and settings to maximize impact. This framework highlights a series of steps, allies, and approaches necessary for unifying and supporting faculty, staff, and students during times of crisis and uncertainty.

Why Us? The Unwritten Role of CTLs

In *Centers for Teaching and Learning: The New Landscape in Higher Education*, Mary C. Wright notes that "CTLs are now playing a broader role on their campuses to support operational needs, strategic aims, and organizational change." Some have successfully "come in from the margins" and lead initiatives with institutional authority. Others choose to occupy the margins as sites of "radical possibility," where relationships, collaboration, and innovation thrive. Still others straddle those lines, holding and offering multiple seats at different tables.[2]

While there is considerable variability in the spaces we select and are selected to occupy, there are certain characteristics that uniquely qualify educational developers to lead in times of crisis. Mary C. Wright, Debra Rudder Lohe, Tershia Pinder-Grove, and Leslie Ortquist-Ahrens present these essential skills as the "Four Rs": Responsiveness, Relationships, Resources, and Research.[3] As we shall see, it is the energy invested into "the basics," including the "Four Rs," that distinguish educational development from other forms or leadership and enables CTLs to lead effectively in times of crisis.

Educational development is inherently an other-directed enterprise. Our service transcends the instrumental rationality of teaching and learning and investigates the conditions necessary for others, including institutions, to succeed. At our best, we work to create a positive campus culture, where trust, belonging, and community thrive. For this to happen, our centers must be safe and brave spaces. We must provide environments and opportunities for colleagues to interact openly and honestly. Like the confidentiality we routinely provide, the places and spaces of educational development exist wherever we and those with whom we interact exist. Especially in times of crisis, we have to meet people where they are (literally and figuratively), knowing that many of the most transformational moments in our careers involve "being there."

In times of crisis, a CTL is a safe harbor, a unifier, an ally, and an advocate. We can pivot instantly to focus on what really matters and even provide hope when it is needed most.

Foundations and Frameworks

Listening is an essential skill, and Margaret Cohen's "Listen, Learn, and Lead" has helped a generation of educational developers avoid the mistake of affixing solutions to problems they know little about.[4] Generally, the argument is that we must listen and learn to lead effectively. When we listen, we must be diligent in our efforts to respect diversity, promote equity, and foster inclusion. As much of our most impactful work occurs when we interact with different populations in their own environments, we must carry that respect with us, mindful of existing and potentially different cultural and communication norms. Here, it is important to recognize the value of allies who we can partner with or defer to based on different levels of entry. Further, "one and done" campus conversations are inadequate: the time, the place, the tone, and the implicit expectations can be exclusionary. Additionally, they can create a façade of democracy and present a false sense of "the" voice of the faculty or the students. In the case of COVID-19, this sensitivity enabled us to gather information about the lived experiences of vastly different populations that resulted in highly differentiated and impactful technological and pedagogical solutions. Similarly, while we were all traumatized by the sudden and tragic loss of four of our students, it would be a mistake to assume that we all processed our trauma identically. Our approach recognized the need for allies and even deference. We strategically mapped out listening, learning, and support sessions through a network of colleagues and realized the value of Rule #1: Don't go it alone. To wit:

- *Work with* tribal representatives, members of Multicultural Affairs, the Women's Center, and others who have existing, deep relationships and communication pathways already in place.
- *Rely on* the strength of the relationships you (should) have developed to realize a shared goal.
- *Accept that* you are not expected to be the expert on all things.
  - In the context of a real-time crisis, it is important to know and amplify the people and units directly related to such events: health centers, counseling services, campus police, and others.
  - While we don't have all the answers, we should know how, when, and where to direct faculty, students, and staff for help, and we should make such information easily accessible from our websites and in our interactions.

To maximize your impact, think about your spheres of engagement:

- *Interpersonally*, we need to be genuinely present. We need to be meaningfully engaged in consultations, exercise respect, listen carefully, and move forward with intentionality and kindness.
- *Organizationally*, we need to know and collaborate with our colleagues. We need to cross-promote services through

multiple highly visible means (web resources, institutionally distributed materials, and the like), and leverage skills to support one another and the goals we share.

- *Internally* (as a center) we need to be mindful of our faculty and academic development responsibilities. We have to maintain our commitment to supporting faculty in ways and on topics that matter to them and to simultaneously support their instructional role, for in times of crisis, this is where we see a direct and literal impact on the learning *and lives* of our students.

An example that has become a case study at Idaho involves the way we progressed from one crisis to another. When COVID first hit, Dr. Kristin Haltinner, professor of sociology, and CETL designed and offered what would become the first in a series of workshops/discussions on "What Do I Tell My Students?" We wanted to promote a pedagogy of care around radical empathy, with the tagline—and goal—of "Empathizing with Students and Building a Community of Support." We were, however unintentionally, linking empathy to hope.

We gathered and shared information on the challenges faced by students (Research and Resources), how to communicate meaningfully with them (Relationships, Research, and Responsiveness), and strategies for promoting belonging, inclusion, and presence (all Four Rs).

This series continued throughout and beyond the pandemic, with subsequent sessions co-facilitated by different units. The more we focused on what ultimately became our version of "The Things We Tell Our Students,"[5] the more a "unifying faculty, students, and staff" theme emerged. We gathered more input and solutions from faculty, students, and staff about the challenges they faced through special programs like our annual Student Success Conference. We pooled together and analyzed the information from our listening sessions, surveys, and events to share what mattered most to our academic community. This became known as the "Three Cs"—another set of "basics" that informed our steps forward:

1. Communication
2. Community
3. Clarity

Gradually, the pandemic waned, and the campus felt vibrant once again. Hugging, smiling, laughing, and walking through "the old arb" (one of two arboreta on campus) returned. Signs would soon appear in building entrances reminding everyone to remove their snowshoes, skis, and ice cleats before entering. Fall recess was on the horizon and with it the coveted break before the mad dash to finals. Then, the unimaginable happened.

The Event that Changed Everything and a Shift

At 11:58 a.m., on Sunday, November 13, 2022, a 911 caller requested assistance for an "unconscious person" on a property near campus. Initially, that was it—police responded to a call about an unconscious person. Later that day, however, the Moscow Police Department issued a press release informing the public that "upon arrival, officers discovered four individuals who were deceased." Moscow police identified the names of the victims, expressed their sorrow for families, friends, and the community, and concluded, alarmingly, by noting that "there is no one in custody" and that "Moscow Police does not believe there is an ongoing community risk."[6]

That last line did not reassure the public in general and our students in particular. Neither did a press release issued on Tuesday, November 15, revealing that "an edged weapon such as a knife was used in the killings" and reminding the public that while no suspects were in custody, there was no risk to the community. Classes were canceled the Monday after the event, and many students understandably sought the comfort and safety of family and friends outside of town.

Although the University of Idaho is the state's Land Grant Institution, it is an intimate campus that prides itself on the fact that students and professors know one another on a first-name basis. Losses do not feel anonymous; they feel personal. The sudden loss of Kaylee, Xana, Madison, and Ethan hit like a ton of bricks. For a moment, everything stopped. Community members were on high alert and locking their doors. Between Sunday and Tuesday, the Center had already been in communication with executive leadership. Referencing our "What Do I Tell My Students?" series and CETL's credibility across campus, we were asked to provide guidance to faculty.

On Monday, the director of CETL, along with Dr. Kelly Quinette,[7] Dr. Erin Chapman,[8] Dr. Casey Johnson,[9] and Dr. Kristin Haltinner,[10] collaborated to produce Teaching and Learning in Times of Crisis. This domain immediately became the official source of critical information for our campus community, so we therefore opened with carefully selected language:

> These are unprecedented times. The tragic deaths of Xana Kernodle, Kaylee Goncalves, Madison Mogen, and Ethan Chapin have shaken our campus to the core, but they have also galvanized our commitment to supporting our students and one another.
>
> Emblematic of this commitment, a group of faculty has developed this guide to teaching and learning in times of crisis. It captures insightful perspectives from our faculty, students, and research.
>
> We are all experiencing this tragedy—and the trauma surrounding it—in real time. We are operating as events unfold and as information becomes available. We are not teaching in the immediate aftermath of a crisis, but literally while it occurs. This document is intended to help us all through this difficult time.

Influenced by the aforementioned work of Chick, Bruff, and Huston and DiPietro in particular, we framed our initial guidelines around "Ten Tips" (the preferred format of our faculty).[11] Our materials were designed to be accessed and shared in multiple formats for multiple different populations, with the overarching message that we are all experiencing this together, in real time, as a community of care. Our Ten Tips for Teaching and Learning in Times of Crisis encouraged faculty to:

1. Think about your class and office hours as a way of being there for your students.

2. Provide time and space to discuss student experiences, perceptions, and concerns.

3. Be flexible with expectations, assignments, and student performance.

4. Remember that this is just one or two weeks of content, but it is one or two weeks that every student will remember

forever . . . perspective is critical. This tragedy is what they will remember forever. How we support our students will be remembered, too.

5. Reconsider grading strategies.
6. Reassure your students that their grades, tests, projects, and learning are not substantially at risk as we struggle with this tragedy. Let them hear it from you, directly.
7. Be mindful of cognitive load during acutely stressful experiences.
8. Focus on what really matters.
9. Acknowledge what's happening and discuss it—resist moving along as if nothing is happening, especially as events are unfolding in real time.
10. Remember that the stress and anxiety students and faculty bring into the learning environment has a significant impact on the learning experience.

Each item included tips for implementation, and all were addressed in different ways in public fora, workshops, and consultations. Through collaboration, this page became a living and evolving portal to *Best Practices for Teaching in Times of Crisis, Supporting Students Experiencing Trauma, A Crisis Resource Directory, Crisis Resource Materials, Altering Instructional Formats to Include ALL Students*, and an archive of presentations, workshops, and materials. Our content and interactions grew and were tailored to the different waves of trauma that time, uncertainty, misinformation, and new information provided.

We coupled scholarship with popular content, such as *Brene Brown on Empathy*, to foster conversation, community, and healing.[12] Members of a *Radical Hope* learning community continued to meet informally, and sometimes simply with screenshots and text messages of profound lines and relevant insights.[13] Professional collaborations frequently morphed into support groups. Allies then are now scholars and practitioners of Trauma-Informed Teaching Practices. We needed and supported one another and still do. Now, our center is more of a hub, a home base, and safe harbor for collaboration, support, and distributed programming.

As a blueprint for supporting teaching, learning, and one another in times of crisis, our experience and actions reflect and validate the Four Rs, plus the underlying need to

- *listen* inclusively and with intentionality;
- *learn* from the diverse array of voices;
- *lead* listening processes and actions based on them;
- *organize* input, ideas, research, and strategies;
- *develop* equitable programs and techniques to reach and teach diverse populations; and
- *share* leadership roles as well as materials.

Associated with this are five key steps to maximizing impact:

1. Call on your allies.
2. Leverage your skills, visibility, and credibility to gain and leverage support from others.
3. Use language and strategies that resonate with your community.
4. Know your field of play and how to play on it.
5. Be open to the radical possibilities, new ideas, and new relationships trying times produce.

Pulling It All Together: Radical Empathy and Radical Hope

Designing, developing, and delivering programs that resonate with your faculty and support them through challenging experiences is one thing, but working with one another on a personal level is quite another. This is where we find the linkage between radical empathy and radical hope. Our experience and process revealed that:

1. We have been engaging in radical empathy all along, but with heightened intentionality during a crisis. We emphasized an approach to education that prioritizes a deep understanding of, and interacting

with, the experiences and challenges of a diverse population of students, faculty, and staff. This form of pedagogy and, I would argue, educational development values active listening, practices cultural humility, relies on collaboration with colleagues with nested expertise in different circles, and promotes sustained engagement.

2. Along the way, we cultivated our own pedagogy of care and kindness, one more keenly aware of the social and emotional development of our students, the impact of crisis and confusion in their lives, the influence of our experiences and behaviors on their performance, and the value of community among faculty, among students, and between faculty and students.

3. All of this reveals what is perhaps the greatest value of our work and our field: fostering radical hope. We are and must be agents of change. While impact-based research routinely focuses on tidy compartments of institutional impact, I implore readers to consider the ways we can foster radical hope—in whatever form it must take—on our campuses. In times of crisis, hope is the hardest thing to find. At the U of I, the forty-seven days of uncertainty ushered in sequential waves of trauma. We adjusted by instituting a daylight-only policy for meetings and events, by hosting campus conversations on topics relating to the crime, and by developing new faculty development tracks dedicated to trauma-informed pedagogy. Our shared experience galvanized our commitment to one another. We reframed and asked out loud, "What are we saying to our students?" and realized in multiple ways that "Pedagogy Cannot Be Neutral."[14] It has to stand for something. *We* have to stand for something. We did and we do.

Conclusion

As I write these closing lines, I am overwhelmed by emotions. The art and architecture students who designed a magnificent and somehow perfectly appropriate Vandal Healing Garden and Memorial completed their work today. I pass this corner of campus—an open green area adjacent to "the old arb"—every day. From day one until today, I have had the privilege of watching these incredible students bring something beautiful to life. Right now, the garden and the structures created within it are suddenly still and silent. I think they are intended to be. They are at once strong and delicate, resilient and graceful, and above all, in harmony with one another. Fitting. They also require care and nurturing, which is also fitting as this is the nature of our work.

While I am hopeful that readers will take something meaningful from the experiences and strategies identified above, I also hope that they will remember the names Madison Mogen, Kaylee Goncalves, Xana Kernodle, and Ethan Chapin and the inestimable value of such knowledge.

Notes

1. Therese A. Huston and Michele DiPietro, "In the Eye of the Storm: Students Perceptions of Helpful Faculty Actions Following a Collective Tragedy," *To Improve the Academy: A Journal of Educational Development* 25 (2007). Nancy Chick, "Teaching in Times of Crisis," Vanderbilt University Center for Teaching (2013), https://cft.vanderbilt.edu/guides-sub-pages/crisis/; Derek Bruff, "Teaching After Charlottesville," Vanderbilt University Center for Teaching (2017), https://cft.vanderbilt.edu/2017/08/teaching-after-charlottesville/.

2. Mary C. Wright, *Centers for Teaching and Learning: The New Landscape in Higher Education* (Johns Hopkins University Press, 2023), 200; Connie Schroeder *et al.*, *Coming in from the Margins: Faculty Development's Emerging Organizational Development Role in Institutional Change* (Stylus Publishers, 2011); bell hooks, *Yearning: Race, Gender and Cultural Politics* (South End Press, 2011); Kay J. Gillespie, "Organizational development," in *A Guide to Faculty Development*, ed. Gillespie, D. L. Robertson, et al. (Jossey-Bass, 2010), 379–96; Emily Gravett and Lindsay Bernhagen," A View from the Margins: Situating CTL Staff in Organizational Development," *To Improve the Academy: A Journal of Educational Development*, 34: 1–2; Laura Cruz et al., *Taking Flight: Making Your Center for Teaching and Learning Soar* (Stylus Publishing, 2020).

3. Mary C. Wright et al., " 'The Four Rs': Guiding CTLs with Responsiveness, Relationships, Resources, and Research," *To Improve the Academy: A Journal of Educational Development* 37, no. 2 (2018): 271–86.

4. Margaret W. Cohen, "Listen, Learn, and Lead: Getting Started in Faculty Development," in Gillespie *et al.*, *A Guide to Faculty Development*, 67–82.

5. Kevin M. Gannon, *Radical Hope: A Teaching Manifesto* (West Virginia University Press, 2020), 28–38.

6. The University of Idaho's main campus is located in Moscow, Idaho.

7. faculty senate chair.

8. faculty senate vice chair and CETL Associate for Diversity and Inclusion in Teaching and Learning.

9. associate professor of philosophy.

10. professor of sociology.

11. Chick, "Teaching in Times of Crisis"; Bruff, "Teaching After Charlottesville"; Huston and DiPietro, "In the Eye of the Storm."

12. Brene Brown, "On Empathy," https://youtu.be/1Evwgu369Jw?si=nLRj4W-KfN8mytkT.

13. Gannon, *Radical Hope.*

14. Gannon, *Radical Hope*, quoted at 31, 18.

References

Brown, Brene. *One Empathy*, located at https://youtu.be/1Evwgu369Jw?si=nLRj4W-KfN8mytkT. 2013.

Bruff, Derek. Teaching After Charlottesville, 2017. Located at https://cft.vanderbilt.edu/2017/08/teaching-after-charlottesville/.

Chick, Nancy. *Teaching in Times of Crisis*, located at: https://cft.vanderbilt.edu/guides-sub-pages/crisis/. 2013.

Cohen, M. W. 2010. *Listen, Learn, and Lead: Getting Started in Faculty Development.* Gillespie, Robertson and Associates, *A Guide to Faculty Development*, 2d ed. Jossey-Bass Publishing.

Cruz, L., Parker, M., Smentkowski, B., Smitherman, M. *Taking Flight: Making Your Center for Teaching and Learning Soar*. Sterling, VA: Stylus Publishing, 2020.

Gannon, K. M. *Radical Hope: A Teaching Manifesto*. Morgantown: West Virginia University Press, 2020.

Gravett, E. O., and Bernhagen, L. "A View from the Margins: Situating CTL Staff in Organizational Development." *To Improve the Academy: A Journal of Educational Development*, V 34, Issue 1-2, 2015. http://dx.doi.org/10.3998/tia.17063888.0034.109.

Gillespie, K. Organizational development. In *A Guide to Faculty Development*, ed. K. J. Gillespie, D. L. Robertson and Associates, 379–96. 2nd ed. San Francisco, CA: Jossey Bass, 2010.

Green, D. A., and D. Little. "Academic Development on the Margins." *Studies in Higher Education* 38, 523–537, 2010.

hooks, b. 1990. *Yearnings: Race, Gender and Cultural Politics*. Boston: South Press.

Huston, Therese A., and Michele DiPietro. "In the Eye of the Storm: Students Perceptions of Helpful Faculty Actions Following a Collective Tragedy." Vol. 25. *To Improve the Academy: A Journal of Educational Development,* 2007.

Little, D., and D. Green. "Betwixt and Between: Academic Developers in the Margins." *International Journal for Academic Development,* 17, no. 3 (2012): 203–15.

Schroeder, C., et al. *Coming in from the Margins: Faculty Development's Emerging Organizational Development Role in Institutional Change.* Sterling, VA: Stylus, 2011.

Moscow Police Department Press Release. https://www.ci.moscow.id.us/DocumentCenter/View/24838/11-13-22-City-of-Moscow-Homicide-Victims.

Wright, M. C., Lohe, D.R., Pinder-Grover, T., Ortquist-Ahrens, L. "The Four Rs" Guiding CTLs with Responsiveness, Relationships, Resources, and Research. To Improve the Academy." *Journal of Educational Development* 37, no. 2 (2018): 271–386.

Wright, M. C. *Centers for Teaching and Learning: The New Landscape in Higher Education*. Johns Hopkins University Press, 2023.

16

Times Like These

Supporting First-Year Students and Contingent Faculty through a Campus Polycrisis

JOSEPH NARDINELLI, JOEL E. R. SMITH, AND MATTHEW AUSTIN

Content Warning: This chapter will revisit a recent on-campus shooting at the University of Arizona (UA). Please be aware that what follows includes reflections on violence and trauma and may be distressing for readers. The impacts of such events can be long-lasting and echo unpredictably. For example, the writing of this chapter occurred at a time of heightened emotions for the UA community, during the shooter's murder trial in June 2024.

Historical Context

Nearly two years earlier, on Wednesday, October 5, 2022, Thomas Meixner—a UA professor and department head—was shot and killed on campus by a former graduate student. While the perpetrator fled and was eventually arrested, UA students, faculty, and staff remained uncertain for hours about their safety. The days and weeks to come were fraught for the UA community as questions and doubts emerged in news stories and two reports about UA leadership's commitment to campus safety. Even though not all campus shootings are preventable, the one at UA may perhaps have been, had leadership not been distracted by two other self-created crises at the time.

That very same Fall 2022 semester also marked the rollout of a brand-new UA General Education program for the first time in over twenty years.[1] This refresh included a reflection- and portfolio-based seminar course for over nine thousand first-year students: "UNIV 101: Introduction to the General Education Experience."[2] The three coauthors of this chapter were part of the small full-time team of contingent UNIV faculty who developed and taught the course, as well as trained and supported over 150 part-time instructors made up of provosts, deans, administrators, librarians, advisors, student affairs staff, faculty from various colleges, and adjuncts. Given UNIV 101's small class sizes (fewer than twenty-seven students) and its goals of introducing new students to the university and promoting metacognition and perspective-taking via reflective writing, our UNIV 101 classrooms became a natural epicenter for difficult conversations and student support during and after the tragic shooting.

Overview

Instead of covering the same ground as the two reports on the October shooting (one internal,[3] one external),[4] we will focus on the steps that our new team of fourteen UNIV faculty took before, during, and after the shooting to best support 150-plus part-time instructors and nine-thousand-plus first-year students.

Along the way, we will frame how the UNIV 101 curriculum, coupled with real-time support for instructors, allowed us to provide simultaneous space for both first-year students and instructors to process what happened. After the shooting, as racial and religious dimensions emerged, our team's previous training in Learner-Centered and Inclusive Teaching and QPR suicide-prevention created a community of practice and a more culturally responsive curriculum to better prepare faculty to support students during a crisis.

These tools are especially necessary since most crises don't appear in a vacuum. On the contrary, one crisis often leads to another (if not directly, then by mistakes that occur when leaders are distracted by a previous ongoing crisis). This dynamic, sometimes referred to as "polycrisis," is often seen in politics, economics, and environmental science but can and should be applied to higher education. By exploring what happened at UA, we hope to offer generalizable and actionable feedback for faculty, staff, and administrators at UA and other institutions.

"Polycrisis" in (and Outside) Higher Education

Over the past decade, UA has reeled from crisis to crisis in an almost vertigo-inducing way. Rather than being an outlier, UA appears to be typical, especially of public institutions that have seen wavering financial support since the 2008 financial crisis.

Meanwhile, "polycrisis" has emerged to become the word du jour at the 2023 World Economic Forum in Davos, Switzerland. In their *Global Risks Report 2023*, the authors define "polycrisis" as a state in which "disparate crises interact such that the overall impact far exceeds the sum of each part," zeroing in on the COVID-19 pandemic, the war in Ukraine, and the global crises in energy, cost-of-living, and climate.[5] And yet, "polycrisis" has not often—by our knowledge—been applied to higher education. At this point, it may be useful to differentiate between *the* polycrisis, which is global, and *a* polycrisis, which can occur at smaller sites.

In the case of the UA, we faced a nested polycrisis that preceded and perhaps even precipitated the breach in public safety resulting in the shooting of Professor Meixner. In 2020, UA faced the largest COVID-era furloughs and pay cuts in the country, in hopes of addressing what appeared to be a $250 million shortfall.[6] Simultaneously, UA was in the process of making a high-upside, high-risk decision to purchase the predatory, for-profit Ashford University, all for a theoretically $1 purchase price.[7] Both these heavily scrutinized decisions proceeded to occupy the UA administration's attention over the next two years, as they faced increasing pressure to reduce the furloughs/pay cuts and justify the acquisition of Ashford (now known as the University of Arizona Global Campus). This scenario formed a textbook polycrisis, as calls from UA's Hydrology and Atmospheric Sciences (HAS) Department to help with an increasingly unhinged graduate student went unheeded for over a year.

Not all gun violence can be prevented on college campuses, and certainly the narrative laid out in this chapter is not meant to suggest a direct causal link between UA's pandemic-era financial challenges and the tragic violence that occurred here. However, the value in interrogating what has happened at UA from a polycrisis-oriented perspective can help faculty, staff, and administrators make sense of the interrelatedness of crises at their own institutions while hopefully offering a path forward. Indeed, as Clara Lachmann notes, it is through the "intersection of diversity," much like the interdisciplinary UNIV instructor team and student-centered approach that we lay out in the following sections, that we might break UA and similar institutions out of their recursive polycrisis loops.[8]

What is UNIV 101?

In Fall 2019, on the doorstep of the COVID-19 pandemic, UA released its $14 million strategic plan—written by McKinsey & Company—that called for a redesign of its General Education program. This resulted in two new one-unit courses focusing on student reflections via a multimodal ePortfolio.[9]

The first of those courses, UNIV 101, rolled out during the Fall 2022 semester, two months prior to the shooting. This student-centered, first-year seminar course introduces first-year students to the goals and expectations of the UA's new General Education program, while simultaneously promoting metacognition and meaning-making through habituated reflection with both in-person reflective activities and out-of-class reflective writing assignments.

Designing a Course to Anticipate the Unforeseen

Given the student-centered and deeply reflective nature of UNIV 101, our classrooms function as an epicenter for conversations about future struggles based on past experiences. For example, three weeks earlier, as students began their UA journey, they completed an in-class activity known as an Academic S.W.O.T. Analysis (strengths, weaknesses, opportunities, and threats). The activity asks students to think about the skills, habits, situations, and circumstances that support their success, as well as the obstacles to their overall well-being and achievement. By reflecting, students identify contingency plans for how they might overcome those obstacles using the campus resources at their disposal.

When discussing potential obstacles to their success as college students, instructors might have expected to see students mention their social lives, familial pressures, and/or financial issues. However, students also identified gun violence as a threat they might encounter on campus. This threat became a reality three weeks later with the October 5th shooting. The nature of the Academic S.W.O.T. Analysis provided an avenue for students to "preflect" while in community with their peers on the real possibility of such a campus crisis. In the days following the shooting, circling back to the Academic S.W.O.T. analysis afforded an opportunity for instructors to process and discuss students' reactions to the shooting.

Reflective Writing and Student Voice

Outside-of-class reflective assignments also played a similar role for students in the aftermath of the shooting. For example, UNIV 101 students aim to align their own interests with the general education courses they might take; they spend roughly one hour over a week tracking and free-writing on what sparks their wonders, interests, and curiosities. In the Fall 2022 semester, this assignment happened to occur the week of the shooting, offering a space for students to share and process their thoughts in real time. One poignant example of this is a UNIV 101 student who wrote their response while receiving text alerts about the shooting, before having received safety guidance from the university: "Am I safe? Why won't the doors lock? What are we supposed to do if the shooter comes into my class? Are we safe being this close to the other building? Why are they letting us out of the building if the shooter is still on campus? How far away should I be standing?"[10] In another example of a student who wrote their reflection in the days after the October shooting, the student reflected, "The main thing running through my head was the shooting earlier this week. I am sure this has been heavy on most people's heads and hearts at the UA. I thought about the fear for my friends in lockdown in surrounding buildings, the sorrow in my heart for Dr. Meixner, and the confusion I had for why it was happening. It is a hard pill to swallow that this is the world we live in."[11] As demonstrated in these two student samples, representing 375 total sections of UNIV 101, one can see how reflection provided a space for first-year students to process the reality of experiencing a campus crisis. Furthermore, giving students the space to process individually and then optionally share within the smaller forum of a UNIV 101 classroom, students serve as expert witnesses in their class communities.

Training and Supporting UNIV Instructors

Another aspect of UNIV 101 that proved beneficial following the crisis pertains to how we facilitate it. Where other large-scale UA general education offerings in writing and languages rely on mixed instructor pools of contingent faculty and graduate teachers, the UNIV part-time instructor pool largely draws from a much more diverse range of educators throughout the UA. In Fall 2022, the vast majority came from faculty and administrative/support staff positions, representing 15 of 21 colleges and over 24 departments/programs. While the full-time UNIV faculty taught around 70 sections of UNIV 101 that semester, over 300 sections were taught by part-time instructors, a massive scaling up as the UNIV program grew beyond its pilot stage of 14 sections in Spring 2022 (see Table 16.1).

As such, in August 2022, the two UNIV course directors were responsible for training the twelve brand-new full-time UNIV faculty who would in turn support and onboard the remaining 140-plus part-time faculty, almost all of whom were teaching UNIV 101 for the first time. Instructors participated in learner-centered and inclusive teaching trainings, a QPR (question, persuade, refer) training for suicide prevention, as well as training on how to use CRM (customer relationship management) software to share progress reports with students and advisors.

Taken together, these various approaches provided UNIV 101 instructors with a strong baseline to design and teach inclusively while also being ready to adapt to emergent situations. No one could have predicted the tragic shooting of Professor Meixner a short two months after these training sessions; nevertheless, the holistic, person-first nature of the trainings was designed to create a resilient and responsive cohort of instructors.

Table 16.1. UNIV Growth from Spring 2022 Pilot to Fall 2022

	Spring 2022 Pilot	Fall 2022 Rollout
Students	332	8,666
Sections	14	375
Instructors	10	156

Source: Tom Murray, email to UNIV faculty, December 19, 2022.

Creating a Responsive Community of Practice

Over the Fall 2022 semester, we noticed outcomes that spoke to these trainings' impact. The greatest area of impact emerged at our various faculty meetings, especially among the small part-time instructor teams that met weekly on Zoom, each led by one of the full-time UNIV faculty. In the wake of the October shooting, these conversations were rarely recorded: this was to respect privacy as instructors took stock of their own raw emotions and responses. In the few cases where documentation was preserved through interfaces like Google Jamboard, responses were recorded anonymously. There were a wide range of sentiments but were largely focused on gratitude for the opportunity to process collectively, the flexibility of time regarding deadlines and class sessions, and most importantly, the sense that UNIV 101 seemed to be one of the few classroom spaces where students could talk to one another and their instructors about what they were experiencing. Furthermore, sharing strategies for communicating after a tragedy modeled for instructors the similarly challenging and difficult conversations they continued having with students.

Empowering Faculty and Students

In the three semesters since the shooting, the UNIV faculty have continued to implement changes meant to promote ready flexibility and inclusive design for instructors. Some of these have been straightforward, such as differentiating the training process for all instructors separate from onboarding for new instructors. Common training focuses on inclusive practices, such as inclusive lesson planning, culturally responsive pedagogy, and techniques to support international students. Further, UNIV faculty have participated in a culturally responsive design institute and developed bilingual sections of UNIV 101 to meet the needs of bilingual first-year students. Such efforts ensure responsive design within UNIV 101 and enable support of experienced and new instructors alike.

Conclusions and Recommendations

While designing course materials and classroom spaces to be more inclusive and culturally responsive *feels* right, these paradigms also ensure that the

UNIV teaching culture will remain shock-resistant in the face of future crises. By creating spaces where instructors feel welcome and included, so too can we foster similar environments for our students. Scaling communities of practice in this way offers abundant support for instructors that can reverberate positively among first-year students, especially in times of (poly)crisis.

At an institution such as UA, where polycrisis has seemed inescapable and often exceeds the capacity of individual instructors to overcome it, we must ensure that students have as much time as faculty to process their feelings and responses to events as they unfold. Courses that emphasize frequent reflection allow for greater self-awareness and critical thinking as students anticipate the possibilities ahead and make meaning of what has—sometimes tragically—come to pass.

But just because "polycrisis" seems to be everywhere doesn't mean it is inevitable. Perhaps the following quote from a UNIV 101 student reflection the week of the shooting makes this point best: "We must acknowledge the problems at hand and face them head on. More than anything, I am very curious about the changes the University will make towards the campus following the event."[12]

It is incumbent on all of us—faculty, staff, and administrators—to prioritize interdisciplinary, diverse teaching teams, facilitate robust and ongoing instructor training, and design curricula that are responsive and student-centered with ample space to reflect. That way, when the unthinkable happens, we will be a more resilient and interconnected community of educators better able to meet the polycrisis head on.

Notes

1. "Curriculum At-A-Glance," University of Arizona General Education, accessed July 10, 2024, https://ge.arizona.edu/curriculum/glance.

2. "UNIV 101: Intro to the General Education Experience," University of Arizona General Education, accessed July 10, 2024, https://ge.arizona.edu/univ-101.

3. Jenny Lee, et al., "OVERSIGHT AND RESPONSE FAILURE: BROKEN TRUST Lessons From the Events Surrounding the Murder of Professor Thomas Meixner," The University of Arizona, Faculty Governance, January 30, 2023. https://facultygovernance.arizona.edu/sites/default/files/2023-02/FINAL_REDACTED_01-30-2023%20-%20SAFETY%20REPORT.pdf.

4. Phil Andrew, "Review of the University of Arizona's Safety and Security Environment," PAX Group, LLC, March 24, 2023. https://www.arizona.edu/sites/default/files/2023-03/PAX_Group_Report_Accessible.pdf.

5. "Global Risks Report 2023," *World Economic Forum* online, January 11, 2023. https://www.weforum.org/publications/global-risks-report-2023/digest/.

6. Steve Jess, "UA Pres. Robbins says economic impact of pandemic 'is dire,'" *AZPM*, April 18, 2020. https://news.azpm.org/s/75582-robbins-briefs-u-of-a-staff-on-pandemic-the-situation-is-dire/.

7. Dan Bauman, "Two Years After Promising a 'Transformational' Partnership, the U. of Arizona and Zovio Part Ways," *The Chronicle of Higher Education*, August 1, 2022. https://www.chronicle.com/article/two-years-after-promising-a-transformational-partnership-the-u-of-arizona-and-zovio-part-ways.

8. See note 6 above.

9. "Wildcat Journey: Driving Student Success for a Rapidly Changing World," The University of Arizona Strategic Plan, accessed July 24, 2024. https://strategicplan.arizona.edu/wildcat-journey.

10. "UNIV 101 Wonder Journal" (digital submission, UNIV 101, The University of Arizona, October 5, 2022).

11. "UNIV 101 Wonder Journal" (digital submission, UNIV 101, The University of Arizona, October 7, 2022).

12. See note 11 above.

Bibliography

Andrew, Phil. "Review of the University of Arizona's Safety and Security Environment," PAX Group, LLC, March 24, 2023. https://www.arizona.edu/sites/default/files/2023-03/PAX_Group_Report_Accessible.pdf.

Bauman, Dan. "Two Years After Promising a 'Transformational' Partnership, the U. of Arizona and Zovio Part Ways," *The Chronicle of Higher Education*, August 1, 2022. https://www.chronicle.com/article/two-years-after-promising-a-transformational-partnership-the-u-of-arizona-and-zovio-part-ways.

"Curriculum At-A-Glance." The University of Arizona General Education. https://ge.arizona.edu/curriculum/glance. Accessed July 10, 2024.

"Global Risks Report 2023." *World Economic Forum* online, January 11, 2023. https://www.weforum.org/publications/global-risks-report-2023/digest/.

Lachman, Clara. "The Polycrisis: Behind the Buzzword." NATO Association of Canada, May 7, 2024. https://natoassociation.ca/the-polycrisis-behind-the-buzzword/.

Lee, Jenny, et al. "OVERSIGHT AND RESPONSE FAILURE: BROKEN TRUST Lessons From the Events Surrounding the Murder of Professor Thomas Meixner." The University of Arizona, Faculty Governance, January 30, 2023. https://facultygovernance.arizona.edu/sites/default/files/2023-02/FINAL_REDACTED_01-30-2023%20-%20SAFETY%20REPORT.pdf.

"Polycrisis." Google Books Ngram Viewer. https://books.google.com/ngrams/graph?content=polycrisis&year_start=1999&year_end=2022&corpus=en-2019&smoothing=3&case_insensitive=false. Accessed on July 31, 2024.

Smith, Joel. "Week 9 Jamboard Session." UNIV 101 Team Meeting, October 17, 2022.
"UNIV 101: Intro to the General Education Experience." The University of Arizona General Education. https://ge.arizona.edu/univ-101. Accessed July 10, 2024.
"UNIV 101 Wonder Journal." Digital submission, UNIV 101, The University of Arizona, October 5, 2022.
"UNIV 101 Wonder Journal," Digital submission, UNIV 101, University of Arizona, October 7, 2022.
"Wildcat Journey: Driving Student Success for a Rapidly Changing World." University of Arizona Strategic Plan. https://strategicplan.arizona.edu/wildcat-journey. Accessed July 24, 2024.

17

Care as Strategy

Lessons from a Center for Teaching and Learning

MOLLY HATCHER AND KAITLYN ROSE FARRELL RODRIGUEZ

The current higher education landscape is fraught with obstacles that threaten the foundations of student learning. As educational developers (EDs), we advocate for evidence-based pedagogical practices that promote meaningful student learning experiences, even in times of long-term and overlapping crises.[1] Recent attacks on higher education put these efforts at risk, harm our teaching and learning communities, and undermine the impact of our work. This chapter shares the experiences of two EDs who have worked together to center care, relationships, and "collective dignity" during difficult times.[2]

Care is embedded in the promise of higher education because it is essential to student learning and the relationship-building and service work that fuel student learning. Yet when there is a disconnect between promise and practice, care also becomes a tool that sustains communities until alignment is restored. Care thus operates as both a sustaining force for healthy learning communities and a healing force when communities are struggling.

In this chapter, we discuss how we implement care to sustain and repair relationships and innovate programming as we work to heal our community at a large, research-intensive public flagship institution. Since 2020, shifting and lacking guidance from our university administrators' has exacerbated negative circumstances caused by pandemic-related work changes; natural disaster responses; reactions to student demonstrations; and widespread staff and nontenured faculty layoffs largely prompted by compliance with our state's recent legislation "relating to diversity, equity, and inclusion initiatives at public institutions of higher education."[3] Budget cuts and campus support unit closures have increased the need for healing care work in our community precisely when we have less energy and fewer resources and staff. By prioritizing our Center for Teaching and Learning (CTL) team's wellness, we have strengthened our work culture, rebuilt trust, faced feelings of fear, and created interrelational support systems. In this chapter, we share strategies we have used with mindfulness about different institutional and organizational types in the hope that others can adapt these strategies to promote care in their unique contexts.

Care as Strategy

EDs are guided by the higher purpose of shaping learning environments that transform students' lives. We collaborate with instructors to support their growth, confidence development, and ability to create valuable learning experiences that center students' voices and needs.

Recent attacks on higher education have spurred many of us EDs to consider the conditions that help us achieve our higher purpose and foster our well-being, such as safety, hope, belonging, and agency. When those conditions are threatened by external forces, where do we turn to ensure our needs are met so we can continue serving our institutions by collaborating with instructors, students, and staff to transform teaching and learning?

One survival strategy we have implemented to navigate this difficult time is to center care in how we treat ourselves, our colleagues, and the people we serve. As Wilson and Richardson argue, care is "an act of resistance . . . because it creates the conditions for well-being, conditions that institutions of higher education (structurally) have yet to create and maintain."[4] While we agree these "conditions for well-being" are rarely baked into institutional structures, we want to be careful about positing care as only an act of resistance. Care is not contrary to higher education aims, but rather integral to and aligned with the purpose of a college education.

In *Teaching to Transgress*, bell hooks professes that effective instruction "cares for the souls of our students" because it provides "the necessary conditions where learning can most deeply and intimately begin."[5] Peter Felten and Leo Lambert (2020) similarly highlight "constellations of important relationships" as foundational to "learning, belonging, and achieving in college" and "essential for persistence and academic success."[6] Learning requires risk-taking, fumbling, and failure, and care is an integral, sustaining ingredient of this vulnerable process.

Centering care in our CTL work thus aligns our organization with high-impact practices and the promise of student success. When external forces disrupt our ability to make good on that promise, implementing care as a strategy helps us weather the storm. Ways we center care include:

- developing ourselves as leaders who prioritize trust-building;
- engaging in activities that restore well-being;[7]
- holding space for naming and facing our fears to regulate emotions;[8]
- building and nurturing campus communities; and
- facilitating conversations that not only lead to specific outcomes, but also "make meaning of our . . . work" using healing-centered facilitation practices.[9]

The following section brings these strategies to life, demonstrating how they create conditions for EDs to both support the promise of higher education for today's students and thrive during times of conflict.

Strategy in Action

Embodying our value of care daily in our CTL internal workplace and external engagements has helped us maintain integrity during challenging times.

CTL Workplace Community

In order to thrive and care for the educators we serve, we prioritize tending to our internal workplace culture. This work is sustained by principles of trust, adaptability, and creativity and takes many forms, including quality time, guided meditations, reflection, and play.

The foundation necessary for this work to matter, especially during times of conflict and uncertainty, is trust. Hemphill (2024) identifies trust as "the bedrock for human coordination, collaboration," and notes that the absence of trust renders us "stuck, unable to act, unable to build, unable to work toward human achievements."[10] Our current CTL leadership onboarded during a time of organizational turbulence. Rebuilding staff trust was key to restabilizing and helped us endure later challenges, including the pandemic and political polarization that has led to higher education attacks.

To foster a culture of trust and a supportive environment, our CTL supervisors embrace weekly one-on-one check-ins with staff as spaces for genuine connection, asking questions to understand motivations and build relationships around shared vision. Rather than issuing top-down solutions, supervisors facilitate collective problem-solving where both parties showcase unique strengths. Supervisors affirm staff insights and achievements and encourage self-reflection so that growth areas often emerge organically from within. This approach models openness to reciprocal learning and growth, reinforcing that all CTL staff have something valuable to learn from one another. This method's effectiveness is especially evident in the mentorship-rich relationships that CTL staff have with student workers, who often stay in their roles until graduation and express gratitude for their CTL experience.

Active listening is a powerful care and trust-building strategy that we implement daily not just in staff/supervisor relationships but as we interact with fellow staff. This takes place in the kitchen when we make shared pots of coffee or in office thresholds. These intentional moments are energizing, especially when reciprocal and bounded appropriately.

Care-driven approaches like active listening also play a large role in all-staff meetings and annual retreats. Weekly meetings create space for managing tactical issues but also offer time to understand each other's values and languages of appreciation so we can collaborate more effectively. For example, we recently completed the CliftonStrengths 34 assessment and dedicated time in team meetings to individually and collectively strategize ways to maximize our unique strengths through collaboration. Building trust together over time allows us to show up wholeheartedly in these interactions, leading to more meaningful relationships and feelings of satisfaction in our work.

Carefully built foundations of trust have also helped us create a safe harbor to explore hard feelings. For us to support educators in providing meaningful student learning experiences during hostile times, we need community conversations that give us space to "name our pain, communicate it to others, and begin creating collective processes that allow us to move closer to healing."[11] In weekly team meetings, we carefully integrate mindful moments like guided breathing exercises and meditation wrappers to help our team get in (and out) of headspaces to process harm. This helps us co-regulate emotions and express valid and varied emotional responses to difficult events. By signaling transitions in and out of these heavy spaces, we support our team in creating and reinforcing boundaries that help us manage emotional overwhelm.

Another tool for processing harm together in team meetings has been reflecting on quotations from inspiring scholars. This semester, we reflected on this quote after learning about legislation restrictions and colleagues who lost their jobs: "facing and opening to the emotional experience of fear allows us to come above the line and access our natural resourcefulness. It calls forth our reason and clarity, courage and compassion. Running away only amplifies the felt sense of being powerless and afraid."[12] Reflections began with individual freewriting/drawing to help ground our own reactions. We then paired up to discuss insights before opening a whole-group conversation. Staff named sometimes all-consuming feelings of fear, dread, and helplessness around not knowing what to do when workshop participants raise "off-limits" topics and the possibility of losing our jobs. These conversations have helped us feel more present with each other and persevere in the face of multiple challenges.

We have also used annual retreat time to make sense of challenges together. This year, we took time to take stock of our current situation, find hope and identify next steps, and celebrate our colleagues' creative strengths. Incorporating play allowed us to implement care as a restorative practice in mission-aligned ways that felt authentic to our community members, who remain eager to feel connected as our campus landscape continues to unexpectedly shift.

For our retreat play activity, we prioritized colleagues' preferences in venue and activity type to honor all perspectives. We solicited activity recommendations in a weekly team meeting, inviting staff to contribute verbally or anonymously in a shared document according to their comfort. From the dozen ideas this exercise yielded, we then designed a voting bracket on a large poster that categorized everyone's contributions, broadly divided into "athletic/physically active" (e.g., curling, mini-golf, go-carts) and "artistic/creative" (e.g., watercolor class, crafting workshop, nature walk), and we facilitated real-time voting at the next team meeting. Colleagues laughed and engaged in friendly competition, marking their choices with brightly colored markers. We left the meeting with not only a winner—mini golf—but also a deeper sense of camaraderie (and a host of ideas for future community-building events!). This activity brought out our team's playfulness and supported relationship-building, as voice and choice were baked into each layer of the process. Folks were excited about the range of options and enjoyed voting at each stage, watching in real-time as winners advanced.

Engaging in trust-building, structured and unstructured time for connection and processing, guided meditation, and collective decision-making have helped our team balance feelings of fear and uncertainty with moments of communal joy, laughter, and play. Many of these strategies can be adapted effectively regardless of team size/resources. Low and no-cost options like retreating at local museums on free admission days or public parks or teambuilding using free strengths-finders like the Adobe Creative Types quiz allow you to tailor to your teams' abilities, preferences, and budget.[13] Creating space for colleagues to suggest options that may not have occurred to you and involving team members willing to facilitate retreat activities by teaching a hobby celebrates diverse team talents in a low-cost, relationship-centered way. The resources we've invested in our CTL culture have created a sustainable wellspring that continually supports our service to the campus teaching and learning community.

Campus Community

After pandemic-related college campus closures in 2020, EDs were on the frontlines of higher education, supporting instructors in pivoting in-person courses to online formats. Our CTL met the moment with resources, consultations, and guidance to university leadership. Simultaneously, we found ourselves extending the caregiving habits we practiced with each other to the people we serve. Leaning into the "temple" function of CTLs, we became a "space where campus teaching and learning communities can find hope and inspiration . . . [in] an institutionally-sanctioned space for exploring pedagogy."[14] We brought care into our work by crafting human-centered newsletters that acknowledged collective grief and facilitating virtual meetings for faculty to build peer-to-peer connection, experiment with digital tools, and process their experiences together. This provided a strong foundation for navigating the current moment when many EDs and instructors feel discouraged, afraid, and exhausted.

We also worked to build trust with our teaching and learning community. We created hallmarks for our one-on-one pedagogy consultations built around respect and human connection, including tenets such as: consultants "approach consultees with humility and curiosity" and "are open to reciprocal learning throughout the consultation." As a result, consultations have become spaces where instructors can share stories of students in crisis and strategize about ways to act within the scope of their roles to offer support. Focusing on care also allows us to emphasize instructors' own wellness needs, emphasizing that student success shouldn't come at the expense of instructors' well-being. We collaborate to design lesson plans that help instructors and students experience collective awe as a class or play together through active learning.

Our commitment to curiosity and attentiveness also informs event-planning practices like incorporating community feedback, protecting time for relationship-building, and pivoting when unexpected situations arise. In Spring semester 2024, for example, we adapted a new transformative teaching event to attend to shifting community needs. About two weeks before the event, approximately sixty staff and nontenured colleagues were unexpectedly fired.[15] Many of them were close collaborators committed to presenting at or attending our event. Their abrupt terminations prompted feelings of grief, fear, and uncertainty about our community's future among remaining staff, faculty, and students. Rather than cancel this opportunity for in-person connection, we reframed a planned museum visit to respond to community needs and center wellness and reflection. The original event was a collaboration with our campus art museum and Disability Cultural Center to facilitate a Universal Design for Learning-inspired gallery tour. We pivoted to facilitate an event rooted in exploration, drawing, and meditation. Participants expressed gratitude for this protected time for emotional processing through sensory engagement. Several participants indicated it was the first time they had felt even a momentary sense of calm since the staff layoffs announcement. According to the emerging field of neuroaesthetics, being in the presence of art even in unstructured, extracurricular ways enriches learning by creating or repairing neural connections.[16] Creating space for healing through beholding art is an act of care that may not prevent systemic or individual harms, but it can offer necessary rest and comfort for those we serve.

Protecting time for wonder and connection has become a hallmark of CTL events, and we find that some of the most healing moments happen during unstructured time. For example, at a faculty event days after the aforementioned layoffs of colleagues formerly appointed in DEI roles, one of our CTL staff connected with a faculty partner about the heaviness they felt. The faculty member shared about a student who was behind in her coursework because she was organizing an affinity graduation event the university had canceled. Holding space for processing concerns about the student led to creative strategizing about alternative assessments that might highlight the skills the student gained through community organizing and event planning. As EDs, we look for ways to reimagine outcomes-aligned assessments that promote experiential learning. Through this unplanned exchange, the CTL staff member provided care and hope for a colleague and her student grounded in pedagogically sound next steps.

Many of these strategies can be adapted to various contexts, including designing events that protect time for unstructured conversations or activate participants' brains through collectively experienced stimuli such as listening to music, appreciating a photograph, or taking campus "awe walks" that are mindful of participants' abilities and interests.[17] Putting care at the center and building trust during tumultuous times has allowed our CTL to cultivate communities of care who help each other process our fears, find hope, and develop solutions that preserve our integrity.

Moving Forward

We hope for a future where the promise of higher education for today's students is more closely aligned with institutional structures, staffing, supports, policies, and practices. For now, we acknowledge that we are in a sustained season of uncertainty with limited agency. What remains in our power is a commitment to care: care as intrinsic to meaningful student learning experiences and as a sustaining, healing force both within our center and in our service of the broader campus community. We are eager to create and nurture cross-institutional relationships and continue finding ways to keep moving forward together.

Notes

1. Kasia Mika-Bresolin, "Pedagogy of Scale: Unmastering Time, Teaching and Living Through Crises," *Educational Philosophy and Theory* 56, no. 4 (2024): 1–15.

2. Sage Crump, "Facilitation as Experiments in Culture Creation," in *Holding Change: The Way of Emergent Strategy and Mediation* (AK Press, 2021), 50–55.

3. *An Act Relating to Diversity, Equity, and Inclusion Initiatives at Public Institutions of Higher Education, S.B. 17*, 88th Texas Legislative Session (2023).

4. Asif Wilson and Wytress Richardson, "All I want to say is that they don't really care about us: Creating and maintaining healing-centered collective care in hostile times." *Bank Street Occasional Paper Series* 43, no. 8 (2021): 79–89, quoted at 80.

5. bell hooks, *Teaching to Transgress: Education as the Practice of Freedom* (London: Routledge, 1994).

6. Peter Felten and Leo Lambert, *Relationship-rich Education: How Human Connections Drive Success in College* (Baltimore: John Hopkins University Press, 2020), 5–7, 17.

7. Wilson and Richardson, "All I Want to Say."

8. Tara Brach, *Radical Compassion: Learning to Love Yourself and Your World with the Practice of Rain* (New York: Rider Books, 2020).

9. Crump, "Facilitation as Experiments."

10. Prentis Hemphill, *What it Takes to Heal: How Transforming Ourselves Can Change the World* (New York: Random House, 2024), 89.

11. Wilson and Richardson, "All I Want to Say," 80.

12. Brach, *Radical Compassion*, 92.

13. "Creative Types," Adobe *Create*. https://mycreativetype.com/.

14. Eli Collins-Brown, et al. "Defining What Matters: Guidelines for Comprehensive Center for Teaching and Learning (CTL) Evaluation. *POD Network* (2018), 8.

15. Mangan, Katherine. "A Slap in the Face: How UT-Austin Axed a DEI Division." *The Chronicle of Higher Education*, 2024. https://www.chronicle.com/article/a-slap-in-the-face-how-ut-austin-axed-a-dei-division.

16. Susan Magsamen and Ivy Ross, *Your Brain on Art: How the Arts Transform Us*. New York: Random House, 2023.

17. Gretchen Reynolds, "An 'Awe Walk' Might Do Wonders for Your Well-being." *New York Times*, September 30, 2020. https://www.nytimes.com/2020/09/30/well/move/an-awe-walk-might-do-wonders-for-your-well-being.html.

18

Dandelions in the Wind

Planting Resilient Seeds during and after a Campus Closure

Heather Keith and Christina Fabrey

On a cool day in May at our small, idyllic New England campus, students, faculty, family, and friends gathered together not only to celebrate our graduates but also to memorialize 185 years of life-changing experiences at this, our college's last commencement. Amidst the usual well-wishing, hat-throwing pomp and circumstance, two moments stood out in this surprisingly joyous and boisterous event. Our faculty marshal, wearing a wreath of dandelions, invited the students, faculty, and staff to throw themselves into the wind like dandelions, spreading the seeds of our college's spirit across the landscape of other campuses and communities. Then a group of students and faculty performed the song "Resilient" by Rising Appalachia, inviting the audience to make a "mighty roar":

> I got my roots down, down, down, down
> Down, down, down, down, down, deep
> So what are we doing here? What has been done?
> What are you gonna do about it when the world comes undone?
> My voice feels tiny and I'm sure so does yours
> But put us all together we make a mighty roar.

Our students and faculty did not disappoint, whooping, yipping, and dancing. Most of the faculty and students had been drawn to work and learn at our small mission-focused college because of our shared and passionate commitment to sustainability and social justice. For many of us, it was a calling and lifestyle. Despite the fact that the closing of our beloved college felt at times like the death of a family member, we were a strong community, prepared to grieve and recover collectively, showing up for one another and for the causes that brought us together.

I am resilient
I trust the movement
I negate the chaos
Uplift the negative
I'll show up at the table, again and again and again
I'll close my mouth and learn to listen.

In 2023 alone, fourteen American nonprofit colleges and universities closed, and the *Hechinger Report* suspects that colleges may now be closing at the rate of one per week.[1] With post-pandemic economic volatility, decreased trust in the value of higher education, increased student debt, and a declining college-age population, we can expect more closures and austerity measures. The authors worked together in a Career, Advising, and Teaching (CAT) Center at a small liberal arts college when it closed in 2019 after almost two hundred years of educating students. Green Mountain College in Vermont was a small bachelor's- and master's-granting institution, which drew stellar faculty to its sustainability and social justice mission. In many ways, the college's values of resilience and community were instrumental in the recovery process for faculty, staff, and students. This chapter explores how to build resilience during such a crisis by focusing on hope and cultivating community through maintaining and creating meaningful traditions while helping to place both faculty and students at other institutions.

No one can doubt that our higher education ecosystem is unstable. With the pandemic, recession, enrollment cliff, threats to academic freedom, and a public less inclined to see the usefulness of a college degree, disruptions to our work abound. Resilience theory calls for us to consider how to mitigate and adapt to disruptions to maintain the important function of higher education institutions. Zolli and Healy frame resilience as "the capacity of a system, enterprise, or a person to maintain its core purpose and integrity in the face of dramatically changed circumstances."[2] Here, we explore some ideas for promoting the resilience of individuals and communities in the face of unusual instability. We also note that our work was part of an upswell of support offered by others on campus and acknowledge that there are many things we could have done differently.

Despite small colleges being essential (to individuals and the wider world), they are endangered. Green Mountain College, consistently ranked (often first) in the top ten colleges for sustainability by multiple outside agencies, was unable to fully recover after the 2008–2009 recession. Burdened with declining enrollment and millions of dollars of deferred maintenance, the Board of Trustees announced the college's closure in January 2019. We have an ache in our hearts just remembering what it felt like to hear that the place many of us considered a second home would close its doors for good, and our community would be disbanded and rootless. As Brittany Carlson notes, "In some ways, a faculty position is 'just a job.' But for many academics, it also becomes an identity and losing it can be traumatic."[3] Green Mountain was the kind of place people raised their kids, bringing them to the office or classroom after school, meeting up with other families to ride bikes on campus or visit the college farm. One of the worst moments for each of us was sharing the news with our elementary school–aged kids. And, of course, we feared our fate in an already difficult academic job market. Would we all be able to regrow roots and thrive in a new environment?

Already known to offer guidance and success strategies to students and faculty, our Career, Advising, and Teaching (CAT) Center was poised to help. As associate dean for teaching and learning (Heather) and associate dean for advising and achievement (Christina), the future plans and care of our students and colleagues became part of our daily roles. The structure of our CAT Center—having career, teaching, and advising professionals working closely together—provided a unique capability to respond to a crisis of this sort. In any given day, we cosponsored workshops in our shared space for various, often mixed, constituencies on how to find meaningful opportunities, whether in advancing one's education or career.

Planting Seeds of Resilience in Our Students

Students were devastated by the news of the college's closure. These emotions lingered throughout the semester while students processed the impact, recognizing the serious disruption to their academic and social lives. Students began to ask questions such as: How do I continue my education and maintain my well-being through this loss? Will I be able to finish my degree on time and on budget? How do I support the community of the college, many who have built their lives around the town? How can I maintain relationships with my friends and faculty beyond closure? The overwhelming truth is that most students at campuses that close give up on their education,[4] and there is significant research in K–12 on the impact of school closure (which is likely similar to college closure), finding increased loneliness, mental health issues, and suicidal risks.[5] The connection between college closure and mental health spurred us to consider new ways of providing student support in the center. After five years of a Title III grant designed to increase success and retention, Green Mountain College embraced a collaborative and holistic approach to supporting students. This ethos resulted in cultivating care and compassion toward student needs and was especially relevant during closure.

After the announcement, the center immediately turned to supporting students in the transition. The center distributed discussion points to faculty, encouraging them to talk about closure in class rather than discounting or ignoring the situation. Providing a sample statement of care, we encouraged faculty to share how they were dealing with the transition, cultivating connection over isolation.

> Sample statement: *I recognize that a college closure has a significant impact on your life and this transition may not be easy for you. Green Mountain College is a special place. The Career, Advising, and Teaching Center has set up several support contacts and events to ease this transition and support you in the steps to completing your degree. I'm passing around information and will send it by email too. Please seek help in planning for your next steps and come talk to me if you are struggling with the transition or completing this course. I want to make sure that you are successful, especially during this stressful time.*

In addition to processing in the classroom, faculty and staff were coached in providing support based on trauma-informed practices (see figure 1), while the center engaged with students in a more targeted capacity. In the midst of chaos, faculty and center professionals allowed the students to see stability in their lives and start to move forward in productive ways (as we found later, many of these practices were worthwhile in a global health crisis, as well). Hope theory, for example, recognizes that hopeful thinkers can navigate challenges easier; more than mere optimism, hope includes strategies to get through the challenge.[6] In integrating trauma-informed practices, we structured events to plant seeds of optimism for the next steps in the students' education but with a clear pathway for how students could intentionally manage the transition (Table 18.1).

Table 18.1. Adaptations of Trauma Informed Practices to Support Students during College Closure

Integrate compassion in the classroom	• Recognize and acknowledge the impact of the crisis • Check in regularly with students and ask open-ended questions around support • Incorporate responsive flexibility
Be aware of the impact on individual student	• Recognize the signs and symptoms of trauma in students • Normalize and validate their experiences • Facilitate coordinated care for students and provide response for healing • Provide venues and space for students feel seen and heard
Offer tools for thinking about and making sense of a new environment	• Open up opportunities for student choice, expression, and support • Engage students in cognitive thinking and planning • Provide digestible information that is timely and relevant • Coordinate resources for support (counseling, advising, financial aid and scholarship, housing, etc.)
Support healing through promoting social networks and resilience	• Ask students what they need for healing and resiliency • Partner with them to support new initiatives based on needs

Source: Substance Abuse and Mental Health Services Administration (SAMHSA). "SAMHSA's concept of trauma and guidance for a trauma-informed approach." (2014). Retrieved from http;//store.samhsa.gov/shin/content/SMA14-4884/SMA14-4884.pdf.

From open-ended dialogue sessions to more structured conversations about teach-out options, the center provided space for healthy processing and relevant and timely information. The center hosted sessions on student resources for transition, each teach-out partner, teach-out information sessions, and social gatherings focused on next steps (Table 18.2). When students expressed interest in having a workshop to write cards to the faculty and staff that they cared about, the center hosted it. Other events included yoga and study break sessions, housing workshops, and advising sessions for international students.

Table 18.2. Student Support Events to Consider in College Closure (List of Organized Events Coordinated by the Center during Green Mountain College closure)

Academic Planning
Academic transition support sessions- credit transfer, transfer of records to teach out partners, housing information and storage
Career Counseling and Advising
Email transfer sessions
Financial Aid and Scholarship Support
Holistic first-year coaching
Special populations advising sessions (International students, students with disabilities, etc.)
Portfolio development
Teach out partners information sessions
Emotional Support
Group counseling
Mental health support
Study breaks and holistic wellness events
Social and Community Events
Affinity groups based on teach out plans
Facilitated discussions on processing college closure
Social opportunities (card making, free hugs, featured meals from their favorite Dining Hall chef, social media groups, photo booths, and closure rituals)*

*Laura A. De Veau, "For Small Colleges, Closure Is the New Disaster Plan." *Medium*, (May 6, 2019)

In nearing the end of the semester, the center helped to prepare students for taking flight, supporting their transition into new environments. The center hosted travel lists for students sharing their new location and providing email contacts for those who wanted to remain in touch. The center partnered with teach-out schools in cohosting social events so that students could begin to build community. The center later encouraged the sharing of travel pictures and stories through social media.

Students explored how to maintain continued connection with each other, including how to maintain rituals and annual reunions, and how to plant seeds of the Green Mountain mission at other institutions. One teach-out partner was consequently inspired to develop the Green Mountain Center for Sustainability at Prescott College and staffed it with Green Mountain College faculty. This center today continues the sustainability mission and traditions of Green Mountain and encourages significant student and alumni input on its activities. Many students consider this new center to be an important legacy of our now-closed campus.

Helping Faculty Take Flight

While much of our work with faculty was around student success and resilience, we also supported faculty holistically. Staff members in our five-year-old teaching and learning center had worked hard to gain the trust of faculty as consultants to their daily work. We leveraged these relationships in providing a safe and productive space for colleagues to discuss career options and make plans. With the help of our in-house career center and the dean's and provost's offices, we offered workshops in updating CVs, cover letters, teaching and diversity statements, launching a job search, and enhancing social media footprints. We also discussed alternative career paths and professional goal-setting and listened as colleagues deliberated between options. The highlight of this time was celebrating successes, and we are happy to report that almost all faculty and staff members found meaningful opportunities to advance their careers at other institutions. While we celebrated when faculty and staff found new career opportunities, we wish that we had been more organized around marking those milestones. Getting an academic job under any circumstances is an achievement, and we could now imagine newsletter blurbs about successes, or sending a note and chocolate when someone got a job offer (chocolate and snacks should not be underrated in a crisis!).

Table 18.3. Faculty and Staff Support Events to Consider in College Closure (List of Organized Events Coordinated by the Center during Green Mountain College Closure)

Career Planning
Workshops on job search, social media footprint, CVs, cover letters, diversity and teaching statements
Peer review of materials
Coaching, with individual consultations and goal-setting
Individual and group conversations about job market challenges
Celebration of successes!
Emotional Support
Individual and group conversations about trauma and grief
Newsletter reminders about wellness
Grading breaks and holistic wellness events
Social and Community Events
Ceremonial closure activities, such as faculty and staff sharing what they would take with them from the experience of the college
Potlucks and parties

As a faculty, we gave ourselves the space and grace to grieve the loss of our campus, making sure to bring as much closure as possible through rituals, such as our illicit tour of the entire campus with a stolen master key (we let our kids climb the clocktower to add their names and dates), and community events, such as a last faculty potluck on a beautiful evening. Now, many of these memories, once bitter, are becoming sweeter. Like Brittany Carlson, we acknowledge that even though we have professionally recovered, success on the job market isn't all positive: "finding a tenure-track job, after facing almost-certain unemployment or underemployment, feels like a miracle at times. But the dislocation and the transition to a new campus will also cause moments of frustration, too."[7] In retrospect, we could have prepared for and normalized this dislocation more. Even years out, it's easy to remember and relive the closure in a way that makes it difficult to fully embrace new roles and communities, and we routinely feel angry and bitter when we visit our former home, which is now a wealthy person's personal private campus (with expensive cars parked on the basketball court and a distillery sales office in our former CAT Center).

We share concerns about the town and wider community as well, since the college was an important part of the local economy and culture and many of our friends and neighbors are still there. Similarly, Carlson notes that survivor's guilt should be acknowledged when some colleagues are more (or more quickly) successful in landing on their feet. Acknowledging our guilt and grief together, as Macy and Johnstone observe in their work on active hope in the age of climate change, is crucial to moving forward and making positive change in the world.[8] They note that grieving helps us come to terms with the idea of starting over, and in the end makes us more adventurous and open to new opportunities for making a difference.

As we noted, many of us have put down new roots. With an intentional focus on resilience, we maintained something of the spirit and mission of the college and the human community. While our ecosystem was disrupted (beyond repair, if we look only at the institution itself), we have individually and collectively returned to functionality in many ways and in different places. This writing team is happy to report that though we are working at different institutions, we are again living in the same neighborhood and working together on publications and other projects! We and our colleagues have used the sustainability and community values of our shuttered campus to begin to re-create meaningful and resilient communities in departments and centers at other institutions—values that can positively impact campuses in other crises, such as in times of austerity, working with contingent faculty, and responding to external threats.

Restoring the Ecosystem

While our focus has been on promoting meaningful transitions to other institutions, we believe it is important for all of academia (whether facing this kind of crisis or blissfully ensconced in institutions with solid endowments and enrollments) to reflect on what we are losing in small, mission-focused, liberal arts colleges. The *Chronicle of Higher Education*'s Scott Carlson writes that "you could see higher education facing a loss of biodiversity—drifting toward a monoculture, as an ecologist might name it, where an environment is shaped to prefer only a handful of dominant, genetically similar organisms. That environment not only lacks the attractive variety of a healthy ecosystem, it is also deprived of the genetic diversity necessary to ward off pestilence and help the whole system evolve."[9] Resilience theory tells us that protecting the ecosystem is key to helping individuals and communities (natural or human) prepare for and recover from disruption. What have we learned from these closures that will help us restore a healthy higher education ecosystem?

The well-being and success of faculty are relevant to this recovery. Even though small colleges are closing or merging every day, we should strive to keep their missions and pedagogies alive via disseminating their ways and values in other kinds of institutions. However, closures contribute to what Eric Zencey called "rootless professors"; while we may teach and praise a cosmopolitan, global outlook in our students (and there are clear benefits of this mindset), there are also community and ecosystemic advantages to learning and living locally, developing connections to the land, and serving local neighbors with our institutions: professors may need to be more "rooted" to do this, rather than "transient exotics."[10] This rootlessness has long been the norm in higher education but has been exacerbated by the campus closure crisis.

So, while we emphasize the need for resilience in our faculty, staff, and students who are uprooted by crises, we must also look more widely at the higher education ecosystem in order to promote a systemic resilience that maintains the variety necessary for our best service to students and communities. In the meantime, we can support our widespread community in sowing the seeds we gathered together in a great college that exists now only in the wind and soil of other campuses.

Notes

1. Jon Marcus, "Colleges Are Now Closing at a Pace of One a Week. What Happens to the Students?" *The Hechinger Report*, May 22, 2024. https://hechingerreport.org/colleges-are-now-closing-at-a-pace-of-one-a-week-what-happens-to-the-students/.

2. Andrew Zolli and Ann Marie Healy, *Resilience: Why Things Bounce Back* (New York: Free Press), 2002. Quoted at 7.

3. Brittany Carlson, "My College Closed. Now What?" *The Chronicle of Higher Education*, July 1, 2024. https://www.chronicle.com/article/my-university-closed-now-what.

4. Marcus, "Colleges are Now Closing."

5. Deni Mazrekaj and Kristof De Witte, "The Impact of School Closures on Learning and Mental Health of Children: Lessons From the COVID-19 Pandemic."

Perspectives on Psychological Science: A Journal of the Association for Psychological Science 19, no. 4 (2024): 686–93.

6. C. R. Snyder, "Hope Theory: Rainbows in the Mind," *Psychological Inquiry* 13, no. 4 (2002): 249–75; Gene M. Alarcon, Nathan A. Bowling, and Steven Khazon. "Great Expectations: A Meta-Analytic Examination of Optimism and Hope," *Personality and Individual Differences* 54, no. 7 (May 2013): 821–27.

7. Brittany Carlson, "My College Closed: Now What?"

8. Joanna Macy and Chris Johnstone, *Active Hope: How to Face the Mess We're in With Unexpected Resilience and Creative Power* (Novato, CA: New World Library, 2022).

9. Scott Carlson, "The Endangered Small College." *The Chronicle of Higher Education*, June 24, 2024). https://www.chronicle.com/article/the-endangered-small-college.

10. Eric Zencey, "The Rootless Professors," *Rooted in the Land: Essays on Community and Place*, ed. William Vitek and Wes Jackson (New Haven: Yale University Press, 2008), 15–19.

19

Collective Lessons from a College Closure

A Conversation Among Colleagues

Kent Andersen, William Tynes Cowan, Louanne Clayton Jacobs, Kevin Shook, and Greta Valenti

> As Chair of the Board of Trustees of Birmingham-Southern College, it is my sad duty to let you know that BSC will cease operations on May 31, 2024. The Board of Trustees voted unanimously today to close the College after a 2024 bill designed to amend the 2023 legislation that established the loan program on which our future depended failed to win sufficient support in the Alabama House of Representatives. Without that funding, the College does not have the resources to continue.
>
> —Rev. Keith D. Thompson '83, Chair, BSC Board of Trustees, March 26, 2024

Institutional Context

Birmingham-Southern College (BSC), a private residential liberal arts institution in Birmingham, Alabama, faced closure three times between December 2022 and spring 2024, eventually ceasing normal operations in May 2024 and closing permanently in July 2024. The college's financial turmoil became public in December 2022 when a state legislator leaked to the press that the private college was pursuing $30 million in public funding from the State of Alabama (Johnson 2022; Associated Press 2022). This funding, the college and press reported, would stabilize finances at the college and allow it to initiate a capital campaign to rebuild the endowment, which had been depleted following at least seven years of structural deficits (Griesbach 2022).[1]

The news coverage emphasized that the college required the state funds to continue operations past the Spring semester of 2023. In response, Alabama legislators crafted the Distressed Institutions of Higher Education Revolving Loan Program, a low-interest state loan program to assist financially distressed colleges ("Alabama Distressed Institutions of Higher Education Revolving Loan Program" 2024).[2] The criteria for the loan matched perfectly with Birmingham-Southern's situation and appeared tailor-made for BSC. The college applied for the $30 million loan in July 2023 (Schwartz 2024).

In October 2023, the state treasurer denied the BSC's loan application on the basis of insufficient collateral, which prompted possible closure for a second time in December of 2023 (Schwartz 2024). Emergency loan funds from other sources enabled the college to remain open at least through spring 2024—with the possibility of continuing operations beyond that date (Griesbach 2023). Almost immediately, BSC's president and board worked with lobbyists to persuade legislators to revise the loan program, this time to be administered by the Alabama Commission on Higher Education rather than the state treasurer. While the revised bill made it through the Senate and passed the House committee, a straw poll in the House in mid-March 2024 made clear that the revised bill would not pass the full house: BSC would not gain access to the requested funds. On March 26, 2024, the chair of the college's board of trustees finally announced closure.

Questions and Reflective Method

Student enrollment had plummeted from 1,058 in 2021, to 975 in 2022, to 731 in fall of 2023, in part because of the financial situation.[3] Prospects looked grim, and at the end of May 2023, nearly 40 of the 101 faculty members departed the college for retirement or alternative employment. Yet some faculty and staff opted to stay. Why? How did we make sense of, cope with, and adapt to the situation? Ultimately, what was it like to experience a college closure? Most importantly, what lessons might be drawn from such an experience for those facing similar circumstances?

Beginning in mid-April 2024, as we prepared for the BSC to close permanently, five of us met regularly to reflect on these questions. The group included a faculty administrator (Kent), an alum and humanities division chair (Tynes), an education professor (Louanne), and two department chairs, one from psychology (Greta) and one from art and art history (Kevin). *We concluded: 1) Blame is a reasonable but pointless impulse in the face of potential or actual closure. 2) The situation requires multiple coping strategies to address the cognitive dissonance of potential and actual closure. 3) In deciding whether to stick it out and/or what to do in the face of closure, each person must gauge their own commitments. 4) And finally, when facing potential closure, leaving the institution is a sound and reasonable option.*

Blame

Trying to assign blame is a natural response to actual or potential closure. We recognized this response as a leading reaction from our colleagues more than ourselves. To be sure, we sought explanations of how the college had reached closure but were not overly concerned with identifying the exact cause or culprit.

> Tynes: One of the differences between this group and those who spent time assigning blame was the level of faith we had in the current leadership. Do we believe they acted in good faith? Do we believe they did everything they could to save the College? We believe so.
>
> Louanne: I am not sure there is a single person at whose feet I can lay blame.
>
> Greta: The information I received during my interview in early 2013 [after financial issues in 2010] made me comfortable that BSC's financial problems were behind them. But I remember being at my first faculty meeting in August 2013 and thinking that things were not as good with the finances

> as I thought had been conveyed to me months earlier. I don't remember thinking anyone had been dishonest, though. There just seemed to be a lack of understanding of how to get to a place of long-term financial stability.

Blame externalizes the problem, distracting one from dealing with the reality of the situation. To be sure, the reality was confusing: on the one hand, the usual rituals of courses and on-campus activities and ample evidence of student success indicated business as usual; on the other hand, knowledge of potential closure indicated otherwise. The contradiction had to be resolved, and some chose to resolve it by searching for someone to blame.

Dissonance

Holding in mind conflicting thoughts produces the negative feeling of dissonance. Dissonance was evoked by observing that colleagues have vastly different beliefs about the likelihood of closure, different levels of faith in the college's leadership, and different reactions to the impending and eventual closure. In the year and a half prior to closure, some colleagues spent their time job hunting and were focused on moving on from BSC. Others were still hopeful and intended to stick it out. We weren't all on the same page.

Dissonance was also evoked in the year leading up to closure as faculty attempted to "live on two tracks": that is, keep going in their current position and, simultaneously, try to rewrite their career paths. We applied for promotions, planned courses, and advised students for future semesters. Additionally, because the college was in the middle of its ten-year reaffirmation, we continued to prepare for reaccreditation and develop long-term plans for improvement. We continued these activities while keeping in mind BSC might not exist and we'd have to find other jobs.

> TYNES: In meetings we started to preface future tense statements with "If we're open" (later condensed to "IWO" and later to a pause and knowing look).

Perhaps the abbreviation of "If we're open" is telling. It was exhausting—impossible—living on two tracks. To the degree that we could acknowledge the alt-universe without dwelling on it, we were able to make it through to the end without checking out, being incapacitated by despair, or fearing we were misleading people. Living on two tracks, while necessary for a time, was not sustainable as it denied one or the other truth.

> KEVIN: I questioned the integrity of recruiting students when the future was uncertain. Realized if I did not, there was no future. Damned if I did, damned if I did not.
>
> More difficult to suppress were feelings of fear. How will I pay my mortgage if the College closes?

> KENT: The first time around (December 2022), I started figuring out options. I talked with a colleague at another institution who wanted to hire me, but she knew that if BSC was going to be open, I'd stick with it. That was the choice I made in April 2023. I couldn't bring myself to apply or search too hard in the interim. I hesitated between the almost-close in December 2023 to the final-we-are-closing in March 2024. Was that denial?

> TYNES: I didn't even look for another job until we got the official announcement of closure. I don't think I was in denial. I was conscious of this alternate life that was unfolding for me, but I couldn't live in both worlds at the same time.

From the perspective of at least some of those who left BSC in May 2023, those of us who stayed might be perceived as being in a state of denial, an unhealthy form of coping. We do not agree that we were in denial; we were willing and able to take a risk. Still, it was not easy to continue doing the job while worrying about the future. So how did we manage to avoid the doom spiral?

Coping

We noted multiple consistencies in our coping strategies: focus on the work in front of us, meet students' needs, and limit the doom scroll of news, social media, gossip, and unfounded conjecture about the college's future.

> Kent: I doubled down on work. I focused on what I could control. I also chose to drown out the noise and focus on what was in front of me. Looking back, I wound up doing too much. That overload really was not a healthy way to cope.

> Louanne: I continued to teach classes and hold office hours and respond to student writing as though nothing had changed. I managed by setting myself daily tasks involved with organizing and packing my office.

> Greta: I was able to continue to be motivated to do my job. I was able to focus both in class and outside of class. At the same time, I tried to be understanding of those whose stress level and financial situation made the situation intolerable to them and could not carry on "business as usual."

Even if we could immerse ourselves in work that remained valuable even as we knew it might vanish, we also sought to avoid triggers that prompted anxiety and sadness.

> Tynes: I even avoided conversations with well-meaning people. Talking about the College's situation was exhausting.

> Louanne: I limited my consumption of news to sources I trusted. I limited discussion of the College's situation to people I knew and trusted. Wearing College gear to the gym invited conversations for which I did not have the bandwidth.

These coping strategies were helpful not only after the closure announcement but also throughout the year that we chose to stay and not to pursue employment elsewhere. We chose to commit to seeing BSC through what we hoped would be just a few more years of financial instability. Given that choice, the work reminded us—and our students—of our purpose and calling, which in itself was healing.

Commitment

Commitment and community were central reasons each of us chose to stay: commitment to students and their well-being, commitment to our work, commitment to colleagues and the campus community, and commitment to a new president who appeared to have the talent and tenacity to address our financial difficulties.

We were committed foremost to the pleasure found in our work, the unique opportunities available at this unique institution, and the personal experiences that connected us to the place. Tynes, an alumnus of the college, had watched one daughter graduate from BSC and was looking forward to the possibility of his other daughter attending.

> LOUANNE: I stayed because these relationships made the threats manageable. I stayed because I have done my best work here and I saw a future that included even better work. I stayed because though the threats loomed, the doors of opportunity continued to open. I stayed because I believed and because that belief was stronger than the specter of closure.

> KEVIN: Sometime in 2008 or 2010, the art students league decided we should have a kickball game between the faculty and the art students. The faculty agreed. We competed on the intramural field. Admittedly, the faculty had to sign a few students as free agents to field a team. However, we liked our chances. It turns out the faculty are very competitive. We lost. I did fear Jim was injured when he went ass over tea kettle attempting to kick a pitch. He missed and did a flip. The art and art history department were special.

We also stayed because we weighed pragmatic personal and professional concerns against the unknown.

> KEVIN: Weighing professional and family concerns: My wife could move and enjoyed looking at real estate in other areas. Two kids in high school, we really did not want to move to a new school before they graduated. Our plan for college was BSC, the tuition benefit is huge.

> KENT: I have been at BSC for 24 years. I said yes when asked. I started as an adjunct and I am now the associate provost. The last one. I'm done with this now, and ready to say yes to something else. What will I say no to?

> KEVIN: I've looked at moving laterally in the art world: graphic design, marketing. I'm not sure that would satisfy me like teaching does.

Put simply, we had committed a ton of time and effort to getting a job that we liked, and we were succeeding at this job. It seems counterintuitive that we would voluntarily leave such a job.

> LOUANNE: I accepted the BSC position because of the emphasis on teaching. At another institution, I was asked to give *a talk* on my research and scholarship; at BSC, I was asked to *teach a class* based on my research and scholarship.

> KENT: Why stay? Inertia. Habit. This was where I was, and I had (mostly) what I needed to feel like I was doing good work. Students. Colleagues I could collaborate with. Challenges that would stretch me but were within reach. Maybe I stayed because I thought BSC could not go on without me. No one else will pick up these materials.

Both the size and the ethos of the college encouraged meaningful collaboration with colleagues and opportunities for expansive scholarship. Commitment to those colleagues and types of experiences served as motivators to remain and hold on to the hope of the future.

> TYNES: I've been writing a lot of recommendation letters recently for my colleagues in the humanities. It is not hard to write positive letters for them. Scratch that. The letter is hard. Making it positive is not. As a result, my attempt to bury myself in my work simply serves as a reminder of the relationships that I'll miss.

> LOUANNE: As we work on this project, I am acutely aware of the loveliness of writing in community with people who I love and respect and will so miss.

Why we stayed might be viewed as irrational: We felt a particular attachment to this place and the people. We loved it here.

Tynes. As an alum, there is a sense of home at BSC and yet there's also a sense of permanence. Maybe that's why I was able to weather the potential closures with a sense of inevitable survival. It is just beyond my ability to comprehend closure.

LOUANNE: I couldn't conceive of a hole on this hilltop not filled by the BSC-ness of this place.

Advice

Dear Colleague at another institution facing similar circumstances:

KEVIN: Determine what is best for you and those around you, focus on your priorities. I came back to my family. My career is on a razor's edge, yet I need a stable foundation for my family. What actions will isolate and protect the kids? At my lowest, my wife was there to support me. The burden and responsibilities do not need to rest on your shoulders.

KENT: Keep your options open and diversify your work. You're going to operate on two tracks. There is this life and this career where you get tenure and do what you are doing for the next 40–50 years. There is also another life where you do an entirely different kind of work, with different people. Broaden your sense of place and purpose when you have the chance. Don't put all your eggs in one basket—I suppose that is what they say.

LOUANNE: In the moment, stop second-guessing yourself. Stop beating yourself up for doing or not doing, saying or not saying. Stop. Stop reading the comments section of each social media post. Move in purposeful ways each day—exercise will burn anxiety and help you think and sleep. Get outside. This thing that is happening will seem smaller when you are in nature. I hope you have sunshine. Sunshine is good.

TYNES: Apply for a job, be ready to leave if you need to, and leave anyway if the tension/anxiety is too much of a downer.

Kevin: I am uncertain of the future. But it helps to break it down into compartments, lists. Establishing a frame helps to build and plan.

Greta: I don't think there's a right answer to whether you should try to leave or take your chances and wait it out. At my college, people responded to the uncertainty in all sorts of ways. But I know this message might not be comforting.

Conclusion

Our observations and experience suggest that the decision to stay or leave was shaped by:

- financial obligations;
- familial responsibilities and support;
- career stage and career flexibility;
- tolerance for uncertainty and ambiguity
- access to and preference for a career in academia as opposed to other sectors;
- connections to current students;
- professional obligations/commitments to the academic discipline; and
- faith in others at the institution to weather and address the crisis.

There is no one best choice. No matter what your decision is, do good work, avoid the blame game, reality test information about the situation and your options, find healthy ways to cope that prioritize your values, and don't undermine the decisions of others—acknowledge that everyone is in a unique situation and may come to different and equally reasonable conclusions.

Notes

1. Rebecca Griesbach, "Losing Birmingham-Southern 'Would Be a Travesty,' Lawmakers Say in Call for $30 Million Bailout." *AL.com*, December 19, 2022.

2. Alabama Distress Institutions of Higher Education Revolving Loan Program, *BHAMwiki*, https://bhamwiki.com/w/index.php?title=Alabama_Distressed_Institutions_of_Higher_Education_Revolving_Loan_Program&oldid=217007.

3. Josh Moody, "Birmingham-Southern Announces Abrupt Closure," *Inside Higher Ed*, March 25, 2024, https://www.insidehighered.com/news/business/financial-health/2024/03/27/birmingham-southern-announces-abrupt-closure.

References

Alabama Distress Institutions of Higher Education Revolving Loan Program. June 5, 2024. BHAMiki. https://bhamwiki.com/w/index.php?title=Alabama_Distressed_Institutions_of_Higher_Education_Revolving_Loan_Program&oldid=217007.

Associated Press. "College Seeks Bailout, Warning It May Close." December 19, 2022. *CBS 42*. https://www.cbs42.com/alabama-news/birmingham-southern-college-seeks-bailout-warning-it-may-close/.

Griesbach, Rebecca. "Losing Birmingham-Southern 'Would Be a Travesty,' Lawmakers Say in Call for $30 Million Bailout." *AL.com*. December 19, 2022. https://www.al.com/educationlab/2022/12/losing-birmingham-southern-college-would-be-a-travesty-lawmakers-say-in-call-for-30-million-bailout.html.

Griesbach, Rebecca. "United Methodists Pledge $2.5 Million to Birmingham-Southern: 'Steady Progress.' " *AL.com*. November 10, 2023. https://www.al.com/education lab/2023/11/united-methodists-pledge-25-million-to-birmingham-southern-steady-progress.html.

Johnson, Roy S. "Birmingham-Southern College in 'Financial Distress,' in Danger of Closing in 2023, Lawmakers Say; School Responds. *AL.com*. December 16, 2022. https://www.al.com/news/birmingham/2022/12/birmingham-southern-college-in-financial-distress-in-danger-of-closing-in-2023-lawmakers-say.html.

Moody, Josh. "Birmingham-Southern Announces Abrupt Closure." *Josh Modo* 2024. https://www.insidehighered.com/news/business/financial-health/2024/03/27/birmingham-southern-announces-abrupt-closure.

Schwartz, Natalie. "A Timeline of Birmingham-Southern College's Failed Bid to Stay Open." *Higher Ed Dive*. March 27, 2024. https://www.highereddive.com/news/a-timeline-of-birmingham-southern-colleges-failed-bid-to-stay-open/698946/.

Part 4

Shared Governance and Organizing for Solidarity

Today, we must all be ready for ideological or financial attacks, whether from within or from without. Regardless of the origin, ensuring a strong, healthy shared governance structure and building a tradition of mentoring our colleagues, sharing solidarity, and organizing resistance are absolute necessities for all of us as we move into an increasingly threatening and uncertain future. We must build the connections among ourselves on our campuses but also reach beyond, to learn from colleagues abroad and to help them as well. On the macro scale, our disciplinary professional organizations might offer this type of connection, as well as advocacy organizations (in particular the American Association of University Professors). But the micro scale remains an essential consideration; our hours and days are spent on particular campuses and with and among specific campus communities. That context is essential as we consider connections and solidarity. We must, as faculty and staff, remember and celebrate that we are a force of labor and a force of good, and that unless we unite to promote the interests of ourselves, our students, and our institutions, we all fail.

20

The Politics of Weakness

Faculty Senate and Faculty Governance in Crisis

Evan A. Kutzler and John LeJeune

The faculty senate, especially in states hostile to public sector labor unions, is the backbone of shared governance in higher education. Town hall meetings can bring faculty into the conversations, but faculty senates confer legitimacy on curricular and other institutional decisions made by noneducators. Yet the university exists as a vibrant decision-making body only in the best of circumstances. In the worst of circumstances, it is a chaotic mess of loosely coordinated initiatives and semifunctional committees. In times of crisis, the faculty senate faces challenges from not only jaded faculty but also from midlevel administrators and the president's cabinet. If university administrators are responsible for creating a healthy environment for shared governance, faculty are responsible for being up to the challenge of making tough decisions. When the institutions of shared governance are weak, so too is the faculty's influence on major issues.[1]

This essay focuses on the Faculty Senate at Georgia Southwestern State University (GSW) during a period of significant change and amid rumblings of greater, perhaps catastrophic, changes to come. Located 2.5 hours south of Atlanta in a town of 15,000 people, GSW is a small regional state university with 2,500 undergraduates and 120 full-time faculty. These small populations mean that even seemingly minor changes have significant effects on students, faculty, and programs. Word travels fast and the same people work together—or against one another—again and again.[2]

The coauthors of this essay served as GSW faculty senate presidents during consecutive academic years. During the 2022–2023 year, Evan Kutzler inherited a faculty senate bereft of bylaws and lacking a positive sense of mission amid controversial administrative decisions that devastated College of Arts and Sciences programs. Meanwhile, a statewide mandate (from the University System of Georgia [USG]) compelled the senate to navigate a policy that threatened to undermine tenure, and it did so without ceding any more ground than required.[3] The following year, USG's so-called ASPIRE initiative pressured universities to deactivate all "low producing programs," threatening every weakened College of Arts and Sciences program. Acquiescing to requests for increased faculty input, the GSW president charged the new senate president, John LeJeune, with cochairing a task force to consider major academic restructuring, with controversial results.

This essay begins from the principle that shared governance is essential to healthy academic functioning. The American Association of University Professors (AAUP) defines shared governance as "the joint responsibility of faculty, administrations, and governing boards to govern colleges and universities," in which the role of faculty is "to have primary responsibility for such fundamental areas as curriculum, subject matter and methods of instruction, research, faculty status, and aspects of student life which relate to the educational process."[4] Achieving this is difficult. Robust institutional practices and productive norms of engagement matter. Cultivating faculty and administrative buy-in requires effective leadership and sacrifice. A senate president's main job involves strengthening faculty institutions, promoting a shared governance culture, and insisting on administrative support beyond the clichés of "faculty-centered" rhetoric spouted by aspiring presidents and provosts.

The Faculty Senate in Crisis

Until 2022, the GSW faculty senate operated mostly by oral tradition. University statutes provided for a senate president, campuswide representation, and issued the charge of crafting policy and advising the president—mostly through standing university committees that reported to the senate. Every faculty member at GSW serves on a standing committee that either mirrors administrative units (e.g., Academic Affairs) or tackles specific curricular and administrative topics (e.g., Faculty Affairs). Committees vary in responsibility and commitment; in light of this variation, the senate overhauled its standing committees in 2018 by eliminating those with the worst reputations (e.g., University and Alumni Affairs) and adding new committees better aligned with faculty governance needs (e.g., Faculty Development).[5] Although the restructuring now limited shared governance to faculty, curricular, and curricular-adjacent matters, it focused attention on issues in their expertise.

Despite reorganization, the reliance on tradition proved an insufficient safeguard for shared governance when major academic decisions were at stake. President Neal Weaver, who received his PhD from the University of Oklahoma in 2005 and served as GSW's president from 2017 to 2024, was skeptical of shared governance. In his short dissertation on regional university presidents, Weaver waxed nostalgic for an era of stronger presidents and described shared governance as a modern barrier to efficiency. Shared governance was something for presidents to endure and survive but not cultivate.[6] Amid the COVID-19 pandemic in the summer of 2020, Weaver announced the closure of the geology and dramatic arts programs without going through the GSW senate or its Academic Affairs committee.[7]

Subsequently, in 2022, Weaver and Provost Suzanne Smith terminated teaching degrees in the College of Arts and Sciences. Since 2003, aspiring teachers had received subject-area degrees from the College of Arts and Sciences and a teaching certificate from the College of Education. A conflict between the School of Education and the College of Arts and Sciences had been simmering for twenty years. Under Weaver and Smith, the administration ceded more control over orientation, advising, and curriculum to the College of Education. In 2022, the Committee on Academic Affairs rejected a proposal to create a new bachelor's of science in education (BSED) program in English. President Weaver, through Provost Smith, responded by insisting that the GSW faculty senate (a) revive a proposal from 2015 for a plethora of new BSED programs, (b) submit the rejected English proposal to the full faculty, or (c) face losing existing programs. Senators decided that they could not revive a proposal from 2015 and, until a proposal passed the Academic Affairs committee, it would not send the item to the full faculty.

That summer, by email, Weaver moved all teaching programs to the College of Education as BSED programs. He reasoned that the BSED programs had been hibernated—not deactivated—since 2003 and did not need faculty or system approval to create programs that had not existed for twenty years. The decision gutted struggling programs in the College of Arts and Sciences. Amid continued objections from senators, Smith and Weaver suggested that the senate overrepresented the College of Arts and Sciences (an artifact of recent college reorganization and hiring priorities) and thus might not represent the will of the faculty on any major decision. It was a low point for shared governance. In a classic example of "weapons of the weak," jaded faculty spread cruel jokes about the administration as well as unsubstantiated rumors of workplace impropriety.[8]

This low point coincided with major faculty handbook revisions mandated by the university system. Changes included new evaluation criteria for faculty in vague categories such as "student success" and a robust posttenure review process. Skeptics claimed that the policy changes meant the end of tenure—indeed, the changes led the AAUP to censure the Georgia system. Senators shared these concerns; nonetheless, a joint subcommittee between Academic and Faculty Affairs guided revisions through the channels of shared governance within the time constraints imposed by the university system. These changes, which matched the existing work portfolio of GSW faculty better than some other state institutions, met the faculty's insistence on peer review and due process. It showed that the GSW faculty senate could resolve the most sensitive issues to the satisfaction of the university system. In fact, in the final conversations, the faculty senate worked directly with the university system to finalize the new policy.[9]

The series of specially called meetings to meet system deadlines, alongside the full faculty approval of the new policies, came and went without major turmoil. The success marked the start of a period of sober reflection and reorganization focused on remaking the senate. One subcommittee proposed the senate's first bylaws to demystify its day-to-day operations and assert itself as the institution and process to best-defend shared governance. For the first time, the senate developed a formula for apportionment, formalized offices, and created meeting norms. Meanwhile surveys gathered data about standing committee workloads and the need for new university committees. The process represented the reemergence of a more energetic senate that began to lead on important issues like the future of the College of Arts and Sciences and diversity on campus.[10]

Building Institutions in a Crisis

The creation of bylaws in 2022 laid the foundation for the senate to pursue three strategic objectives in 2023. Increasing faculty access and input into the senate's policy agenda became a top priority. The senate implemented its first all-faculty survey in the fall of 2023 with administrative, academic, faculty affairs, and student affairs questions. Senate subcommittees reviewed the responses, identified priorities, and forwarded action steps to standing committees. The senate also added public address as a standing agenda item and created an online message form and email address for archiving communications.

Rapprochement and constructive engagement with the administration became a second objective. In a one-on-one summer meeting, President Weaver agreed to attend senate meetings and have the senate communicate his remarks in detail. Encouraged to send major academic concerns through shared governance channels, President Weaver brought two substantive academic issues before the senate in the fall of 2023, including concerns about how to academically address waived SAT-ACT requirements for incoming first-year students.

Objective three sought to improve the institutional functioning of the senate and its standing committees. Amending bylaws to cover procedural gaps, the senate recommitted itself, in alignment with the Georgia Open Meetings Act, to the timely posting of meeting agendas, summaries, and minutes, and eventually required standing committees to commit to the same. These measures increase the transparency and visibility of shared governance procedures at all levels.

The biggest test of the summer rapprochement came at a town hall meeting. On November 29, 2023, President Neal Weaver requested that a task force cochaired by the senate president and new GSW provost, Jill Drake, answer the question, "What are the implications to realigning our academic colleges from four to three to allow for moving the academic priorities needle?" Weaver wanted specific recommendations on reorganization. The long initial meeting focused on fourteen so-called low-producing programs and a system-wide threat that these "LLPs"—almost all in the College of Arts and Sciences and many affected by the earlier decisions about education—risked deactivation. In early 2024, a system-wide "Academic Strategies and Programs for Institutional Relevance and Excellence" memo, the so-called ASPIRE document, signaled the imminent massacre of College of Arts and Sciences programs and ramped up the pressure on GSW's Academic Reorganization Committee. "If a program's three-year rolling average has been below thresholds for two consecutive years," the document stated, "it is assumed that you are deactivating the program." At a small meeting that same month, Weaver confirmed that his reorganization vision centered on partitioning Arts and Sciences courses while reiterating that he would respect the task force's recommendation.

The reorganization committee, on paper, marked a great advance in shared governance for the university.[11] President Weaver framed it as a response to unique opportunities to address major challenges, such as ASPIRE, offered by enrollment growth and high-level retirements. He also called it a response to faculty complaints. Indeed, more than anything else in the 2023 survey, faculty wanted greater input into major decisions.

In practice, the experiment suffered from debilitating flaws. Weaver justified March 15, 2024, as the deadline on the grounds that the university needed to write a job description to replace a retiring dean. Factoring the December break, this deadline gave an unwieldy committee of faculty, deans, and other administrators a mere two months to formulate, research, and write a formal recommendation about dissolving the university's largest school and restructuring the other three. A lack of clarity regarding ASPIRE also hindered the committee. To what extent should ASPIRE and the future of GSW's fourteen LPPs inform the recommendations? Despite the LPPs' central role in Dr. Weaver's town hall and all common sense that these were intertwined issues, mid- and upper-tier administrators frequently suggested decoupling the problems. Looming administrative changes threatened the viability of any committee recommendation: on February 22, 2024, the University of Texas System Board of Regents named Dr. Weaver as the sole finalist for president of Stephen F. Austin State University.

Old issues also emerged on the reorganization committee, which did not engender mutual trust between faculty and administration. The large committee divided labor between a faculty-centric "Academic Programs Subcommittee" and a dean-centric "Finance + Administration" subcommittee. The former, chaired by the senate president, submitted meeting reports, research summaries, data files, and comparative assessments of reorganization models, while the latter submitted a single PowerPoint summary showing how dissolving the College of Arts and Sciences would affect the budgets and workloads of administrators. The summary offered no judgment of that model's comparative strength in part because it provided no alternative four-college model for comparison.

The reorganization committee's tense final vote on March 15 further muddied shared governance. Ahead of time, one dean improperly instructed a faculty member to vote for three colleges. At the urging of the provost, the final vote was secret. By a 10–6 majority, the committee recommended that GSW pursue a three-college model that eliminated the College of Arts and Sciences. The faculty were shocked. On March 28, a reorganization committee member spoke during public address, asking "what case has been made" that a three-college model would meet the stated objectives of reorganization, since no other member had made that case on the record. He also requested submitting the question to a faculty vote. Dr. Weaver, who had accepted the new job, said he would not make any decision about reorganization, leaving the whole exercise in limbo.

The legacy of this committee was not a happy one and left feelings back where they were in the fall of 2022, albeit with a much stronger faculty senate. The absurdity of the assignment, the mixed messaging and high anxiety surrounding LPPs, and, perhaps most disturbingly, the uncanny coordination behind the vote for three colleges, revived old sour tastes and seemed to confirm longstanding suspicion of a rigged game. In response, the senate president announced at his last general faculty meeting that transparency would constitute the center of his 2024–25 agenda as past president, starting with the Office of Academic Affairs and, more specifically, the meetings of the Deans' Council, an institution hitherto closed to the faculty. Not only the senate, but also the administration, must be accountable for compliance (or lack thereof) with open meetings and records laws.

Coda: Four Suggestions for Effective Shared Governance

Our experience suggests the following rules to protect and enrich institutions of shared governance.

Rule 1: Know the rules. University officials are bound by the rules of their system, university statutes, and internal bylaws and handbook policies. Chairs and officers who do not read and study the rules end up deferring to administrative authority or make mistakes. Faculty must know the rules and insist on them. Mini-handbooks can be especially useful for informing chairs about basic procedures.

Rule 2: Create records. Shared governance requires that actions accord with the rules, that historical statements align with facts, and that what happens, how, and by whom is documented. Protect shared governance by creating and referring to as complete a historical record as possible. At the senate and committee level, this protection means collecting, cataloging, and publishing agendas and minutes. At a university level, it means insisting that informational documents, meeting agendas and minutes, and other decision-making processes housed in "administrative" halls be made public in accordance with local open meetings and open records laws. Always ask for *something* in writing. Always.

Rule 3: Insist on the truth. Administrators tend to exaggerate good news where it reflects well on their performance, and to emphasize bad news only when it absolves them of personal responsibility. The senate must be an institution of facts, not propaganda. A critical function of senate meetings is to formalize communication with administrators regarding serious matters. The senate, in turn, must also acknowledge and address its own missteps past and present.

Rule 4: Take responsibility. Shared governance becomes most salient in crisis. Don't wait. University statutes typically empower the senate and its committees to craft policies in a plethora of areas. Listen to your faculty. Seize the power of initiative—or risk ceding it.

Notes

1. Peter D. Eckel, "The Role of Shared Governance in Institutional Hard Decisions: Enabler or Antagonist?" *Review of Higher Education* 24, no. 1 (Fall 2000): 15–39; Michael T. Miller and Julie Caplow, eds., *Policy and University Faculty Governance* (Greenwich, CT: Information Age Publishing, 2003); Michael T. Miller et al., "Debate and Discourse: The Role of the Faculty Senate on the Modern American Campus," *Journal of Higher Education Theory and Practice* 16, no. 3 (2016): 22–29.

2. "GSW Fact Book," accessed July 16, 2024, https://www.gsw.edu/institutional-research/fact-book; University System of Georgia, "Georgia Southwestern State University," accessed July 16, 2024, https://www.usg.edu/institutions/profile/georgia_southwestern_state_university.

3. Giulia Heyward, "Georgia's University System Takes on Tenure," *New York Times*, October 13, 2021.

4. American Association of University Professors, "Shared Governance," accessed July 16, 2024, https://www.aaup.org/programs/shared-governance/faqs-shared-governance.

5. Faculty Senate, minutes, February 23, 2018, March 30, 2018, GSW.

6. Neal Weaver, "Presidential Leadership: A Phenomenological Study of the Leadership Experience of Oklahoma's Regional University Presidents" (PhD Diss., University of Oklahoma, 2005), 3, 39–40, 123.

7. Faculty Senate, minutes, February 26, 2021, GSW.

8. Teacher Education Council, minutes, February 7, 2003, Registrar's Office, GSW; GSW General Faculty Meeting, May 1, 2015, https://www.gsw.edu/faculty-

resources/general-faculty-meetings/minutes/m05012015.pdf; Committee on Academic Affairs, minutes, February 11, 2022, GSW; Faculty Senate, minutes, April 29, 2022, GSW; Neal Weaver, email and attachment to Rachel Abbott, et al., June 20, 2022; Cheri Paradise, email to Evan Kutzler, October 22, 2022; Bryan Davis, email to Evan Kutzler, October 26, 2022; James C. Scott, *Weapons of the Weak: Everyday Forms of Peasant Resistance* (New Haven, CT: Yale University Press, 1987).

9. Colleen Flaherty, "University System of Georgia Censured over Tenure Changes," *Inside Higher Ed*, March 6, 2022; General Faculty Meeting, minutes, October 13, 2022, GSW.

10. Faculty Senate, minutes, October 22, 2022, November 17, 2022, February 23, 2023, March 30, 2023, GSW.

11. The most comprehensive record of this committee's proceedings is John LeJeune, "Record of the Proceedings of the GSW Academic Reorganization Examination Committee, Fall 2023-Spring 2024: A Faculty Senate Report," March 26, 2024, GSW.

21

The Being Human in STEM Initiative

Campus Transformation through Crisis

SARAH L. BUNNELL, SHEILA JASWAL, MONA WU ORR, SHU-MIN LIAO, AND ZACHARY WATSON

Much attention is being paid to college campuses across the United States right now. As students protest against national and international harms and campus leaders are interrogated by politicians, many are asking: What is the purpose and value of higher education today? And is it irreparably broken? We see this moment not as an indication that higher education is in disrepair but rather that it is being called to embody its core mission: to step into complex campus dynamics as teaching and learning opportunities and to help students do the same.

How can we approach tense moments on our campuses as collaborations rather than contestations, as curious conversations rather than entrenchments, as avenues for reaching out rather than retreating in? Our students will be launching into a world in which they must navigate society's most "wicked" problem: living with and learning from folks with drastically different values and motivations than their own.[1] If we want our students to engage with their future communities in productive, curious, and collaborative ways, we must teach and model how to do so when they are with us now.

We write as members of a campus whose students, in the not-so-distant past, occupied the library for a four-day sit-in, referred to as the

"Amherst Uprising."[2] When such a protest occurs, institutional leaders get to work, but they are often doing the wrong kind of work. They put great energy toward *managing the protest*—diffusing the disruption and crafting institutional messaging. But the protest is not the crisis. Rather, the protest is a marker of underlying crisis conditions that have been allowed to fester on a campus and now, because they have not been attended to, or have bubbled-over. A protest indicates deferred maintenance of the needs of a community.

A powerful outcome that emerged from the uprising was "Being Human in STEM," or HSTEM, a framework and a course that has now become a nationally recognized approach to humanizing undergraduate education. We have written elsewhere about the student learning outcomes emerging from this course.[3] Here, we turn to transferable tools for responding to campus crises; of note, these tools explicitly seek to address the disconnects that students identified as the underlying crisis conditions in our community. HSTEM is a a model of how staff, faculty, and students listened and partnered to bring about inclusive changes in undergraduate science education in response to student protest. Our campus had underlying crisis conditions to which attention had not been adequately paid: an institution that had dramatically diversified its student body but not its pedagogies, structures, and values. As a window into this moment, we share the voice of one student protester from that time:

> Coming to college, I was again "the other." My blackness was acknowledged, but it was and still is at a price. I am reminded every day I am a working-class woman of color . . . If I walk even ten feet outside at night alone, I get a gut-wrenching feeling that I'm not going to make it to my final destination. I didn't even realize it was fear until someone put a name to it on Thursday. This is supposed to be my home nine months out of the year. I should not fear for my body or my life walking around my "home." The reason I chose to come to Amherst was because I wanted to be a name and not a number, but my name has become a number to make the school look "diverse." (Anonymous, personal communication, letter to STEM departments from a current undergraduate student, November 2015)

Across those four days, student protesters had a clear message, which we summarize as:

1. We do not feel that we belong or matter at Amherst.
2. Faculty, staff, and administrators are not listening.
3. Even when we do share our concerns and experiences, the College does not take us seriously, and may even retaliate in response.
4. Many faculty, staff, and other students don't realize their own role in maintaining harmful systems, policies, and practices at the College.
5. Decision-making at the College is top-down and unilateral. There is no space for us to meaningfully contribute.

In this essay, we first introduce the HSTEM tools that instructors across the country have employed to humanize classroom and laboratory spaces, and then we share practices that can be used, within or separate from an HSTEM course, to help each of us build, develop, and refine these tools in our own teaching contexts. It's our hope that these approaches help you, your students, and your campus build capacity to step into crisis moments with greater empathy, humanity, and agency.

Essential HSTEM Tools for Being Human in Crisis

Emerging from the November 2015 Amherst Uprising, the HSTEM course began as a special topics course the following spring, codesigned by Sheila Jaswal and nine students. The HSTEM essential tools for responding to campus crises, which are also the core pillars of the course, are: (1) Building Community, (2) Listening, (3) Validating, (4) Reflecting, and (5) Partnering.

In recent interviews with nine faculty and staff HSTEM cofacilitators at Amherst (IRB #23-013) the importance of these tools pervaded their reflections. Through the HSTEM process, instructors develop transferable strategies for engaging with campus conflicts and for proactively creating healthier learning communities. In terms of building community, one instructor shared, "If we want to have a truly inclusive environment, we have to think about what we are doing to prepare our students, what we are doing to support our students, and what we are doing to make our students feel like we actually want them to be there." Another instructor spoke about the power of experiencing belonging at the college for themselves, through HSTEM: "Being Human in STEM has made me feel belonging here at Amherst in a way that nothing else I've done here has . . . [it] clarified for me why I love teaching at an undergraduate place like this."

As faculty and staff in HSTEM learn to listen actively, they develop new insights. One instructor shared that they now "realize what a difference there is between the student experience for so many of our students and what we intend." Relatedly, faculty and staff reflected on the importance of learning to validate the experiences of others, especially when these experiences differ from one's own, and to model that process for students. As a result of HSTEM, one instructor is working to build "a culture of being open to the idea that other people's experiences might be different from ours" in all of their courses. This instructor states that they pursue this learning goal by being "more open and exhibit[ing] a little bit more vulnerability about my own experiences."

Multiple cofacilitators shared how they had become more reflective about their teaching practice as a result of HSTEM. One spoke about how they now respond to conflict with a mental script: "Let's just pause a minute, and think about, 'What is the context for this [point of conflict]? Let's be curious, rather than judgmental, about what's happening here.' " As a result, this instructor now feels they are able to "intervene gently" with individuals across campus when disagreements emerge. Finally, facilitators said that as a result of positioning oneself as a partner and co-learner in the HSTEM classroom, they are now able to be a "better mentor for colleagues," appreciating that "everybody will find their own way; it doesn't have to be my way." As more members of our campus community teach and learn in the HSTEM course, the implications of HSTEM's impacts on teaching and learning at Amherst have only continued to spread.

Developing Your HSTEM Toolkit

We've articulated five tools for a human-centered, partnership-focused response to campus crisis. You may be wondering how to develop these skills in yourself, your colleagues, and your students. In the context of a course, the Being Human in STEM book outlines each module and provides a list of example readings, activities, and facilitator guides (all of the facilitation guides for these practices are available for free and downloadable from the Being Human in STEM Routledge website, under

"Supporting Materials").[4] We also routinely build mentoring networks across institutions (so please reach out if you are interested in joining). That being said, we also recognize that developing a full HSTEM course in your institutional context may be disruptive or impractical at this time; as such, in many of our recent workshops, we've focused on the practices that you can embed and adapt in your work with students across contexts. We turn to those now.

Building Community

The first step is to intentionally build what Arao and Clemens referred to as "brave spaces," which they contrast to safe spaces.[5] Here, we briefly describe one practice that our students consistently point to as meaningful for their sense of community: the "Humanizing the Professor" activity.[6] By way of brief summary, you first let students know that you recognize and appreciate them as whole, complex humans and that you want them to see you as the same. Then you describe your own journey in academia and the challenges or barriers you faced along the way. This activity positions the instructor not as an infallible expert but as someone who is human, learning, and growing. Many students will see aspects of themselves reflected in your narrative, which can help to build trust and connection between yourself and those students (Solanki and Xu 2018; Stout et al. 2011); all students will benefit from knowing that who they are matters both inside and outside of the classroom.[7]

Learning to Listen

Hearing and listening are quite distinct acts: Hearing is an automatic and often subconscious process. Active listening demands focused attention. Our students consistently report on the value of learning how to actively listen to one another and the power of being actively listened to. This active listening exercise is deceptively simple and can be adapted and integrated into a single class, workshop, or lab. Students are first arranged in pairs, and each partner takes two minutes to respond to a reflective prompt such as, "What is something that you are proud of this semester, and why?"[8] The listening partner does not provide feedback beyond simply thanking their partner for sharing. Next, in groups of four, each student shares not a verbatim report of what was shared, but rather what they heard their partner communicate that they care about and value. Finally, the whole class debriefs the process and what they learned from the experience. Students repeatedly report drawing on this tool beyond the classroom, in their interactions with teammates, family members, and others.

Validating the Experiences of Others

One of the more challenging yet essential components of humanizing conflicts is to authentically value and appreciate experiences that differ from our own. When this step is skipped or done performatively, more harm is committed, and trust can be broken. Some examples include: administrators who seek stakeholder feedback and then move forward with an initiative in active opposition to this feedback—or student groups bringing forward a list of demands that only center their own experiences. One practice that can help develop our validation skills is a meta-reflection activity.[9] In HSTEM, students consistently write individual reflections to readings, thinking deeply about their own points of connection to the material and questions of interest to them. To help them move from self-focus to a broader validating stance, a subset of students then reviews all the reflections for each module, identifying themes and points of tension that have collectively emerged from the reflections. Importantly, students are instructed to notice, not analyze or make value judgments about, the nature of these themes, and share these observations with the broader class. In this way, students practice adopting the mental framework that we shared above: "Let's be curious, rather than judgmental, about what's happening here."

Meaningful Reflection

One powerful learning outcome for HSTEM students and facilitators alike is how much they learn about themselves and others. To see campus crises as opportunities for growth, we need to open ourselves to learning what each experience, especially heavily contentious ones, can teach us about ourselves and about the people in our community. To practice iterative reflection, we recommend our signature assignment called "Telling your HSTEM Story."[10] At the beginning of the semester, instructors and students create representations of their experiences in STEM to date, including the positive and negative factors that have shaped their experience. Midsemester, we revisit and expand these stories; at this point, students have spent many weeks engaging with the empirical literature on the experiences of others in STEM and dialoguing with the other members in class; they incorporate what they have learned into a more layered, nuanced understanding of their experience. Finally, at the end of the term, students again revisit this assignment, this time focused on their hoped-for future relationship with, and impact on, STEM, including strategies they will use to bring that vision to fruition.

Inclusive Partnership

HSTEM coursework culminates in students' final project proposals, which attempt to address areas of continued need in STEM. The campus community is invited to provide feedback on these proposals, and students must draw on their HSTEM toolkit to partner with staff and administrators to identify avenues for their projects to be integrated into ongoing and future campus initiatives. A consistent challenge is that students are on campus for four short years: They understandably desire changes to happen quickly but often lack institutional historical knowledge and context. We intentionally structure partnership work to attend to this challenge: First, preliminary assignments ask students to actively research what has already been done by past students in HSTEM and by others in the campus community. Recently, this effort has taken the form of interviewing past HSTEM students and experienced facilitators. Second, we work with students to explicitly develop skills of reaching out to others as meaningful partners; this work includes how to think expansively about potential partnerships and how to frame project proposal presentations to campus stakeholders as authentic invitations for collaboration.[11]

HSTEM Tools in Action: Responding to Crisis

The HSTEM tools were put to the test in spring of 2020; when COVID forced everyone into isolation midsemester, we employed listening, validating, and reflecting exercises in small group breakout rooms at the start of each virtual class session. The HSTEM tools served as a mechanism for maintaining the positive and brave community we had established earlier in the term. Building on this strong foundation, students were then able to do meaningful and productive work even during this tumultuous time. For the final class project, many students contributed essays, artwork, or infographics to a creative "Zine," while others produced workshop plans for campus partners to readily integrate HSTEM principles and content into their programming and practices, such as first-year orientation programming, STEM departmental seminars, and approaches to structuring office hours. The quality of the process and products created during this ongoing crisis was a testament to the efficacy of the HSTEM model in creating a community resilient enough to weather a crisis that expanded beyond the classroom walls.

After George Floyd's murder, alumni of the HSTEM Spring 2020 class again sprang into action. Five biology majors from the class wrote to their department, expressing care, providing resources and concrete steps that the department could take, and urging further action. A number of biology faculty have supported HSTEM and been early adopters of HSTEM practices into their courses; as such, the department was primed to respond to these students with listening, validating, reflecting, and a commitment to ongoing partnership. In their publicly available statement, they write: "Our work has been guided from within and by important help from Biology alumni and HSTEM students, including several valued letters to our department that share lists of action items . . . We are committed to working towards these goals and to continuing collaborative work to the betterment of all involved with Biology at Amherst" [see https://www.amherst.edu/academiclife/departments/biology/equity-inclusion].

At the same time, HSTEM alumni from other STEM majors also partnered with faculty to co-design and facilitate gatherings to align with the #ShutDownSTEM movement. This effort was a powerful moment of meaningful, inclusive partnership for our campus, which resulted in dramatic shifts in STEM curricular and institutional structures, especially because these shifts occurred at the same time that institutional leadership was advancing other antiracist campus efforts. Outcomes included the creation of student-faculty-staff DEI departmental committees, the addition of a DEI-focused course requirement to majors, and the public posting of departmental DEI goals and commitments.

Conclusions

It's our firm belief that the HSTEM course, as a response to the Amherst Uprising, has primed our campus to respond to future crises in collaborative and human-centered ways. We have established a history of inviting our campus community into partnership, to work together to address underlying crisis conditions. At the same time, we have established trust in each other's good intentions. We recognize that as humans, we get things wrong, we misstep, and we say the wrong thing, but the HSTEM tools provide pathways for us to navigate those moments with grace while learning how to do better by and for each other. We hope that the ideas we've shared in this essay provide a framework for other campuses to do the same.

If we actively listen to one another, seek to value one another's voices and experiences, and look for avenues of partnership, we can be human through crisis, together. In doing so, we can build healthier and more responsive campus communities.

Notes

1. Johanna Lönngren and Katrien Van Poeck, "Wicked Problems: A Mapping Review of the Literature." *International Journal of Sustainable Development & World Ecology* 28, no. 6 (August 2021): 481–502

2. Sarah Bunnell, Megan Lyster, Kristen Greenland, Gabrielle Mayer, Kristen Gardner, Tanya Leise, Thea Kristensen, Emma D Ryan, Richmond Ampiah-Bonney, and Sheila S Jaswal, "From Protest to Progress through Partnership with Students: Being Human in STEM (HSTEM)." *International Journal for Students as Partners* 5:1 (May 2021), 26–56; Sheila Jaswal, "Being Human in STEM: Moving from Student Protest to Institutional Progress." *Diversity & Democracy* 22, no. 1 (2019): 21–24.

3. Sarah Bunnell, Sheila Jaswal, Megan Lyster. *Being Human in STEM: Partnering with Students to Shape Inclusive Practices and Communities* (Stylus 2023); Bunnell, et al., "From Protest to Progress"; Jaswal, "Being Human in STEM."

4. Bunnell et al., *Being Human in STEM*. The website address is https://www.routledge.com/Being-Human-in-STEM-Partnering-with-Students-to-Shape-Inclusive-Practices-and-Communities/Bunnell-Jaswal-Lyster/p/book/9781642672299

5. Barbara Mae Gayle et al., "Safe Spaces, Difficult Dialogues, and Critical Thinking." *International Journal for the Scholarship of Teaching and Learning* 7, no. 2 (July 2013).

6. Bunnell et al., *Being Human in STEM*, Appendix B.

7. Sabrina M.Solanki and Di Xu, "Looking Beyond Academic Performance: The Influence of Instructor Gender on Student Motivation in STEM Fields," *American Educational Research Journal* 55, no. 4 (August 2018): 801–35; Jane G. Stout et al., "STEMing the Tide: Using Ingroup Experts to Inoculate Women's Self-Concept in Science, Technology, Engineering, and Mathematics (STEM)," *Journal of Personality and Social Psychology* 100, no. 2 (2011): 255–70.

8. Bunnell et al., *Being Human in STEM*, 60.
9. Bunnell et al., *Being Human in STEM*, 61–63.
10. Ibid., Appendix O.
11. See Bunnell, et al., *Being Human in STEM*, 48–49.

References

Bunnell, Sarah, Sheila Jaswal, Megan Lyster. 2023. *Being Human in STEM: Partnering with Students to Shape Inclusive Practices and Communities*. First edition. Sterling, Virginia: Stylus. https://www.routledge.com/Being-Human-in-STEM-Partnering-with-Students-to-Shape-Inclusive-Practices-and-Communities/Bunnell-Jaswal-Lyster/p/book/9781642672299

Bunnell, Sarah, Megan Lyster, Kristen Greenland, Gabrielle Mayer, Kristen Gardner, Tanya Leise, Thea Kristensen, Emma D Ryan, Richmond Ampiah-Bonney, and Sheila S Jaswal. 2021. "From Protest to Progress through Partnership with Students: Being Human in STEM (HSTEM)." *International Journal for Students as Partners* 5, no. 1 (May): 26–56. https://doi.org/10.15173/ijsap.v5i1.4243.

Gayle, Barbara Mae, Derek Cortez, and Raymond Preiss. 2013. "Safe Spaces, Difficult Dialogues, and Critical Thinking." *International Journal for the Scholarship of Teaching and Learning* 7, no. 2 (July). https://doi.org/10.20429/ijsotl.2013.070205.

Jaswal, Sheila. 2019. "Being Human in STEM: Moving from Student Protest to Institutional Progress." *Diversity & Democracy* 22, no. 1: 21–24. https://web.archive.org/web/20200717012735/https://www.aacu.org/diversitydemocracy/2019/winter/jaswal

Lönngren, Johanna, and Katrien Van Poeck. 2021. "Wicked Problems: A Mapping Review of the Literature." *International Journal of Sustainable Development & World Ecology* 28, no. 6 (August): 481–502. https://doi.org/10.1080/13504509.2020.1859415.

Solanki, Sabrina M., and Di Xu. 2018. "Looking Beyond Academic Performance: The Influence of Instructor Gender on Student Motivation in STEM Fields." *American Educational Research Journal* 55, no. 4 (August): 801–35. https://doi.org/10.3102/0002831218759034.

Stout, Jane G., Nilanjana Dasgupta, Matthew Hunsinger, and Melissa A. McManus. 2011. "STEMing the Tide: Using Ingroup Experts to Inoculate Women's Self-Concept in Science, Technology, Engineering, and Mathematics (STEM)." *Journal of Personality and Social Psychology* 100, no. 2: 255–70. https://doi.org/10.1037/a0021385.

22

Recruiting and Retaining a Diverse Faculty

Mari Elise Ewing and Andrea Overbay

Faculty, staff, and administrators often retreat to their silos and react defensively in times of crisis. This response robs the community of the opportunity to join disparate ideas and perspectives to creatively solve the problem at hand. Austin College is not immune to the many challenges facing higher education, and recently, we (like many other institutions) have struggled with the recruitment and retention of diverse, nationally trained faculty members. As our student body increasingly changes, we recognize that an engaged and diverse faculty body is critical to student success.[1] It's also key to fostering a thriving community for our college and the surrounding area.

Austin College is a liberal arts college located an hour north of Dallas in Sherman, Texas. As with many higher education institutions,[2] several faculty members have left our institution post-COVID. Excluding retirements, approximately 12 percent of the tenured or tenure-track faculty have left since 2020. Each faculty member who left had a different reason for doing so. Some departed because they could not see a future in academia, while others left because they did not want to live in a semirural region in a conservative state currently attacking diversity, equity, and inclusion (DEI) initiatives, reproductive rights, and the rights of migrants. While we cannot know how many potential faculty members are simply choosing not to apply to our open positions, we have had several failed faculty searches since 2020. As suggested above, this situation is not unique to any one higher education institution. If these circumstances were not enough of an uphill battle, the cost of housing in the area has increased dramatically in the last few years. We can no longer entice prospective and current faculty members with a lower cost of living, especially in the fast-growing communities between Sherman and the greater Dallas-Fort Worth metroplex.[3]

Because we recognize it's the people on the ground who make decisions in challenging times, we feel it is important to explain who we are. We have both been faculty members at Austin College for over a decade. While we share a similar personal background of growing up as white women from lower-middle-class families in rural areas, our professional experiences differ. Mari Elise is an environmental studies professor with expertise in resilient systems. She has served as chair of the executive committee of the faculty, member of the crisis management task force, and member of the faculty compensation committee. Andrea is a mathematician and the director of the Johnson Center for Faculty Development and Excellence in Teaching. She has served as chair of the teaching evaluation task force and on two iterations of the campus committee for DEI, codeveloped well-being programs for employees and students, and co-organized an antiracist white allyship faculty learning community for staff and faculty. This range of experiences positions us to see the different threads of a solution to our challenge and weave them together into a cohesive whole.[4]

In reviewing our values of commitment to our mission, collaboration, communication, connection, and transparency, we realized upholding these values (not *even* in times of crisis[5] but *especially* in times of crisis[6]) opened pathways for us to address the problem of recruiting and retaining faculty. Below are some of those pathways: (1) strengthening our shared governance model, (2) creating a responsive faculty development program, and (3) supporting campus and community connection and wellbeing.

Strengthening Shared Governance

While shared governance has always played a crucial role at Austin College, it has morphed over the years to meet the changing needs of the institution. Central to this model is the role that the executive committee of the faculty (FEC) plays in communicating between the faculty and administration, setting priorities through the faculty meeting agendas, and executing those meetings. The FEC meets regularly with the vice president of academic affairs (VPAA) and president of the college. Upholding existing, effective policies and procedures while working to improve ineffective ones via this mutual commitment to communication and a strong shared governance model is a time-tested way to address problems in higher education,[7] including the recruitment and retention of faculty. We provide three examples below:

With the support of the administration, the faculty convened a diverse group to create a faculty compensation structure in 2016. The structure articulated shared values on compensation and increased equity and transparency for current and prospective faculty. The faculty compensation committee initially worked to eliminate two major problems of inversion and compression. More recently, the committee's work has focused on adhering to the structure despite the dual pressures of budget constraints and further salary differentials. While imperfect, the structure gives faculty increased confidence in the compensation process and has improved pay equity.

In response to COVID's impact on our institution, the VPAA and faculty convened a Crisis Management Task Force to review early COVID responses, fortify effective procedures, and identify better responses for future crises. One of the task force's first steps was to request a change to the original charge, adding a focus on preparedness and not solely response. In the crisis management literature, response (postcrisis) measures are often inadequate if not preceded by preparedness (precrisis) measures. In other words, crisis management is proactive work.[8] Two faculty members on the task force familiar with the crisis management literature recognized and repaired this initial oversight.

Finally, during one of their monthly meetings with the president in 2022, the FEC suggested two ideas to ease the housing burden for new faculty—adding to the supply of college-owned faculty housing and securing favorable interest rates with local lenders. The college had torn down several college-owned houses during the previous decade with no plan to replace them. Importantly, four of the five members of the FEC at the time had benefited from college housing in their early years at the college. We therefore knew well the benefits afforded by college-owned houses, namely building community relationships and saving money for down payments. The board of trustees approved the suggestion, and new employee housing became available in the fall of 2024.[9] Slightly more favorable interest rates are also now available. As highlighted in the summary below, the generation of these ideas was the result of creating spaces for connection, communication, and collaboration.

Creating a Responsive Faculty Development Program

In addition to a strong faculty governance model, an agile and responsive faculty development center is central to recruiting and retaining faculty members. The Johnson Center for Faculty Development and Excellence in Teaching has been part of the Austin College community for well over a decade and is a faculty-driven initiative. The center is led by a director, chosen from the faculty, who works with a steering committee of five elected faculty representatives. The Johnson Center provides a wide range of programming including new faculty orientation, weekly lunch discussions, faculty reading groups, sponsored lecture series, peer class visits, and a staff class visit program.[10] The steering committee aims to create programming that is responsive to the needs of the faculty, and with the support of the broader faculty community and VPAA, we foster an active, vibrant faculty development center that is both a selling point and resource for current and prospective faculty and is a second pathway to addressing the problem of recruiting and retaining faculty. We provide two examples below:

When the Johnson Center assumed responsibility for new faculty orientation in 2016, the steering committee designed a program with four learning goals. New faculty members will (1) experience the culture of liberal arts teaching and learning at Austin College, (2) meet their new faculty peers and other staff and faculty, (3) receive the most important tips and information to get them to midsemester, and (4) learn about important policies and information related to their employment. After orientation, new faculty programming continues with a monthly new faculty lunch series. We use this time to build connections between new faculty members and the broader community, to educate new faculty members about resources and opportunities on campus, and to invite new faculty into conversation and problem-solving. By providing time and space for communication and connection, we learn more about the challenges facing new faculty members, which allows us to create responsive programming and support.

To further foster collaboration and communication, the Johnson Center sponsors reading groups that meet once a semester and more intensive faculty learning communities that meet several times throughout the academic year. As with all Johnson Center programming, these faculty initiatives are responsive to our community's needs. Most recently, we had faculty learning communities about difficult dialogues in 2016, the scholarship of teaching and learning in 2018, and antiracist white allyship in 2021. These learning communities encourage interdisciplinary conversations among faculty members and educate the faculty broadly on topics pertinent to our community. Often, it is in these learning communities that a new understanding of college problems and creative solutions arise. We also recognize that these communities benefit from more voices and that it is important to remain open to changing logistics should the need arise. For example, when we realized that more than fifty faculty members and many more staff members wanted to participate in the antiracist white allyship community, the single learning community grew into a campus-wide program consisting of several smaller communities with twelve members each, cosponsored by the Johnson Center and Staff Council.

Supporting Connection and Wellness on Campus and Beyond

Social connection can have positive impacts on health,[11] foster a sense of well-being, and prevent burnout.[12] Just as we are committed to educating "the whole student" as part of the Austin College mission, we recognize that educating and supporting staff and faculty members as "whole people" is central to recruiting and retaining faculty. Creating and strengthening programs that support the well-being of community members is central to our mission and is a third pathway to addressing the problem of recruiting and retaining faculty. We provide three examples below.

Thanks to the connection and communication already in place on campus, the Johnson Center, Staff Council, and Human Resources collaborated to create a well-being program. The Johnson Center provides sessions about well-being, finding joy in academia, and avoiding burnout as part of the weekly lunch series; Staff Council sponsors a wellness day for all staff and faculty twice a year; and Human Resources provides equipment and support for free staff and faculty yoga classes twice as week as well as additional resources and support through our *Live Well* program.

Supporting faculty grant writing and increasing communication and connection among campus offices has also been vital to addressing the crisis of faculty recruitment and retention. Without an enthusiastic, helpful grants-writing office on campus, we would not have had the resources for furthering social justice conversations. These conversations brought together the people who generated the housing and lending ideas. Another way we strengthened these connections is through the executive committee of the faculty (FEC) meeting with various vice presidents on campus. Broadening FEC conversations to include not only the VP of academic affairs but also the VPs of business affairs, student affairs, institutional advancement, institutional enrollment, and others has deepened our understanding of the work of others on campus and the ways in which we might work together to face myriad campus issues.

To this point, we have focused on college-specific challenges. Taking an outward focus helps us to see broader community challenges and opportunities. Austin College is part of the Texoma community, an interstate region comprising eight counties in Oklahoma and Texas along the Red River and Lake Texoma. The region is historically impoverished and relatively rural, with most of the population concentrated in Grayson County. Grayson County is the home of Austin College and is experiencing increasing poverty rates[13] and food insecurity among schoolchildren.[14] The region is also rapidly changing. Construction of multibillion-dollar semiconductor manufacturing facilities (Dallas-based Texas Instruments and Taiwanese-based GlobalWafers) is underway in Sherman, promising jobs and increased tax revenue.[15] However, the strain on housing and supporting services, including freshwater and other natural resources, seems underappreciated. While the college is a regional partner in guiding this economic development, some faculty worry the community has not fully considered the long-term social and environmental impacts. Having served on many faculty searches, we are mindful of making the Texoma community a more desirable place to live and work. In our experience, relying on our proximity to a major metroplex does not foster local community building. More fully integrating the college into regional conversations might lead to more thoughtful development and better outcomes for the college and Texoma community.

Austin College has long worked to provide integral services to the Texoma community. For example, Austin College's Social Entrepreneurship for Poverty Alleviation (SEPA) is a decade-old program that pairs Austin College students with local nonprofit agencies to work on grant-writing projects each summer.[16] Additionally, as the recipient of a generous Mellon grant, "Pathways to a Just Society," the college launched social justice and public humanities internships with benefits to the local community.

More recently, the college started a new physician's assistant program to address the scarcity of health services.[17] While the college tries to make community connections, some of the opportunities are underutilized. We worry that one reason some promising programs fail to maximize their impact is because of insufficient communication regarding their availability and desirability. Recruiting and retaining faculty might not always require new initiatives but instead better ways of connecting faculty to existing underutilized initiatives. In other words, taking an inventory of existing opportunities and then finding ways to connect faculty to those opportunities is beneficial for faculty, students, and the community.

Summary of the Toolkit

These pathways to address the challenge of recruiting and retaining faculty create a community where more faculty and staff have a role in generating solutions. Moreover, these pathways are not separate but frequently merge. It's in these intersections that we generate the best ideas. For example, the new employee housing and lending rates came about in a small group discussion with three faculty members belonging to historically underrepresented groups and one white, male, full professor. Three of us—director of faculty development, chair of the executive committee of the faculty, and social justice learning community cofacilitator—had a conversation with the senior faculty member who suggested the initial idea. Here's what we learned: Conversations that bring together individuals with different experiences and roles on campus can generate good ideas. These conversations only happen when we practice our values—commitment to our mission, collaboration, communication, connection, and transparency—and turn abstract ideas into actionable solutions.

Transferable Lessons

While we recognize that each institution is unique with different challenges and resources, components of our experiences can transfer across those differences. Here's what we recommend: (1) Survey multiple audiences to learn what historically worked and/or is currently working for your institution; (2) identify the existing lines of communication at your institution and use those to your advantage; (3) leverage the existing structures (faculty governance, centers for teaching and learning, new faculty orientation, committees on campus) to open further lines of communication so more voices and perspectives can be heard; (4) increase the transparency and ownership around decision-making to create space for more openness, trust, and even vulnerability; (5) recognize the strengths and needs of your surrounding community; (6) connect with local leaders to collaborate on deliberate planning for the future. No single campus alone can provide all the resources to give faculty members a sense of belonging, but strengthening connections to the surrounding community is a step toward making the college more attractive to faculty.

What's Next?

During the 2024–2025 academic year, Austin College hired more than a dozen new tenure-track faculty members. This cohort will be the first to benefit from the new housing and other initiatives on campus. Time will tell whether these initiatives will succeed in retaining these new campus members. However, now is not the time to sit back and wait to see what happens. Using the existing lines of communication, the college can create spaces for honest discussion of how those new members are doing. Do they feel a sense of belonging? Do they have the resources they need to be successful? Do they feel a connection to the campus and Texoma community? And if not, we can remind new faculty how to connect to the pathways described above: shared governance, faculty development, and community connections. For example, the new faculty lunches provide an excellent opportunity to engage new faculty members in these pathways. By extending these same conversations across career stages, we can help rejuvenate and retain all faculty.

Notes

1. Gary Rhoades, *Faculty Engagement to Enhance Student Attainment* (Washington, D.C.: American Council on Education, 2012), https://www.acenet.edu/Documents/Faculty-Engagement-to-Enhance-Student-Attainment—Rhoades.pdf.

2. College and University Professional Association for Human Resources (CUPA-HR), "Higher Ed Workforce Turnover: Multi-Year Data," accessed February

19, 2025, https://www.cupahr.org/surveys/workforce-data/higher-ed-workforce-turnover/.

3. Shannon Pettypiece, "The affordable housing shortage is reshaping parts of rural America." NBC News, November 29, 2024, https://www.nbcnews.com/politics/economics/affordable-housing-shortage-reshaping-parts-rural-america-rcna181700.

4. We feel uniquely qualified to share our experiences and knowledge in this chapter because of the various ways in which we have served our institution. However, we recognize we offer only two perspectives among the many individuals who contributed to this work. We distributed a draft of this chapter to the vice president of academic affairs and divisional deans to make sure we could share it with others.

5. American Association of University Professors (AAUP), *Principles of Academic Governance during the COVID-19 Pandemic* (Washington, D.C.: AAUP, 2020), https://www.aaup.org/news/principles-academic-governance-during-covid-19-pandemic.

6. American Association of University Professors (AAUP), *Report of AAUP Special Committee: Hurricane Katrina and New Orleans Universities* (Washington, D.C.: AAUP, 2007), https://www.aaup.org/report/report-aaup-special-committee-hurricane-katrina-and-new-orleans-universities.

7. American Association of University Professors (AAUP), *Statement on Government of Colleges and Universities* (Washington, D.C.: AAUP), https://www.aaup.org/report/statement-government-colleges-and-universities.

8. Chris Wuthrich, "Review of Campus Crisis Management: A Comprehensive Guide to Planning, Prevention, Response, and Recovery," *The Review of Higher Education* 31, no. 2 (2008): 255–56. https://dx.doi.org/10.1353/rhe.2007.0069.

9. "Austin College Announces New Employee Housing Development," *North Texas e-News,* October 15, 2023, https://www.ntxe-news.com/cgi-bin/artman/exec/view.cgi?archive=95&num=135204.

10. "Johnson Center," Austin College, accessed February 19, 2025, https://www.austincollege.edu/johnson-center.

11. Julianne Holt-Lunstad, "Social Connection as a Critical Factor for Mental and Physical Health: Evidence, Trends, Challenges, and Future Implications," *World Psychiatry: Official Journal of the World Psychiatric Association (WPA)* 23, no. 3 (2024): 312–32, https://doi.org/10.1002/wps.21224.

12. United States Department of Health and Human Services (HHS), *The U.S. Surgeon General's Framework for Workplace Mental Health and Well-being* (Washington, D.C.: HHS, Office of the U.S. Surgeon General, 2022), https://www.hhs.gov/surgeongeneral/reports-and-publications/workplace-well-being/index.html.

13. Harold Todd, "As Texas' Rate Tends Downward, Poverty Rate up in Grayson County," Texoma Council of Governments, October 31, 2018, https://

tcog.com/news/news-articles/2018/10/as-texas-rate-trends-downward-poverty-rate-up-in-grayson-county/.

14. Brynne Herzfeld, “Sherman Denison ISDs Providing Free Meals for all Students,” *KTEN News,* updated May 9, 2024, https://www.kten.com/sherman-denison-isds-providing-free-meals-for-all-students/article_6615b435-9569-527d-b787-6e60907f125d.html.

15. Michael Mooney, “North Texas’ ‘Silicon Prairie’ Gets Billions in New Investment,” *Axios,* August 7, 2023, https://www.axios.com/local/dallas/2023/08/07/texas-semiconductors-chips-sherman.

16. “SEPA Program Highlights,” Austin College, accessed February 19, 2025, https://www.austincollege.edu/details/~board/program-highlights-short/post/sepa.

17. Leigh Ellen Romm, “New Master’s Degree Helps Meet Growing Healthcare Need,” *AC Magazine*, February 16, 2024, https://acmagazine.austincollege.edu/2024-issue/new-masters-degree-helps-meet-growing-healthcare-need/.

23

Mentoring Squares

Establishing a Peer Mentoring Program to Support Non–Tenure Track Faculty

RYAN RIDEAU AND DANA GROSSMAN LEEMAN

For about the past decade, the challenges and inequities associated with Non–Tenure Track Faculty (NTT) positions have been well documented. NTT faculty are required to fulfill many of the same functions as their tenured peers; however, because of their rank they are often deprived of respect, recognition, professional development funds, or political agency within their units and absented from critical decision-making processes that greatly impact their professional roles and responsibilities. There is, in effect, a system of structural inequity whereby NTT faculty feel marginalized and subordinate to tenured faculty: undervalued, overcommitted, underpaid, and without options for professional advancement.[1] Chronic feelings of invisibility and lack of belonging, feeling unaffirmed by department chairs, program directors, or colleagues, and the scarcity or nonexistence of support systems and clear pathways to career advancement have led to many contingent faculty exiting the academy, and others contemplating departure despite their devotion to teaching, their disciplines, and their learners. NTT faculty often comprise the majority of student-facing faculty because they teach and advise students. As a result, faculty turnover deleteriously impacts the creation of an environment that hurts student learning and deprives students of developing long-term and meaningful relationships with faculty members, something vital for their academic success. This represents a crisis moment across higher education that directly impacts the ability of institutions of higher education to fulfill their most basic educational mission.

We have noticed many of these trends at our institution, which is an R1, private, and highly hierarchical institution in the northeastern United States. Over the past several years, through institutional climate surveys, programmatic feedback forms, and individual conversations, NTT faculty at our institution have disclosed that they feel unable to identify and work with a consistent mentor and feel devalued within their departments. Most mentoring efforts are targeted at full-time, tenure-track faculty, which is a source of emotional and existential pain; NTT faculty can request mentors but there is little formalized support for their work. Typically, senior faculty are overcommitted and unable to perform mentoring functions or are never incentivized to do so. Thus, many junior NTT faculty go several years at the institution without the oversight, support, or guidance of more seasoned faculty except in summative ways relating to merit increases or promotion.

Overview

In an attempt to address this problem, we created the Mentoring Squares Program in the fall of 2023. In this chapter, we provide you with a step-by-step guide that outlines our process for designing this program from concept to execution. We also offer lessons culled from our reflections. We conclude with practical tips and words of encouragement for those who wish to try this program at their home institution.

Context for Creating This Program

In the fall of 2023, we created the Mentoring Squares Program as a peer-mentoring program for NTT faculty members in response to the dearth of consistent, reliable support systems and mentoring networks for NTT faculty. Mentoring Squares was adapted from the peer-observation-of-teaching model, Teaching Squares, developed by Anne Wesley of St.

Louis College in the 1990s.[2] In Wesley's model, a teaching square consists of four faculty who observe one another's classroom teaching. After these visits, they debrief the session from a stance of curiosity and respect about their colleague's classroom culture and pedagogic methods. Feedback is formative and supportive.

Similarly, Mentoring Squares consist of groups of (ideally) four NTT faculty members who come together with shared concerns, needs, goals, experiences, and practical wisdom. They meet regularly, about twice a month, to provide compassionate thought partnership, and at times guidance, to one another. In helping one another, they are also helping themselves. The program thus becomes a mutual aid system.[3] Participating faculty come from a multitude of disciplines and from across the professional lifespan. Some are newly hired faculty in their first job following graduate school, while others are veteran faculty members. Each "square" works together to support its members and their aligned objectives.

Program Logistics

What follows is the process we created to build the Mentoring Squares program. We hope this outline will be a helpful resource for institutional leaders interested in replicating it.

Step 1: Stakeholder Engagement

Given all we knew about the experiences of NTT faculty members, we decided we needed to increase our efforts to support them. Initially, we reached out to members of our Faculty Senate to get feedback on our proposed program to support NTT faculty. We presented our ideas for a highly structured faculty development program, consisting of a series of skill-development areas. One faculty member suggested we meet with NTT union representatives to gain their feedback and support. This suggestion was particularly important given that the union was in the process of negotiating a new contract with the university. We heeded this advice and decided to convene a group of NTT faculty members to discuss potential programming from our offices.

To set the stage for this meeting, we reached out to the faculty member who suggested that we meet with union representatives to engage her assistance in contacting individual union leaders. She issued a call to union stewards to gauge their interest in working with us. Several agreed to serve as an advisory group for the program. We also invited groups of NTT faculty to meet to ascertain their needs. We hosted the first meeting before faculty concluded their work at the end of the academic year because many NTT faculty are not paid over the summer, and we did not wish to ask them to work without compensation. In this first conversation, there was ample representation across disciplines and career lifespan and we focused on their concerns as NTT faculty members. As the conversation ensued, we became acutely aware that NTT felt neglected by their departments and by the university at large and were frustrated by the lack of mentoring and support structures.

We hosted a second, smaller meeting with six faculty members from the advisory group to specifically conceptualize the program. The advisory group members were very clear that they did not want another typical faculty development program because they could participate in programs hosted by our respective offices to fulfill these needs. They wanted a space in which to build community and share ideas. One of the members suggested the Mentoring Squares model, which was then agreed upon by the group.

Step 2: Recruitment Strategies

Recruitment followed construction of the program format. We asked our advisory group to assist by sending program information to union members. Then we announced the program on our university announcement forum and in the Center for Teaching newsletter. These strategies helped to bring together a modest-sized cohort of twenty-one participants for our inaugural semester.

Step 3: Forming Groups

After we had participants sign up, we needed to match them. Matching groups proved to be one of the most difficult tasks due to the demanding schedules of many participants. When we solicited applicants for the program, we asked participants to specify their availability, identify their goals for participating in the program, and indicate whether there were individuals with whom they would like to be matched. We tried to honor individual preferences for matches and create squares with individuals who had similar goals. Ultimately, however, availability and scheduling constraints proved to be the crucial factors in assigning individuals to squares—there were some squares where individuals had different goals but had to be matched because of scheduling imperatives. Although it was not ideal, we had few options. These groups concerned us, and we were more vigilant toward them due to the greater potential for them to be unsuccessful. When creating groups, we tried to assign individuals from different departments because we were mindful that individuals from the same department would not have the opportunity to expand their networks of support into other areas of the university.

Step 4: Creating and Sharing a Program Guidebook

Although we wanted to ensure flexibility regarding how the faculty participants used their time together, we wanted to provide guidance for the squares: so we created a guidebook. We started by defining mentoring, emphasizing its collaborative nature as a shared learning experience that enables mutual growth. The guidebook included information about the program, anticipated logistical matters such as frequency of meetings, a process for reimbursement of their expenses, and program expectations. Finally, it included a section about meetings with suggestions for their time together that could benefit all participants and build upon their collective wisdom.

Step 5: Group Meetings

Once groups were formed, we sent participants the guidebook and reached out to encourage them to begin meeting. Creating a sense of community was essential to the success of this program and one of the greatest draws for faculty engagement. While we wanted to ensure as much flexibility as possible for participants, we believed that the ability to establish a community of support by meeting in person was critical. To this end, we created a small pot of funds to encourage squares to meet in person, funded through the Office of the Provost. We allocated $100 for each square to use for their in-person meetings for the semester. This money could be used on a single meal, coffee, or over multiple meetings. We understood that schedules, timing, and faculty who lived in cities across the country might prevent some squares from meeting in person, but we thought providing some funds would encourage those who could do so.

Step 6: Following Up with Groups

Once groups began to meet, we emailed them every two to three weeks to check on their progress. This check-in was done to ensure they were meeting, capture feedback about their experiences, and offer support for individuals in need. Most groups communicated with us and updated us about their progress. Only on rare occasions did individuals or groups reach out for additional support. For the most part, it was wonderful to receive emails indicating that faculty were meeting regularly and enjoying their time with one another. For example, one participant emailed the following, "Thanks so much for checking in! We had our second meeting today and had a great discussion about how to respond to student feedback and manage end-of-the-semester class emergencies." Most of these emails were short but confirmed that groups were meeting or indicated a need for support from us.

Program Facilitators' Roles

For both of us, this program was much more hands-off than other faculty development offerings we normally facilitate. Our role was to create the logistic and administrative support, communicate our interest in how the groups were doing throughout the semester and offer guidance to the squares, or to any individual faculty members who were experiencing challenges with their squares.

In addition to email communication, we scheduled two in-person luncheons: the first to launch the program and the second to come together at the end of the academic year. The purpose of these larger gatherings was to reinforce that they were part of a broader community that existed beyond their squares, provide social time, share themes that were emerging from their conversations, and gauge how impactful the squares were for these small groups. When faculty were unable to attend in person, we hosted each meeting as a hybrid experience for ease of accessibility.

The final task involved the processing of funds reimbursements to participants for meeting in person. Participants shared receipts with us, and we coordinated with finance administrators to process their reimbursements. Overall, our principal role was to serve as conveners and handle administrative aspects of the program. We were not involved in the planning or participation in their meetings.

Lessons Learned

In this section, we provide an overview of some of the lessons we learned after running the program for its first year.

Stakeholder Engagement is Critical

Stakeholder engagement was crucial to ensuring the success of the program, as it helped us gain credibility and trustworthiness with NTT faculty. Given that NTT faculty feel they lack agency and visibility, centering their needs about the scope of this program and what it ultimately would and would not be was critical. Further, in conversations with the faculty senate and then relatedly in advisory meetings, it became clear that our initial idea of providing faculty development offerings was not what they wanted. Had we not heeded their advice, we would have created a program that did not meet NTT faculty needs, and it would most likely have failed.

Involve Faculty in Recruitment

We believed that it was essential to engage faculty to recruit their peers for the program, and it was so helpful that we will reprise this practice by soliciting participation from past participants and asking them to help recruit new ones. Secondly, we will put out an open call for participants. We learned from our inaugural experience that faculty are the best advocates for one another, so hearing about opportunities from their colleagues can have a far greater impact. When we transition to the spring semester, we will not open the program widely but ask current members to invite new members to the group to respect the communities that were built. We did so in the spring semester for our pilot, and it seemed to work well in ensuring the continuity of groups. Clearly, in both stages of recruitment, faculty will play a vital role in bringing new members to the program, which is essential to building authentic communities of shared learning.

Provide Funds to Support In-person Activities

In our interactions with the faculty participants, we routinely heard about the importance of the funds we provided to in-person gatherings. Many groups did not use all or any of their funds. Yet they consistently remarked on how this small gesture made it appear that the administration cared for them. For those who did use the funds, they mentioned that meeting off-campus allowed them to feel comfortable getting to know one another. One challenge was that we did have some groups with participants from different campus locations and one faculty member who lived out of state. Because of such challenges, these groups could not meet in person and were unable to utilize this benefit. Next year, we will explore the possibility of providing these participants with a gift card for a food delivery service so that all of the participants consistently feel cared for through this small perk.

We recognize that some colleges and universities may not have the funds to provide $100 per square. This fund can certainly be a smaller amount if needed as it still sends a signal of care for NTT faculty. The program can still run even without this type of appropriation, so lack of funding need not be a deterrent to starting a mentoring squares program. If, however, funds are available, we encourage you to take advantage of them, as our experience underscores how important they can be.

Address Faculty Concerns and Disappointments

As befits its nature as a pilot, the program had its flaws. One challenge arose when some faculty had different goals from other members of their square. This occurred in one instance but serves as a useful example. Initially, the faculty member approached us about how to get what she needed from the group, saying she felt her group was unresponsive to her. We both sat down with her and brainstormed strategies. She seemed to appreciate our suggestions and tried to implement some of the ideas we shared. However, these new ideas did not yield the outcome she hoped. We offered to move her to another group, but ultimately, her schedule for the next semester was incompatible and she elected to withdraw from the program. There will always be individuals who benefit more from this program than others or have expectations that cannot be met. We learned the importance of ongoing check-ins with participants that enabled us to address any challenges or conflicts that arose, even if the efforts were ultimately unsuccessful.

Prioritize Individuals' Goals and Interests in Matching

As previously mentioned, matching was one of the most difficult aspects of the process. In the first semester, we matched groups based on goals, interests, and scheduling constraints. Yet scheduling became the overriding factor. This led to groups with mismatched goals, and in a single case, an overrepresentation of group members from one department. These groups did encounter challenges. During the second semester, after a few new members joined, we added them to groups that aligned with their interests and let the groups work out their own schedules. This solution was easier with a small number of new members. No groups were able to meet because of scheduling. We suspect that when filling out the form, some participants only listed the times they preferred to meet and not their full availability. In the future, we will try to align group members by shared goals and interests. We will continue to ask about availability; however, we will prompt them to list times when they have obligations that are inflexible such as teaching, office hours, or family obligations. We anticipate that this approach will give us more flexibility and clarity as we match participants according to the alignment of their goals and interests.

Practical Strategies and Words of Encouragement

When we established this program, we believed it could serve as a model for how to effectively bring faculty members together. In a moment when faculty may feel a greater sense of isolation, where many campus relationships are fractured because of rank, diminishing resources, and global and political instability, many people are seeking greater connection. This program was an easy way to facilitate those connections among faculty that had tangible effects on their work. Additionally, Mentoring Squares are relatively simple to replicate and not burdensome for administrators. Moreover, facilitating this program is gratifying, and, we believe, a vehicle for organizational and cultural change. Mentoring Squares does require coordination and intentional communication with the participants. If a square is experiencing interpersonal conflict, or members are struggling to effectively use their time together, we offer to meet with them. However, once the program is established, it is relatively self-sustaining. Thus, it serves as a relatively easy way to address an important and deeply challenging systemic problem—especially acute in our current moment—that affects many of our colleagues and their sense of well-being as professionals and human beings.

Notes

1. Adrianna Kezar and Cecile Sam, "Institutionalizing Equitable Policies and Practices for Contingent Faculty." *The Journal of Higher Education* 84, no. 1 (2013): 56–87.

2. Neil Haave, reprinted from "Teaching Squares: A Teaching Development Tool," *The Teaching Professor* 28, no. 10 (2014): 1.

3. Dominique Moyse Steinberg, *A Mutual-Aid Model for Social Work with Groups* (London: Routledge, 2014), 21.

24

Where Are the Faculty?

Reflections on Higher Education's Labor Movement and the Role of Faculty in Wall-to-Wall Organizing

DYLAN M. HARRIS AND JON SHEFNER

The Struggle for Higher Ed

In response to COVID-19, faculty scrambled to make their courses accessible and impactful. Staff, many of whom were considered essential workers, were simultaneously responsible for maintaining the core operations of the university while being thinned due to budget cuts. Students were forced off campuses and expected to keep up their coursework, all while paying record-high rates of tuition. At the same time, the number of high-paying administrative positions continued to explode, and structures for shared governance were hollowed out, leaving, in many cases, a shell mechanism for greenlighting administrative decisions.[1]

These inequalities have extensive roots that have only deepened since 2020. Our work has been dragged into an ongoing culture war, and the future of academia is being actively contested in highly publicized (and politicized) legislative efforts. However, our work is also being contested in lesser-known spaces: departmental meetings, one-on-ones with our students, and, critically, conversations with one another. It is within this context of uncertainty and frustration that a growing labor movement for higher ed has emerged.[2] In the past four years, we have seen dozens of strikes, walkouts, sit-ins (and, critically, wins), all of which have been the result of diverse and strategic coalition building between university workers. However, faculty members are largely absent from many of these coalitions. In this chapter, we ask—*why? Where are the faculty members?*

Outside of administration, tenured and tenure-track faculty are among the highest-paid, most secure, longest-serving members of the university workforce. Further, faculty often serve on committees with direct access to university decision-makers and, in many cases, are among those making decisions. Yet, from our shared experience, we find faculty are often missing from picket lines and union meetings. If they are present, they are often in supporting roles rather than organizing on behalf of their own struggles. Here, we build from our experiences as faculty organizers in United Campus Workers (UCW), a growing wall-to-wall union present in several premajority (e.g., without collective bargaining) states across the US Southeast and Mountain West, to discuss why faculty may be missing and to make the case for their involvement. In short, we need faculty in the labor movement more than ever.

Situating Faculty in Wall-To-Wall Unions

Aside from being critical sites for labor studies, universities have been key sites for workers' struggles, resulting in powerful coalitions with well-established labor organizations such as United Auto Workers (UAW), the Service Employees International Union (SEIU), and the Emergency Workers Organizing Committee (EWOC) to name a few. However, within these coalitions, university workers are often divided by types of employment: graduate students, post docs, adjuncts, staff. This organizational philosophy has been in place for decades, resulting in some important wins, but ultimately, in our view, pitting workers against one another. This antagonism is not generative of a larger labor movement, which is why we are both committed to UCW's wall-to-wall organizing model. The idea is to build workplace solidarity across job classifications, putting into perspective that many of the issues we face—dwindling public funds, for example—impact us all, albeit in different ways. Rather than struggling for resources among ourselves, we want to struggle together, pointing fingers up instead of across.

Nearly all of UCW's locals are in states without legislation protecting collective bargaining rights. Critically, we believe that the lack of collective bargaining, while generative of a more grassroots labor movement within our universities, also contributes to what we see as structural barriers within our organizing work. While faculty have been less present at strikes over the past four years, there are prominent examples where faculty stood shoulder-to-shoulder with other university workers on the picket line, such as the successful strike at Rutgers University in 2023, which brought together three distinct unions (Bowman 2023). However, in our experience in universities in states without collective bargaining, where, to be clear, there are still active campaigns to address ongoing inequalities in our work, faculty are much less involved. While we are committed to the wall-to-wall model, we also understand its challenges, which are exacerbated within premajority states.

Faculty Work—Our Place in the Struggle for Higher Ed

According to the AAUP's 1966 *Statement on Government of Colleges and Universities,* "The faculty has primary responsibility for such fundamental areas as curriculum, subject matter and methods of instruction, research, faculty status, and those aspects of student life which relate to the educational process" (AAUP 2025). Whereas faculty being responsible for research and education may be intuitive, it is the latter part of this statement—that faculty are responsible for the conditions of student learning—that highlights the broader role of faculty within the university, showing that matters beyond research and teaching, such as budgets and infrastructure planning, should also be within the purview of faculty.

And yet, so much of the anti-higher-ed discourse cropping up in the US, with a concentration in southeastern states where UCW is active, is targeting the primary role of faculty. Legislation targeting tenure, in states such as Georgia, Florida, and South Carolina, explicitly removes faculty governance from the process, shifting it instead into the hands of board members or elected politicians.[3] As a result, the so-called academic freedom granted to faculty to conduct research freely is severely curtailed and policed. Similarly, legislation meant to undermine teaching on Critical Race Theory, such as Tennessee's Divisive Concepts Law (SB 2290, 2022), and to block efforts to build diversity, equity, and inclusion on campuses, such as Alabama's Anti-DEI Law (SB 129, 2024)—also including language regarding gendered bathrooms—clearly take power away from faculty.

While it is important to recognize that many faculty members are fighting back, they are simply not as present within the growing higher ed labor movement as they could—or, arguably should—be, given that much of the emerging discourse against higher ed in the US is directly antagonistic toward faculty work. Moreover, faculty—compared to students and staff—have more protection from being fired, and they often have more access to decision-makers. In other words, faculty have the most to gain and the least to lose from actively organizing to fight against the growing discourse.

With all that is developing, why are faculty members more comfortable taking a backseat position or not showing up at all? Further, why have faculty been reluctant to join a wide front of university workers? We think that the answers lie in professors' socialization into their roles; their structural positions, and how that limits their and others' actions; and organizers' inability to recognize and conceptualize how to work through the internal hierarchies intrinsic to higher ed. Professors aren't socialized to think of themselves as workers but more as independent scholars (Perry 2014). Although many of us hew to progressive politics, we still hold to our intellectual status in ways that limit our conceptualizations of how we might work in our own interests. Many of us form centers and institutes, or work within departments in ways that push forward our collective intellectual interests; however, that does not translate into an internal solidarity based on our similarity as workers that can push forward our collective material interests. The lack of internal solidarity stands in profound contrast with our common expressions of external solidarity. Again, we often speak out in support of our students, or the less protected workers on campus, whether they are underpaid, overworked, or disrespected. But few of us have been able to think of ourselves in class terms as experiencing grievances that can be addressed collectively.

This inability to imagine a political alternative is due to our structural and ideological position in the university. Simply put, professors' roles are glorified and celebrated in ways that differentiate us from other workers, even if we are not compensated in ways that reinforce that isolation. These structural barriers are even more exaggerated in research-intensive universities, in which the coin of the realm is research production and innovation. This prioritization helps professors separate themselves, but it also provides a structural barrier, an intrinsic hierarchy, that wall-to-wall labor organizing has yet to sufficiently address. Factories and construction sites have internal hierarchies, certainly. Laborers are thought of differently than carpenters or electricians, but the commonality of their work and the organizing that tends to their needs limit the hierarchy as expressed ideologically and materially. The opposite is true in the academic workplace. Tenure-track and tenured professors are perceived—by themselves, staff, and instructors—as more hierarchically elevated, often in a largely insurmountable way. It is not that staff do not get promoted, or that instructors, on occasion, never enter the tenure track. Certainly graduate students may join the ranks of the tenure-seeking. But as much as the principles behind tenure can and should be defended, it and other characteristics reinforcing the perception and reality of the higher education labor hierarchy have not been coherently addressed by labor organizers. The outcome is a partial solidarity, in which professors may be willing to support others without organizing around their own grievances, on one hand, and other university workers may not organize around professor's grievances, on the other. However, we believe this division could change in time.

The Promises and Challenges of Wall-To-Wall Organizing

In many ways, the wall-to-all model for organizing is counterintuitive to decades of labor activism in higher ed, which has followed more closely to what may be considered craft or trade unionism. Faculty and grad students have long had their distinct unions. Take the AAUP, for example. The AAUP has historically represented faculty, and tenure, as outlined in the 1940 *Statement of Principles on Academic Freedom and Tenure*, is considered a gold standard within AAUP policy. However, nearly 70 percent of all faculty members held contingent positions in 2021, compared to 47 percent in 1987, meaning the majority of faculty members do not have—and statistically will not receive—tenure.[4] As a result, there has been a rise in contingent faculty unions, which often strategize tactics in opposition to tenured faculty, reinforcing the harmful hierarchies that characterize higher ed.

Opposing this tactic, focusing instead on building solidarity across job classifications, is what we see as the promise of wall-to-wall organizing. Antagonisms and class-based divisions run deep in academia. Despite its challenges, we are committed to the philosophy of wall-to-wall organizing, and we believe the relative absence of faculty within UCW is generative for understanding the broad contours of faculty organizing in higher ed. Here, we share two examples from our work as faculty organizers that highlight both the promise and challenge of wall-to-wall organizing, emphasizing the role that faculty have played in specific wins. However, we also want to highlight how, and in what ways, these wins, while important, also depended upon and deepened structural hierarchies within our universities.

The Fight for $15 at UCCS

In fall 2021, UCW members at the University of Colorado-Colorado Springs launched a campaign to raise the campus minimum wage to $15/hr. After a yearlong slog through impacts of COVID-19 on campus, as well as record-high inflation rates in Colorado Springs (higher, on average, than in other large cities in Colorado), UCCS—the only campus within the University of Colorado system that did not have a $15/hour minimum wage—was struggling to maintain employees on campus, which had cascading impacts across campus affecting nearly every university worker. Further, the longtime justification for paying university workers less at UCCS, that the cost of living was cheaper than at other CU campuses, was simply no longer true. UCW-CO began collecting signatures to petition for a higher minimum wage on campus, and, after getting more than twelve hundred people to sign, we were successful. However, the circuitous path to success highlights both the strengths of the wall-to-wall organizing model as well as what we see as the broader and ongoing issues underlying faculty organizing.

Initially, the petition was seen by most as an effort to raise the minimum wage for students. However, UCW-CO used this perception as a tactic to inform people that many staff and instructors made less than $15/hour, and that the pay inequities at UCCS, compared to the other campuses, left many workers' pay far below the increasing costs of living. This discussion galvanized workers across job classifications to share the petition through shared governance structures (e.g., faculty assembly, staff assembly, and student government). As the petition gained momentum, we garnered media attention, which caught the eye of upper-level administrators (Shinn 2021). Administration, through UCCS spokesperson Chris Valentine, spoke to local reporters, suggesting that upwards of 464 current positions would need to be cut to increase the minimum wage

(KOAA 2021). It was apparent that this figure was untrue, which further galvanized university workers.

In spring of 2022, the petition was delivered by a coalition of students, staff, and faculty, and, by the end of the summer, there was a promise to increase the minimum wage. While this campaign was certainly a win, and though it brought together workers across job classifications, its success depended, in part, on faculty members signing the petition as supporters. Once the petition was delivered, however, faculty within UCW largely went back to their daily routine instead of articulating their own grievances, which, we argue, follows suit with some of the broader reasons why faculty are difficult to organize. In short, many of them do not feel like they need to, and yet, as noted above, many of the issues facing higher ed currently directly impact faculty.

Outsourcing Victory at UT Knoxville

In 2015, then-Governor Bill Haslam announced his intention to seek privatization alternatives for physical plant workers across Tennessee's universities and colleges, and in its state parks (Hill 2015). Outsourcing, of course, threatened the pay, security, and medical, pension, and tuition benefits of loyal university workers. Corporations soon recognized there was little money to be made at the state parks, but the vultures circled the universities as clear profit centers, with the UT Knoxville prize seen as the most valuable. A two-year struggle ensued, with many of the characteristic mobilization strategies. But this struggle was defined by an important cross-job category participation, and successful outreach to a variety of additional stakeholders, including the faith community, local small businesses who contracted with higher education, and legislators.

Recruitment quickly soared among physical plant workers, and streetside demonstrations and petition campaigns followed. Participation soon widened beyond these staff members; non-tenure-track and tenure-track professors alike joined, perceiving threats to their work environment. Those focused on teaching were concerned about the cleanliness of their classrooms as speed and number of rooms attended were likely to substitute for quality attention. Women faculty members and graduate students who often worked late were concerned about the potential revolving door of workers and the threats that could potentially pose to their safety. Researchers who used complex technology were concerned that the excellent care their tools received would diminish with an outsourced workforce. Vendors who contracted with the university worried they would be replaced, as large janitorial companies would rely on their own suppliers who could sell more bulk at lower prices.

We began street and campus demonstrations, wrote letters to the editor, met with campus administrators, and met with legislators, resulting in a letter of opposition addressed to the governor. Despite his clear alliance with the governor and a Board of Trustees that favored privatization, the president of the UT system said the decision would be each campus's unique right. Once the chancellor of UT Knoxville rejected outsourcing, campuses in both that system and the other Tennessee higher education system followed suit. Despite retaliation and punishment, victory was won after two exhausting years.

What was the lesson? With careful organization, enormous energy, and hard work, the harm done to one sector of workers could be generalized as harm to all—and to wider stakeholders. The hierarchy intrinsic to the university did not matter. How can we take that lesson and apply it to our wall-to-wall union? So far, we have not been able to do so. Shortly after this victory, UCW-TN began to prioritize organizing by job classification, reducing contact among all workers, and, in our view, diminishing solidarity.

Conclusions—Building Faculty Solidarity

Like our students and our staff colleagues, we sell our labor in order to live within a capitalist society, and, as such, we also have grievances. Further, while the emerging discourse against higher ed in the US impacts all university workers, these impacts directly challenge faculty members' abilities to do our jobs well: to teach what we know and to contribute to society through research. And yet, as we have articulated in this chapter, faculty, in our shared experience, are among the most difficult university workers to organize. Here, we have outlined some ideas as to why this may be the case, and we have offered examples of how wall-to-wall solidarity *can* work. However, we have also shown that—even with wins—faculty are often missing. It is our hope that the explanations and examples we offer are useful to others for framing our positions as workers, as members of a broader community of workers who need to, more than ever, organize to beat back the evolving and insidious narrative against higher ed.

Notes

1. Megan Zahneis, "Shared Governance Was Eroding Before Covid-19. Now It's a Landslide, AAUP Report Says." *The Chronicle of Higher Education,* May 26, 2021. https://www.chronicle.com/article/shared-governance-was-eroding-before-covid-19-now-its-a-landslide-aaup-report-says.

2. Ryan Quinn, "Report: Higher Ed Unions and Strikes Surged in 2022, 2023." *Inside Higher Ed,* September 1, 2023. https://www.insidehighered.com/news/quick-takes/2023/09/01/higher-ed-unions-strikes-surged-2022-2023.

3. Matt Krupnick, "Attacks on Tenure Leave College Professors Eyeing the Exits," *The Center for Public Integrity,* December 19, 2023, https://publicintegrity.org/education/academic-freedom/attacks-tenure-college-professors-exits/.

4. Glenn Colby, "Data Snapshot: Tenure and Contingency in US Higher Education," *AAUP* 2023, https://www.aaup.org/article/data-snapshot-tenure-and-contingency-us-higher-education#:~:text=Nearly%20half%20(48%20percent)%20of,39%20percent%20in%20fall%20198.

References

American Association of University Professors (AAUP). Statement on Government of Colleges and Universities, 2025. https://www.aaup.org/report/statement-government-colleges-and-universities.

Bowman, E. The Rutgers University faculty strike is over, for now, after a deal is reached. *NPR.* April 15, 2023. https://www.npr.org/2023/04/15/1170284149/rutgers-university-faculty-strike-ends-tentative-deal.

Hill, H. "Campus Workers, Students to Protest Haslam Privatization Proposal." *The Daily Beacon,* 2015. https://www.utdailybeacon.com/news/campus-workers-students-to-protest-haslam-privatization-proposal/article_e95715bc-51f0-11e5-915c-8bbfeaea90c1.html.

KOAA. "UCCS Student workers, Staff Push for $15 Minimum Wage." KOAA, 2021. https://www.koaa.com/news/covering-colorado/uccs-student-workers-staff-push-for-15-minimum-wage.

Perry, D. M. "Faculty Refuse to See Themselves as Workers. Why?" *The Chronicle of Higher Education,* 2019. https://www.chronicle.com/article/faculty-refuse-to-see-themselves-as-workers-why.

Shinn, M. "UCCS Students Fighting for Higher Wages Amid Tight Labor Market." *The Gazette,* 2021. https://gazette.com/news/education/uccs-students-fighting-for-higher-wages-amid-tight-labor-market/article_29a2cc72-56c9-11ec-b705-a36a7a13a679.html.

25

Academics of the World, Unite!

On the Importance of Internationalism in Addressing Campus Crises

Anne-Laure Amilhat Szary and Myriam Houssay-Holzschuch

Neoliberalization, bureaucratization, and fascist attacks on higher education are international issues. We are all fighting the same beast; it takes on different shapes according to our varied national contexts, and it often pits us against one another. For example, French universities are being undermined under the pretense of becoming more international and adopting so-called best practices from the US and the UK—which are, in fact, their worst practices. The right, extreme right, and so-called left-wing universalists (people who claim to be left-wing but are exploiting secularism to advance racist and Islamophobic agendas) perversely use tactics borrowed from US neo-conservatives to attack scholars because our work is "too American" or *wokiste*, a pejorative Francization of the term "woke," that vaguely points to any research on gender and racial discrimination.[1] We face attacks not only for our ideas but also for our international connections.

However, just as international connections are turned into a cause for attack, so might they be a source of strength. Fighting back needs to be globally organized and locally rooted to effectively address the specific shape these attacks take. Fortunately, this challenge is not new—it's the very same one that workers faced when capitalism expanded. The answer lies in international solidarity, specifically emancipatory internationalism.[2] "[The] internationalization [of higher education] needs a morality, a direction, which would not only be most evident in curriculum but also present in structures and administrations."[3] Furthermore, internationalism offers a framework and resource for "politicizing the construction of solidarity" (Featherstone 2012, 246). This "labour of connection" (Featherstone 2012, 63) is needed before, during, and after a crisis: Shared references, repertoires of actions, and networks can be mobilized for a local fight, which in return nurtures the collective horizon.[4]

While French universities mostly remain public, with little student selection and extremely low tuition, they have undergone two decades of brutal neoliberal reforms, in contrast to their public-service ethos.[5] Direct political attacks from the government started under Macron's presidency. Despite masquerading as liberal, he accused academics working on racial and gender discrimination of "breaking the Republic in two."[6] His accusations were followed by attacks by two ministers (Blanquer for Education and Vidal for Higher Education and Research) who engaged in a public crusade against "islamoleftism," a fantasized alliance between leftists and Islamists. This direct assault on critical academia from the top levels of the government opened the gates: It normalized a far-right discourse that had been on the rise since the 2002 presidential election but was still frowned upon. Open racism and xenophobia, especially against postcolonial minorities, have become mainstream and receive active support from national media.[7] The increasing visibility of postcolonial minorities, who are pushing back against the violent consequences of French universalism and secularism, has triggered a backlash. In this context, researchers studying topics such as "identity politics," "communities," racial or gender discrimination, or intersectionality have become frequent targets.

We, and especially one of us, have been the direct targets of these national attacks during the Sciences Po Grenoble affair.[8] We want to share our experience in fighting back through this essay in the spirit of internationalism, hoping that doing so can help others. We detail the forms our resistance took and the array of tools we used, organized chronologically: immediate reactions, midterm actions, and long-term ways of resisting.

Moreover, our means of action and capacity to access and use tools of resistance are deeply rooted in who we are. Being aware of our standing and the (material, social, psychological, etc.) resources our positionality offers is a precious primary tool. We are two internationally connected full professors in critical geography, oddities in the French context. We have both served on the board of PACTE, one of the main social sciences research centers in France: Anne-Laure as head, Myriam as a member. The board's decisions were collectively made and remarkably horizontal among its nine members (three administrators and six elected scholars). On a personal level, we are two white women from antiauthoritarian family backgrounds. This positionality has provided us with strength, confidence, intellectual and political tools, and an acute awareness that lines were being crossed, fueling our determination to fight back. *No pasarán.*[9]

When the Crisis Comes: Holding the Line

When discriminatory remarks were made during a violent exchange involving students, we simply had to intervene between two colleagues to protect both the students and the targeted colleague. We were the only responders, acting with the small collective then leading Pacte, one of France's biggest research centers in social sciences.[10] This simple act unleashed a torrent of vitriol: the government, national media, and anonymous online haters threatened Anne-Laure's professional position and responsibilities, her scientific reputation, and her life with sexist, Islamophobic, and antisemitic attacks.

To withstand this onslaught at its peak, we found strength in small, trusted local collectives, starting with the PACTE board, with whom we experienced the crisis. Community proved to be a powerful and immediate tool, especially with people who quickly grasped the nature and gravity of the crisis. Practically speaking, community meant being physically close, meeting often (e.g., we held crisis meetings every morning at 7:30 before our work days began), always being available for one another, sharing our vulnerabilities and pain, and even just weeping together. Such collectives functioned not only as emotional support but also as a trusted operations room to analyze the situation, assess options, and act strategically. They helped us fight the isolation, including by our institutions, and the individualization of targets. Also, the unfailing personal support from our dismayed families and loved ones, to whom we had to first explain the stakes, took a harsh toll on them. As their support was intrinsically private, it could not counter the sheer public nature of the attacks.

These experiences are why the spontaneous direct support (e.g., phone calls) from scholars we did not know but who had been targets before was a great help.[11] These calls marked an early expansion of our toolbox, an expansion that was also geographical as support for us became national and international. Scholarly solidarity (internationalism!) from individuals or associations kicked in, either spontaneously or through pressure applied by us through prior networks or by our international friends and colleagues. Comrades in positions of power mobilized the French professional association of geographers and the representative twenty-third section of the Conseil national des universités, while others worked through sympathetic specialty groups to influence the International Geographical Union. National and international professional associations and societies publicly expressed their support, and disseminated information through social networks, disciplinary listservs, and websites. Their support mattered not only emotionally but also because it rightfully conveyed that the assault was directed not just against an individual but against the social sciences as a whole. These professional associations further reaffirmed Anne-Laure's scientific credentials, which many mainstream media outlets had dismissed as "mere activism." In addition, this support gave us institutional leverage to directly challenge our employers (i.e., the university and the CNRS), which, in the context of increased competition among neoliberalized universities and a xenophobic, Islamophobic government, had prioritized securing access to public funding over publicly supporting us.

In short, the toolkit we used during the crisis integrates and articulates multiple dimensions that enhance its effectiveness. It is multiscalar, mobilizing both places and networks across local, national, and international levels. The support systems we benefited from were both physical and virtual, informal and institutional, and these dualities are crucial.

We want to underline the importance of the preexisting conditions that underpinned our resistance and endurance. They had been built up over years through our education and careers. We never imagined that these academic bonds would be called upon to face such a crisis. Professional friendships with (unexpected) political benefits bring joy and should be cultivated.

Midterm: Regaining Control

Beyond the frenzied days of the crisis, when we were more reactive than proactive, we tried to regain control by developing a midterm action plan that used the media, labor law, and legal action against the attackers.

We developed a media strategy through trial and error. The silence that our institutions required of us and that we initially respected was a profound mistake, as it allowed a fascist narrative to dominate the mainstream media without a counterdiscourse. We first reached out to journalists who shared our ethical standards, and whose publications accurately reflected the events as we lived them:[12] Anne-Laure gave a video interview to *Mediapart* a few weeks after the attacks.[13] We then learned to navigate less-friendly press arenas by communicating with journalists specializing in higher education issues to share our side of the story. This approach was relatively successful: several prominent liberal newspapers shifted from moral panic to becoming allies. We avoided right-wing media, as they would have likely twisted and exploited our stories. We also worked to disseminate our account of the attacks and the results of our scholarship within and beyond the institution: to students, wider audiences at public events, and family and acquaintances. For instance, Myriam delivered a series of talks at a "Popular University," a nationwide network of associations for popular education, where attendees earnestly asked to know more about what they initially perceived as the "new totalitarianisms"[14] like feminism, antiracism, etc.

We used all available resources of a rather protective labor law, with support from our (leftist) unions. First, we asked for the *protection fonctionnelle*, a mechanism by which the state covers legal costs for civil servants attacked in the line of duty. This protection was granted to Myriam as she was listed by right-wing groups, and to Anne-Laure, because of the death threats that our unsupportive university could not deny. Second, Anne-Laure successfully fought for the health consequences of the attacks to be recognized as a "work accident." Her main goal was to establish a crucial juridical precedent and place the responsibility for the consequences on the university as employer. Thus, the costs of medical care were covered, and the long-term health impact was officially recognized.

Taking the various attackers to court was the last part of this midterm strategy. Some of the attacks could be prosecuted as felonies, including death threats, defamation, and sexist hate speech. Despite significant foot-dragging by the university, which led to some charges being dropped on formal grounds,[15] three trials were held or are ongoing. One has already resulted in senescent fascists[16] being convicted and fined for their death threats. Another, unfortunately, exonerated the former minister of higher education for abusing her power. The judgment for the last case, accusing the media mogul who made Anne-Laure's name public of sexist defamation, is still pending. Anne-Laure's decision to sue the attackers was based on several considerations: a precondition was that, with the *protection fonctionnelle*, her legal costs would be covered by the university. This precondition is crucial, as the French judicial system typically awards only modest sums if the lawsuit is won—a couple thousand euros at most, less than the cost of hiring a lawyer. Most importantly, she realized that her situation was that of a canary in a coal mine: political attacks on scholars by the government, the media, and social networks are on the rise. She acted on principle to again create a legal precedent. She already succeeded with the first lawsuit: French law, previously inadequate in dealing with electronic publication, now recognizes that comments on an internet post can be subject to liability. The decision for the second lawsuit did not set, as hoped, a precedent about ordinary sexism in the media as courts increasingly share a right-wing ideology; however, they officially acknowledged the condescension of the attackers, who were quite surprised to have to defend themselves. Her choice of a well-known lawyer, recommended by one of our early supporters, and of pursuing the proceedings in Paris, was strategic—they ensured visibility and politicization. She was also confident in her strength and courage to go to court. At the same time, she was aware of the drawbacks: the personal and emotional impact of the lawsuits on her, the personalization of the debates, even though she pursued wider impact, the likelihood of becoming a public figure, and the time the lawsuits would take, repeating trauma exposure and delaying closure. She discovered that public hearings, beyond court decisions, bring two benefits: publicly and formally presenting one's account counteracts previous silencing; and placing the reconstituted facts within systems of domination allows one's personal case to apply to broader political claims. Both are healing and bring closure.

In short, effective midterm strategies entail mobilizing existing media, unions, and legal and judiciary resources. While these strategies can be shared internationally, the specific shape they assume is reterritorialized, as these resources vary and are context-specific: national, state, federal, and so on. Moreover, information about and access to these resources often requires complex networks, built over time.

Going for Structural Change

The third part of our toolbox deals with long-term actions for structural change. We focused on building alternatives by fostering, through an interdisciplinary conference entitled *Et maintenant on fait quoi?* (What do we do now?), a positive vision for what we want the university to be. The conference featured panels on work conditions at different universities in France and Europe, scholarly analyses of the evolutions of the French tertiary education system, presentations on the responsibilities of scholars concerning the climate crisis, and several workshops. One workshop developed criteria for a "Grenoble ranking," a noncompetitive alternative to the Shanghai ranking. Another used theater forum to explore how and when we could or should work with, without, or against the institution. Yet another workshop asked participants to write thwarted love letters to the university, which were later published as the open-access *Dictionnaire amoureux et néanmoins critique de l'université*.[17] The idea behind the dictionary was to help faculty and staff reclaim and rebuild a common language beyond the bureaucratic Newspeak of acronyms and excellence, as well as explore their romantic-turned-toxic relationship with academia. The *Dictionary*'s first letter is "Adieu," and letters are interspersed with short, poetic, aphorisms such as "Accomplices wanted by prisoner, for escaping Excel cells."[18]

We also created, participated in, and supported various collectives—the association of heads of research units[19] for institutional work, collective blogs (e.g., the widely read *Academia*[20]) to raise awareness, and an antifascist league[21] to produce resources (e.g., documentation, potential safe places) for future targets and allies. All these tools have unfortunately become necessary due to the deterioration of the political situation in France, as is the case elsewhere, underscoring the need for such collectives to be international.

Academics of the world unite! Internationalism is not just the moral direction Byram offered to meet the challenges of higher education's internationalization; it is a political imperative in the face of a neoliberalization of academia and a fascization of governments and societies around the world. It serves as an effective tool and an increasingly necessary practical refuge.

> The dawn dares when it rises. To strive, to brave all risks, to persist, to persevere, to be faithful to oneself, to grapple hand to hand with destiny, to surprise defeat by the slight terror it inspires, at one time to confront unjust power, at another to defy drunken triumph, to hold fast, to hold hard.[22]
>
> —Victor Hugo, *Les Misérables* (1862), Book 1, "Marius," Chapter 11

Notes

1. M. Alex Mahoudeau, *La Panique woke. Anatomie d'une offensive réactionnaire* (Textuel, 2022).

2. Fred Halliday, "Three Concepts of Internationalism." *International Affairs* 64, no. 2 (1988): 187–98; David Featherstone, *Solidarity: Hidden Histories and Geographies of Internationalism* (London: Zed, 2012).

3. Michael Byram, "An Internationalist Perspective on Internationalisation," in *Educational Approaches to Internationalization Through Intercultural Dialogue. Reflections on Theory and Practice*, ed. Ulla Lundgren, Paloma Castro and Jane Woodin, Internationalization in Higher Education (London: Routledge, 2020), 15–26.

4. Featherstone, quoted at 246 and 63.

5. Renaud Le Goix, Myriam Houssay-Holzschuch, and Camille Noûs, "Multiple Binds and Forbidden Pleasures: Writing as Poaching at French Universities." *Environment and Planning A: Economy and Space* 54, no. 7 (2022): 475–1485.

6. *Le Monde*, June 11, 2020, https://www.lemonde.fr/politique/article/2020/06/10/il-ne-faut-pas-perdre-la-jeunesse-l-elysee-craint-un-vent-de-revolte_6042430_823448.html.

7. Claske Dijkema, "Being Black but Not Black? Diasporic Identities in France, across the Atlantic, and across the Mediterranean," *Geographica Helvetica* 77, no. 4 (2022): 499–504.

8. An accurate summary (in French) of the crisis can be found on *Mediapart* (https://www.mediapart.fr/journal/france/110321/accusations-d-islamophobie-la-direction-de-sciences-po-grenoble-laisse-le-conflit-s-envenimer), or for free on Ibos's blog, https://blogs.mediapart.fr/edition/fac-checking/article/140421/sciences-po-grenoble-un-repaire-d-islamogauchistes.

9. "They will not pass," the antifascist motto from the Spanish Civil War partisans.

10. Pacte (https://www.pacte-grenoble.fr/en) is a mixed research unit (UMR-5194) specializing in the social sciences. It is affiliated with France's National Centre for Scientific Research (CNRS), Université Grenoble Alpes (UGA) and Sciences Po Grenoble, School of Political Studies, Université Grenoble Alpes.

11. In turn, we now fulfill that role for others.

12. Mahoudeau, *La Panique woke.*

13. See https://www.mediapart.fr/journal/france/060521/sciences-po-grenoble-un-crash-test-du-debat-public-pour-2022.

14. An expression often used in right-wing media and by their authors.

15. We therefore highly recommend not only using existing institutional support but also carefully following through all steps to ensure the institution does not let these matters slide, intentionally or not.

16. See https://www.mediapart.fr/journal/france/130123/sciences-po-grenoble-dix-personnes-condamnees-pour-avoir-menace-de-mort-une-enseignante-islamo-gauchiste.

17. Freely available at https://emofq-grenoble.ouvaton.org/pdf/dictionnaire-amoureux.pdf.

18. "Prisonnier cherche complices en vue évasion cellule Excel."

19. Assemblée des Directeurs de laboratoires, https://adirlabos.wordpress.com.

20. https://academia.hypotheses.org.

21. The Coordination Antifasciste pour l'Affirmation des Libertés Académiques et Pédagogiques (CAALAP), https://www.caalap.com/ and https://blogs.mediapart.fr/caalap.

22. "L'aurore ose quand elle se lève. Tenter, braver, persister, persévérer, s'être fidèle à soi-même, prendre corps à corps le destin, étonner la catastrophe par le peu de peur qu'elle nous fait, tantôt affronter la puissance injuste, tantôt insulter la victoire ivre, tenir bon, tenir tête (. . .)."

References

Byram, Michael. 2020. "An internationalist perspective on internationalisation." In *Educational Approaches to Internationalization through Intercultural Dialogue. Reflections on Theory and Practice*, edited by Ulla Lundgren, Paloma Castro and Jane Woodin, In Internationalization in Higher Education, 15–26. London: Routledge.

Dijkema, Claske. 2022. "Being Black but not Black? Diasporic Identities in France, across the Atlantic, and across the Mediterranean." *Geographica Helvetica* 77, no. 4: 499–504. https://doi.org/10.5194/gh-77-499-2022.

Featherstone, David. 2012. *Solidarity: Hidden Histories and Geographies of Internationalism*. London: Zed.

Halliday, Fred. 1988. "Three Concepts of Internationalism." *International Affairs* 64, no. 2: 187–198. https://www.jstor.org/stable/2621845.

Le Goix, Renaud, Myriam Houssay-Holzschuch, and Camille Noûs. 2022. "Multiple Binds and Forbidden Pleasures: Writing as Poaching at French Universities." *Environment and Planning A: Economy and Space* 54, no. 7: 1475–85. https://doi.org/10.1177/0308518x221116114.

Mahoudeau, M. Alex. 2022. *La Panique woke. Anatomie d'une offensive réactionnaire*. Paris: Textuel.

Coda

Resistance Is *Not* Futile

Lisa M. Di Bartolomeo and Kevin M. Gannon

This volume represents the beginning of a discussion about the crises facing American—and, indeed, international—higher education, but it is only that: a beginning. Much remains to be examined, and many more institutions than what we could include in this book still have stories to tell. Even as we began receiving excellent essays from our contributors, fresh incidents, closures, and threats to higher education were daily headlines. Most notably, as this manuscript moved through the editing process, campus protests and—in many institutions—heavy-handed responses by administration and local law enforcement called the very foundations of both civil discourse and academic freedom into question. From community encampments springing up on campus, to the ongoing litany of program and personnel cuts everywhere, it is daunting even to try to keep up with the seemingly never-ending stream of bad news for higher ed, and we occasionally doubted the wisdom of attempting to capture some of the threats to what for many of us is more than a job but also a passion and a life's work.

But the bad news doesn't have to be overwhelming. Dealing with the polycrisis eroding the success of and trust in higher education isn't easy, but it's not hopeless, as many of this volume's essays demonstrate. We can strategize by building communities, galvanizing opposition, girding shared governance structures. We can evince solidarity—among faculty (across all classes, from part-time adjuncts to veteran tenured professors), among staff (often forgotten in the struggle), and among students. We can build support networks to help soften landings for those ejected from academia, to aid in healing from campus trauma, to foster the resilience that enables us to weather the ongoing storms and the climactic events still to come.

The topics included in the present volume collectively offer hope and a path forward. Some of our essays suggest ways to resist "culture war" attacks on teaching and curricula, especially DEIJ work, whether that opposition is at the immediate campus level or at a broader statewide—perhaps even national—level. Some detail strategies for handling closure, whether of an entire campus or of multiple programs. Other chapters provide models for organizing and developing campus solidarity, whether across campus groups or within them, as well as ways to build community on campus, nurturing resilience or developing strategies of care. Some essays help us contextualize what is happening in the U.S. with what is happening abroad, specifically in France, as well as to the many international students hosted in the U.S. Finally, many of the essays stem from the unthinkable: campus closures, horrific campus attacks and tragedies, or drastic program cutting. Although the original impetus of this book was the "academic transformation" in 2023 that left West Virginia University a diminished version of itself and a diminished option for its mostly under-resourced Appalachian students, as editors we quickly realized that many campuses are beset by crisis and that it behooves us all to understand those crises before they arrive on our doorsteps like harbingers of doom—or in the guise of national educational consultants.

The United States and other countries face a rising tide of mistrust in higher education: a wave that often coincides with a rising tide of fascism and authoritarianism. It is no accident that higher education is under attack from the very people who seek to decimate civil society and civil liberties, to reduce the pool of eligible voters both in numbers and the information available to them. Educated and informed voters stand up to authoritarian, or would-be authoritarian, regimes, so it is logical that education must be one of the first bricks to remove in the bulwark against such totalitarian impulses. Those of us in higher education must continue to fight, no matter how exhausted we may be. Scholars of fascism warn us not to surrender our agency—and certainly to not do so in advance—and it is that clarion call to arms that animates this book.

The crises in higher education are not going away anytime soon; but then again, neither are we. If we stand together, we stand a chance. And thanks to the contributors to this volume, we have a well-stocked toolkit we can deploy on our campuses to fight back. Sometimes we will lose, as we ultimately did at West Virginia University and elsewhere. But sometimes we win. And we have to keep trying to win. It is our hope that the readers of this collection find new energy and inspiration after reading the essays within, and, thus fortified, continue to stand with the deeply entrenched values embodied in a liberal arts education. Each of us must stand up, on our home campuses and at the ballot box, if we are to have any hope of ensuring that the promise of higher education is kept: for its practitioners, its students, and its societies. The survival and continued success of higher education depends on all of us. We hope that each of our readers finds comfort, hope, and a call to action in our collection.

Contributors

Christian Adams Born in Clarksburg, WV, Christian Adams is a student, organizer, and co-founder of the West Virginia United Students' Union, which played an active role on campus during the so-called "Academic Transformation" process.

Kent Andersen held various positions at Birmingham-Southern College prior to its closure in 2024. For twenty years, he was a staff member of the Associated Colleges of the South (ACS) Teaching and Learning Workshop, a one-week intensive workshop for ACS faculty. He currently teaches graduate courses in the Office of Interdisciplinary Graduate and Professional Studies at the University of Alabama at Birmingham.

The **anonymous** author of the WVU Facts report was a tenured professor at WVU, laid off along with many others as part of the Gordon Gee administration's vandalism of the institution. They were a founding member of WVU's short-lived AAUP chapter, and a member of the West Virginia Campus Workers AFT Local. They do not forgive and they do not forget.

Emil Asanov is a PhD candidate in curriculum and instruction (second language education major) at Florida State University. His background is in teaching and researching less commonly taught languages, particularly Russian; English as a second language; second language pedagogy and methodologies; and teacher education. Emil is also interested in qualitative inquiry, qualitative methodologies, and arts-based research.

Matthew Austin is an assistant professor of practice in the W.A. Franke Honors College and Office of General Education at the University of

Arizona. In his role, he teaches two bookend courses in UA's General Education Program, working with students across campus departments along their undergraduate careers. His scholarly interests focus on the role of student voice in curricular iteration at the university level.

Sarah L. Bunnell is the director of the Center for the Advancement of Teaching and Learning at Elon University and an associate professor of psychology. She is past president of the International Society for the Scholarship of Teaching and Learning, an ISSOTL Distinguished Service Award winner, and a Gardner Institute Russell Edgerton Innovation Fellow. A coauthor of *Being Human in STEM* (2023), Sarah is passionate about building student-faculty-staff partnerships to enhance teaching, learning, and thriving across educational spaces.

William Caraher teaches in the Department of History and American Indian Studies where his specialty is the archaeology of Greece, Cyprus, and contemporary America. His latest books are *The Archaeology of Contemporary America* (2024) and *Beyond Icons: Theories and Methods in Byzantine Archaeology in North America* (2025) coedited with Dar Brooks Hedstrom and Kostis Kourelis.

Andy J. Carr is a PhD student studying politics at The New School for Social Research and holds a JD from UC College of the Law, San Francisco. His work on the First Amendment has appeared in *UC Law Constitutional Quarterly* and the *Washington & Lee Journal of Civil Rights and Social Justice*, among others.

Lisa M. Corrigan is a professor of communication and director of gender studies at the University of Arkansas. She is the author of *Prison Power: How Prison Influenced the Movement for Black Liberation* (2016) and *Black Feelings: Race and Affect in the Long Sixties* (2020) as well as the editor of *#MeToo: A Rhetorical Zeitgeist* (2021). She is a contributor to *The Nation* and cohosts the popular podcast, *Lean Back: Critical Feminist Conversations* with Laura Weiderhaft.

William Tynes Cowan is professor emeritus of English, Birmingham-Southern College. He received his BA in English from the College in 1985 and returned to teach for twenty-two years, including a nine-year stint as English department chair.

meaghan davis (she+they) is a passionate cocreator of liberatory spaces, committed to reimagining higher education by pushing the boundaries of what is possible. Currently, she is working at SUNY Farmingdale to cobuild a transformative first-year experience that centers students as they navigate the awesome, critical, and formidable transition to college. In 2024, meaghan completed their doctoral dissertation, *Cocreating Liberatory Spaces in Higher Education,* positing the Model for Liberatory Spaces in Higher Education.

Lisa M. Di Bartolomeo remains Singer-Hill Professor Emerita of Humanities at West Virginia University, where she ran the Russian program until the Department of World Languages was eliminated in 2024. Having received her undergraduate degree from WVU, she earned an M. Litt. at the University of Glasgow as WVU's first British Marshall scholar, before earning her Ph.D. in Slavic Languages and Literatures at the University of North Carolina at Chapel Hill. She now works for a national environmental organization.

Camille Engle is an English studies graduate student at Ball State University. She is currently writing her thesis on Christian asceticism as a means of resistance to overconsumption and hypercapitalism.

Mari Elise Ewing is an associate professor of environmental studies at Austin College. She teaches courses on systems thinking including resilient systems, food systems, and environmental justice. As director of Austin College Thinking Green (THINK), Mari Elise collaborates with students, staff, and faculty to help reduce the college's environmental impact.

Christina Fabrey is the director of the Student Success Center at Virginia Tech University. She is a Professional Certified Coach through the International Coaching Federation and a Board Certified Coach through the Center for Credentialing Education. As a coach trainer and mentor, Christina has trained hundreds of higher education professionals in coaching skills over the last decade. Her edited anthology, *Coaching in Disability Resources: From Transitional to Transformational,* was published in May 2023. She is the author of numerous book chapters and articles focusing on holistic student support, peer education, coaching, and neurodiversity coaching.

Kaitlyn Rose Farrell Rodriguez (she/hers) is a faculty development specialist at UT Austin's Center for Teaching and Learning who continues to draw from her graduate student development background to support instructors at every career stage. She facilitates the CTL's theater- and arts-based pedagogy program (Longhorns Play), and her current research explores relationship-rich pedagogy; effective approaches to teaching during challenging times; strategies for enhancing both student and instructor engagement and well-being; and ways to design accessible, human-centered, equitable experiential learning opportunities.

Sheron Fraser-Burgess is professor emeritus of Social Foundations of Education/Multicultural Education at Ball State University. She also serves as a lecturer in the doctoral program in educational leadership at the University of Pennsylvania Graduate School of Education.

Kevin M. Gannon is director of the Center for the Advancement of Faculty Excellence and professor of history at Queens University in Charlotte, NC. He is also the author of *Radical Hope: A Teaching Manifesto* (2020).

Kathleen Gray is a higher education optimist who believes we can make our institutions into the joyful, collaborative, sustainable, and successful communities we want them to be. With over twenty years of experience as a sociologist, faculty member, and administrator, she is currently the associate provost of learning and student success at Baruch College, a constituent college of the City University of New York system.

Jennifer Grouling is a professor of English at Ball State University. Her research focuses on higher education and writing program administration, particularly the training and labor or graduate teaching assistants. She currently serves as the copresident of Ball State's AAUP advocacy chapter.

Dylan M. Harris is an assistant professor of geography and environmental studies at the University of Colorado–Colorado Springs (UCCS). His work focuses on the stories we tell (and don't tell) about socioecological change, focusing specifically on the procedural justice elements of climate and energy justice. He is interested in work that exists at the intersection of change, drawing from what he terms experimental and speculative political ecology to critically study the unequal power structures informing many "transition" projects (e.g., carbon offsets) while also aiming to disrupt them, pointing toward more equitable possibilities, through interventionist research. He is a member of both United Campus Workers and the AAUP, and he is on the national coordinating organizing committee for the newly founded Higher Ed Labor United.

Molly Hatcher is assistant vice provost and director of the Center for Teaching and Learning at the University of Texas at Austin. She leads a dynamic team dedicated to fostering a vibrant culture of teaching and learning at UT by partnering with instructors, students, and staff to enhance learning experiences. She is also coeditor of *Preparing for College and University Teaching: Competencies for Graduate and Professional Students.*

Matthew R. Hotham is an associate professor of religious studies at Ball State University. His in-progress book manuscript, *Pig Fat, Goat Blood, and Dog Hair: Animals, Islam, and American Anxiety about Religious Difference*, investigates the relationship between Islamophobia, affect, and human-animal relations. He is vice president of the Ball State Chapter of the American Association of University Professors.

Myriam Houssay-Holzschuch is a French geographer whose research focuses on urban spaces, with a particular emphasis on issues of spatial justice, urban inequalities, and the ways in which social dynamics shape the experience of the city. She has extensively studied cities in South Africa, particularly Cape Town, exploring how apartheid's legacy continues to affect urban segregation and access to space. Her work often intersects with critical geography and is now exploring issues in critical epistemologies and pedagogies. She and her coauthor are both affiliated with Université Grenoble Alpes, CNRS, Sciences Po Grenoble, Pacte, Grenoble, France.

Louanne Clayton Jacobs taught for sixteen years at Birmingham-Southern College as a professor of education. Following her tenure at BSC and the shuttering of the institution, she has returned to her roots in K-12 public education and now teaches English Language Arts at i3 Academy Middle School in Birmingham, Alabama.

Sheila Jaswal is a professor of chemistry and a member of the Program in Biochemistry and Biophysics at Amherst College. She leads a team of undergraduate researchers in applying experimental and computational approaches to study protein folding and serves as the chair of the Protein Society's Diversity Equity and Inclusion Committee. Also a coauthor of

Being Human in STEM, Sheila founded the "Being Human in STEM" (HSTEM) course with students in 2016. She has also cofacilitated the HSTEM course at Amherst with more than twenty faculty and staff colleagues from the arts, humanities, social sciences and natural sciences also supporting the national network of over a dozen institutions now offering their own HSTEM courses.

Heather Keith is executive director of faculty development and professor of philosophy at Radford University. She is the coauthor of *Intellectual Disability: Ethics, Dehumanization, & a New Moral Community* and *Lives and Legacies of People with Intellectual Disability*, co-editor of *Pragmatist and American Philosophical Perspectives on Resilience*, and author of numerous articles and book chapters on American philosophy, ethics, environmental philosophy, feminist theory, Asian and comparative philosophy, philosophy of pop culture and sports, and high impact practices in teaching and learning.

Evan A. Kutzler is associate professor of history at Western Michigan University where he teaches US history and public history. He is the author of multiple book-length projects, including *Living by Inches: The Smells, Sounds, Tastes, and Feeling of Captivity in Civil War Prisons* (2019).

Sean Davis Lawrence Sean Lawrence is assistant professor of history at West Virginia University where his teaching and research focus on the entangled environmental histories of modern Europe and the Middle East. He is an active member of the National Humanities Alliance and an advocate for broad humanities education in West Virginia and beyond.

Dana Grossman Leeman directs the Center for the Enhancement of Learning and Teaching at Tufts University. Before coming to CELT in 2020. Dana was on faculty at the Simmons University School of Social Work for twenty-five years, during which she helped launch two online degree programs in clinical social work and behavior analysis. She was the inaugural associate dean for online education for the School of Social Work, and appointed as the Inaugural Provost Faculty Fellow for Online Education, providing professional development to all faculty teaching in six online master's programs across the university. She holds an MSW from Boston University School of Social Work and a PhD in clinical social work from Simmons University.

John LeJeune is a professor of political science at Georgia Southwestern State University in Americus, GA. His interests include political theory, political violence, and chess.

Shu-Min Liao is an assistant professor of mathematics and statistics at Amherst College. She earned her PhD from Pennsylvania State University in 2009. Shu-Min is an active member of the American Statistical Association Committee on Statistics and Disability (CSD) and Justice, Equity, Diversity, and Inclusion (JEDI) Outreach Group. She also served as an inaugural Faculty Fellow for the Amherst College Center for Teaching and Learning and has twice cofacilitated HSTEM courses.

Lindsay Stallones Marshall (she/her) is an assistant professor of history at Illinois State University. Her research focuses on Native North American history, especially the creation and perpetuation of settler colonial public memory through history education. She also researches the environmental history of human-equine relationships with an emphasis on interdisciplinary and decolonial methodologies.

Joseph Nardinelli is an assistant professor of practice in the W.A. Franke Honors College and Office of General Education at the University of Arizona. His primary areas of teaching have been in writing composition, reflection-based portfolio curation, and food culture and pathways, especially in and around Tucson, Arizona. Joseph's scholarly interests focus on culturally responsive pedagogy, borderlands writing, and organizational theory.

Mona Wu Orr is an assistant professor of biology and a member of the Program in Biochemistry and Biophysics at Amherst College. She earned her PhD in biological sciences from the University of Maryland, College Park, and completed her postdoctoral training at the National Institutes of Health. Mona is dedicated to advancing our understanding of bacterial physiology through innovative research and student mentorship and is deeply invested in creating supportive STEM communities in and out of the classroom.

Andrea Overbay is an associate professor of mathematics at Austin College. She served as director of Austin College's Robert & Joyce Johnson Center for Faculty Development and Excellence in Teaching during the COVID-19 pandemic. Andrea is also a registered yoga teacher (500 RYT) with

Yoga Alliance and regularly teaches yoga classes for the Austin College employee well-being program.

Ryan Rideau is the program director for faculty development and mentoring at the Massachusetts Institute of Technology (MIT). AT MIT, he enhances faculty success at all levels by supporting and scaling faculty mentorship and graduate advising programs and additional faculty advancement programming over a range of faculty career levels.

Sara Rzeszutek is the director for faculty advancement in teaching excellence and professor of history at Quinnipiac University, where she leads initiatives that help faculty translate strong pedagogy into student success. She is the author of *James and Esther Cooper Jackson: Love and Courage in the Black Freedom Movement* (2015) and "Taking a Thematic Approach with the History of Fun" in *Designing Introductory History Courses for Student Success* (2024).

Jon Shefner is the Herbert Family Professor of Excellence in the Department of Sociology at the University of Tennessee, where he is also director of the Community University Research Collaboration Initiative (CURCI). The author and editor of many books and dozens of articles on austerity, protest, and organizing, Jon has been active in social movements, labor organizing, and community organizing for over forty years. Jon is a twenty-plus-year member of United Campus Workers of Tennessee, the Southeast's first UCW.

Kevin Shook is an artist and was a professor of art at Birmingham-Southern College for nineteen years. Originally from northeast Ohio, he graduated with an MFA in printmaking from the University of Delaware. He currently is creating and teaching art in the US Southeast.

Brian Smentkowski is vice president and chief academic officer for the University of Alaska system. Prior to coming to Alaska, he was director of the Center for Excellence in Teaching and Professor of Political Science at the University of Idaho.

Joel E. R. Smith is an assistant professor of Practice in the W.A. Franke Honors College and Office of General Education at the University of

Arizona. He teaches undergraduate seminars on reflective writing, ePortfolios, and the Gen Ed Experience, and his scholarly interests are in writing studies, shared governance, and nontenure-track activism.

Winston Smith, originally from Virginia, is a cofounder of West Virginia United Students' Union and political science student at WVU. He, along with the rest of the Students' Union, won the Mother Jones Hellraiser Award from the WV Mine Wars Museum in 2023. He continues to pursue organizing in the state of West Virginia.

Anne-Laure Amilhat Szary is a French geographer working on territorial governance and borders. Her work offers insights into borders' complex, political, social, and cultural dimensions. She critically investigates the intersection of space and art at, around and against borders, notably in Latin America. She and her coauthor are both affiliated with Université Grenoble Alpes, CNRS, Sciences Po Grenoble, Pacte, Grenoble, France.

Greta Valenti was an associate professor of psychology at Birmingham-Southern College; she spent eleven years there. She holds a PhD in psychology from Ohio State University and currently works as a researcher at the University of Alabama at Birmingham.

Luke Waltzer directs the Teaching and Learning Center at the CUNY Graduate Center, where he supports graduate students in their teaching across the City University of New York system. He teaches courses in the Interactive Technology and Pedagogy and Digital Humanities Programs, is codirector of the Mellon Foundation-funded CUNY Humanities Alliance, principal investigator of the Google.org-funded Critical AI Literacy Institute, and Director of Community Projects for the CUNY Academic Commons.

Zachary Watson is currently the Being Human Academic Fellow in the Chemistry Department at Amherst College. He earned his BA from Amherst College in a student-created interdisciplinary major, Equitable Museum Design, which fuses science, art, and critical pedagogy to create exhibition spaces that challenge traditional scientific narratives and engage diverse audiences. Through his experiences in genomics research, art, teaching, and community science, Zac hopes to reshape science education to be critically reflective and community-responsive.

Christine Zabala-Eisshofer (she/her) earned her PhD in education at the University of Colorado, Boulder. Her research focuses on university diversity initiatives, institutional diversity rhetoric, and the impact of policy on higher education. She is currently a visiting assistant professor at the University of Iowa in the Higher Education and Student Affairs Program.

Index

www.ingramcontent.com/pod-product-compliance
Lightning Source LLC
LaVergne TN
LVHW100518110826
845146LV00002B/683

* 9 7 9 8 8 5 5 8 0 5 7 8 9 *